Research Methods in Legal Translation and Interpreting

The field of legal translation and interpreting has strongly expanded over recent years. As it has developed into an independent branch of Translation Studies, this book advocates for a substantiated discussion of methods and methodology, as well as knowledge about the variety of approaches actually applied in the field. It is argued that, complex and multifaceted as it is, legal translation calls for research that might cross boundaries across research approaches and disciplines in order to shed light on the many facets of this social practice. The volume addresses the challenge of methodological consolidation, triangulation and refinement. The work presents examples of the variety of theoretical approaches which have been developed in the discipline and of the methodological sophistication which is currently being called for. In this regard, by combining different perspectives, they expand our understanding of the roles played by legal translators and interpreters, who emerge as linguistic and intercultural mediators dealing with a rich variety of legal texts; as knowledge communicators and as builders of specialised knowledge; as social agents performing a socially situated activity; as decision-makers and agents subject to and redefining power relations, and as political actors shaping legal cultures and negotiating cultural identities, as well as their own professional identity.

Łucja Biel is Associate Professor and Head of Corpus Research Centre at the Institute of Applied Linguistics, University of Warsaw, Poland, where she teaches and researches legal translation. She is Secretary General of the European Society of Translation Studies (EST) and editor-in-chief of the *JoSTrans Journal of Specialised Translation.* She has participated in a number of internationally and nationally funded research projects on legal and institutional translation. Her research interests focus on legal/EU translation, legal terminology, translator training and corpus linguistics. She has published over 50 papers in this area, e.g. in *The Translator, Meta: The Translators' Journal, The Interpreter and Translator Trainer, Fachsprache, LANS-TTS* and a book *Lost in the Eurofog. The Textual Fit of Translated Law* (Peter Lang, 2014).

Jan Engberg, PhD is Professor of Knowledge Communication at the School of Communication and Culture, University of Aarhus, Denmark. He teaches legal as well as financial translation at BA and MA level, as well as other branches of text-oriented foreign language skills. His main areas of research interest are the study of translation and mediation of knowledge in the field of law, texts and genres in the academic field, cognitive aspects of domain-specific discourse and the relations between specialised knowledge and text formulation as well as basic aspects of communication in domain-specific settings. His research focus is upon communication and translation in the field of law. He is editor-in-chief of the international journal *Fachsprache* and member of the editorial or advisory boards of a substantial number of international scholarly journals.

M. Rosario Martín Ruano is Associate Professor at the University of Salamanca, Spain, where she is a member of the Research Group on Translation, Ideology and Culture and where she currently leads the research project entitled VIOSIMTRAD ('Symbolic Violence and Translation: Challenges in the Representation of Fragmented Identities within the Global Society', FFI2015–66516-P; MINECO/FEDER, UE). Her research interests include legal and institutional translation, translation and ideology, and gender and post-colonial approaches to translation. She has published widely on these issues, including a number of books and co-edited collective volumes, as well as more than 50 chapters and articles in journals such as *The Interpreter and Translator Trainer (ITT), TTR, JoSTrans, Linguistica Antverpiensia*, etc., and in volumes by Routledge, Multilingual Matters, John Benjamins, St Jerome, etc. She is a member of the editorial board of *Perspectives, Estudios de Traducción, Clina* and a reviewer for a number of specialised journals (*Target, Meta, JoSTrans, Language and Intercultural Communication, MonTI*, etc.). She has been a practising translator since 1997.

Vilelmini Sosoni is Assistant Professor at the Ionian University, Greece. She teaches legal and economic translation as well as other branches of specialised translation. She has participated in a number of internationally and nationally funded research projects on legal translation and translation technology. Her research interests lie in the areas of legal and institutional translation, corpus linguistics, intercultural communication and translation technology. She has published widely on these topics, including articles in journals such as *Perspectives, JoSTrans, mTm, Journal of Language and Law*, etc. and in volumes by Routledge, John Benjamins, Springer, etc. She is a member of the editorial board of *JoSTrans* and *Intercultural and Intersemiotic Translation.* She has been a practising translator since 1997.

Law, Language and Communication

Anne Wagner
Université du Littoral Côte d'Opale, France
Vijay Kumar Bhatia
formerly of City University of Hong Kong

This series encourages innovative and integrated perspectives within and across the boundaries of law, language and communication, with particular emphasis on issues of communication in specialized socio-legal and professional contexts. It seeks to bring together a range of diverse yet cumulative research traditions in order to identify and encourage interdisciplinary research.

The series welcomes proposals – both edited collections as well as single-authored monographs – emphasizing critical approaches to law, language and communication, identifying and discussing issues, proposing solutions to problems, offering analyses in areas such as legal construction, interpretation, translation and de-codification.

Synesthetic Legalities
Sensory Dimensions of Law and Jurisprudence
Edited by Sarah Marusek

Legal Persuasion
A Rhetorical Approach to the Science
Linda L. Berger and Kathryn M. Stanchi

International Arbitration Discourse and Practices in Asia
Edited by Vijay K Bhatia, Maurizio Gotti, Azirah Hashim, Philip Koh and Sundra Rajoo

Phraseology in Legal and Institutional Settings
A Corpus-based Interdisciplinary Perspective
Edited by Stanislaw Gozdz Roszkowski and Gianluca Pontrandolfo

Fiction and the Languages of Law
Understanding Contemporary Legal Discourse
Karen Petroski

For more information about this series, please visit: www.routledge.com/Law-Language-and-Communication/book-series/LAWLANGCOMM

Research Methods in Legal Translation and Interpreting

Crossing Methodological Boundaries

Edited by Łucja Biel, Jan Engberg, M. Rosario Martín Ruano, and Vilelmini Sosoni

Routledge
Taylor & Francis Group
LONDON AND NEW YORK

First published 2019 by Routledge

2 Park Square, Milton Park, Abingdon, Oxon, OX14 4RN
605 Third Avenue, New York, NY 10017

Routledge is an imprint of the Taylor & Francis Group, an informa business

First issued in paperback 2020

British Library Cataloguing-in-Publication Data
A catalogue record for this book is available from the British Library

Library of Congress Cataloging-in-Publication Data
Names: Biel, Lucja, 1974– author.
Title: Research methods in legal translation and interpreting : crossing methodological boundaries / Lucja Biel, Jan Engberg, Rosario Martâin, and Vilelmini Sosoni.
Description: Abingdon, Oxon [UK] ; New York, NY : Routledge, 2019. | Series: Law, language and communication | Includes bibliographical references and index.
Identifiers: LCCN 2018052675 (print) | LCCN 2018055536 (ebook) | ISBN 9781351031226 (ebook) | ISBN 9781138492103 (hardback)
Subjects: LCSH: Law—Translating. | Law—Language. | Semantics (Law) | Court interpreting and translating. | Law—Interpretation and construction. | Translators—Legal status, laws, etc. | Translating and interpreting.
Classification: LCC K213 (ebook) | LCC K213 .B54 2019 (print) | DDC 418/.0334—dc23
LC record available at https://lccn.loc.gov/2018052675

ISBN: 978-1-138-49210-3 (hbk)
ISBN: 978-0-367-73000-0 (pbk)

Typeset in Galliard
by Apex CoVantage, LLC

Contents

Contributors

Carmen Bestué is a trained Attorney and a Lecturer in Translation from English into Spanish at the Autonomous University of Barcelona. She holds a J.D. degree in Law from the University of Barcelona, a University Degree in comparative law from the University of Paris II, Pantheon-Assas, and a PhD in Translation Theory from the Autonomous University of Barcelona. From 2003 to 2016 she was the Director of the Postgraduate Degree in Legal Translation at the Autonomous University of Barcelona. She has published many articles in translation journals as well as a monograph entitled *Los contratos traducidos* [Translated contracts].

Łucja Biel is Associate Professor and Head of Corpus Research Centre at the Institute of Applied Linguistics, University of Warsaw, Poland, where she teaches and researches legal translation. She is Secretary General of the European Society of Translation Studies (EST) and editor-in-chief of the *JoSTrans Journal of Specialised Translation.* She has participated in a number of internationally and nationally funded research projects on legal and institutional translation. Her research interests focus on legal/EU translation, legal terminology, translator training and corpus linguistics. She has published over 50 papers in this area, e.g. in *The Translator, Meta: The Translators' Journal, The Interpreter and Translator Trainer, Fachsprache, LANS-TTS* and a book *Lost in the Eurofog: The Textual Fit of Translated Law* (Peter Lang, 2014).

Jan Engberg, PhD is Professor of Knowledge Communication at the School of Communication and Culture, University of Aarhus, Denmark. He teaches legal as well as financial translation at BA and MA level, as well as other branches of text-oriented foreign language skills. His main areas of research interest are the study of translation and mediation of knowledge in the field of law, texts and genres in the academic field; cognitive aspects of domain-specific discourse and the relations between specialised knowledge and text formulation as well as basic aspects of communication in domain-specific settings. His research focus is upon communication and translation in the field of law. He is editor-in-chief of the international journal *Fachsprache* and member of the editorial or advisory boards of a substantial number of international scholarly journals.

Justyna Giczela-Pastwa is a translation researcher and translator trainer, currently working as an Assistant Professor at the University of Gdańsk. She was a Visiting Lecturer at City University London (MA in Legal Translation) from 2012 to 2014. She holds a PhD in Linguistics, Postgraduate Diploma in Legal and Business Translation (University of Gdańsk), and an MA in Music (Academy of Music in Gdańsk). She is the head of Specialized Translation Training Research Group, University of Gdańsk; an external collaborator of the Corpus Research Centre, University of Warsaw, and an expert in the Polish Normalisation Committee. Her academic interests include legal translation, specialised inverse translation, corpus translation studies and translator training. She co-edited the volume entitled *Norm-Focused and Culture-Related Inquiries in Translation Research* (Peter Lang, 2016).

M. Rosario Martín Ruano is Associate Professor at the University of Salamanca, Spain, where she is a member of the Research Group on Translation, Ideology and Culture, and where she currently leads the research project entitled VIOSIMTRAD ("Symbolic Violence and Translation: Challenges in the Representation of Fragmented Identities within the Global Society", FFI2015–66516-P; MINECO/FEDER, UE). Her research interests include legal and institutional translation, translation and ideology, and gender and post-colonial approaches to translation. She has published widely on these issues, including a number of books and co-edited collective volumes, as well as more than 50 chapters and articles in journals such as *The Interpreter and Translator Trainer (ITT)*, *TTR*, *JoSTrans*, *Linguistica Antverpiensia*, etc., and in volumes by Routledge, Multilingual Matters, John Benjamins, St Jerome, etc. She is a member of the editorial board of *Perspectives, Estudios de Traducción, Clina* and a reviewer for a number of specialised journals (*Target*, *Meta*, *JoSTrans*, *Language and Intercultural Communication*, *MonTI*, etc.). She has been a practising translator since 1997.

Mikhail Mikhailov is Professor of Translation Studies (Finnish and Russian) at the University of Tampere, Finland. During his academic carrier he has worked as a lecturer in Moscow Linguistic University (1986–1994), as a researcher at the Institute of Russian Language of the Russian Academy of Sciences (1994–1999), and as a researcher, lecturer and acting professor at the University of Tampere (1999–). He was appointed full professorship as of 1.1.2014. Mikhail Mikhailov compiles and collaborates in the compilation of multilingual corpora and develops web-based corpus software. His research covers corpus-based translation studies with a particular focus on parallel and comparable corpora, terminological studies and translation technologies. He works mainly with Russian-Finnish and occasionally with Russian-English data. He is one of the authors of the book *Corpus Linguistics for Translation and Contrastive Studies* (with Robert Cooper) published by Routledge in 2016.

Sylvie Monjean-Decaudin is Professor at the Sorbonne University (France). She holds a doctorate in French law from the University of Paris X (2010) and a doctorate in Spanish law from the University of Malaga, Spain (2010). Her thesis on, *The translation of law in judicial proceedings—a contribution to the study of legal linguistics,* was awarded the Research Prize of the National School for Magistrates (*Prix de la recherche de l'École Nationale de la Magistrature*) in 2011 and published by French legal publishing company Dalloz in 2012. She founded the CERIJE (*CEntre de Recherche Interdisciplinaire en JuritraductologiE*), which is the first interdisciplinary research centre dedicated to "juritraductology", in 2012.

Esther Monzó-Nebot is an Associate Professor at the Translation and Communication Studies Department, Universitat Jaume I. She is the director of the master's program "Research in Translation and Interpreting", and coordinates the research group "Translation and Postmonolingualism" (TRAP) and the legal and administrative language section of *Revista de Llengua i Dret/Journal of Language and Law.* Between 2013 and 2015 she was a Professor in the Sociology of Translation and Interpreting at the Department of Translation Studies of the University of Graz, Austria. Before that period, she had worked as a translator at the World Trade Organization, the United Nations and the World Intellectual Property Organization. Her PhD thesis (2002) explored the professional practice of sworn translators in Spain, combining textual and sociological approaches. Her current research focuses on the uses of translation and interpreting in managing diversity and intercultural and intergroup relations using mainly psychosocial approaches.

Karolina Nartowska (PhD) is an interpreting researcher, trainer and practitioner. She completed her postgraduate translation studies (German, Polish) at the UNESCO Chair, Jagiellonian University. She holds a PhD in Interpreting Studies from University of Vienna. Her research explored the role behaviour of court interpreters in criminal proceedings in both Austria and Poland. Her academic interests focus primarily on community interpreting, role(s) of interpreters in institutional settings, the power of interpreters, and ethical standards. She has written several publications on court interpreting and she is an international trainer providing presentations on court interpreting in cooperation with TEPIS.

Mariana Orozco-Jutorán is a professional translator and a Senior Lecturer in Translation from English into Spanish at the Autonomous University of Barcelona since 1996. She holds a PhD in Translation Theory, for which she received the Best Doctoral Thesis Award in 2005. She has been involved in several funded research projects and is currently a member of two research groups: TRAFIL (Translating Remote Philosophies to Facilitate Understanding), MIRAS (Intercultural Mediation), as well as the LEXTRA (Legal Translation Studies) research network. She has published a book and more than 30 articles in international translation journals and book chapters in publications by John Benjamins, Multilingual Matters, Gunter Narr and others. She is a member of the editorial boards and scientific committees of journals such as

Perspectives or *Hermeneus*. As a professional translator, she has worked in a wide range of areas over the last twenty years.

Gianluca Pontrandolfo is currently Adjunct Lecturer at the University of Trieste (IUSLIT, Department of Legal Language, Interpreting and Translation Studies), where he teaches general and specialised translation from Spanish into Italian. He combines his activity as freelance translator with his academic and research projects. His research activity focuses on translation-oriented legal terminology and phraseology, from a contrastive (Spanish, Italian, English) and corpus perspective. In line with his PhD thesis, which deals with a quali-quantitative study of legal phraseology in a trilingual corpus of criminal judgments (COSPE), his publications mainly focus on the relationship between language and law. His research interests also include specialised genres, textual analysis applied to translation, translator training and corpus linguistics. He is a member of the Research Centre on Languages for Specific Purposes (CERLIS) of the University of Bergamo.

Joëlle Popineau-Lauvray is currently working as an Assistant Professor in translation studies at the University of Tours, France. She also teaches classes in juritraductology at the Faculty of Law, University of Tours. She holds a Doctorate in Linguistics and Computer-aided Translation (1992) and a Maîtrise in Specialized Translation (University of Lorraine, France) (1986). Her academic interests include linguistics, translation studies and didactics. She is a full accredited researcher at the Laboratoire Ligérien de Linguistique (a CNRS joint research unit); she is the Chair of CerLiCO, a French linguistics society.

Fernando Prieto Ramos is Full Professor of Translation and Director of the Centre for Legal and Institutional Translation Studies (Transius) at the University of Geneva's Faculty of Translation and Interpreting. With a background in both translation and law, his work focuses on legal and institutional translation, including interdisciplinary methodologies, international legal instruments and specialised terminology. Former member of the Centre for Translation and Textual Studies at Dublin City University, he has published widely on legal translation and has received several research and teaching awards, including a European Label Award for Innovative Methods in Language Teaching from the European Commission, an International Geneva Award from the Swiss Network for International Studies and a Consolidator Grant for his current project on "Legal Translation in International Institutional Settings" (LETRINT). He has also translated for several organisations since 1997, including five years as an in-house translator at the World Trade Organization (dispute settlement team).

Miia Santalahti is a University Instructor and PhD student at the University of Tampere, Finland. She teaches translation and interpreting in the language pairs Russian-Finnish and English-Finnish, and is working on her doctoral dissertation on the topic "Language of treaties – language of power relations? Manifestations of power relations and impacts of translation activity in bilateral treaties between Finland and Russia/USSR and Finland and Sweden". She is also a seasoned translator specialised in marketing texts, contracts and official documents.

Juliette Scott is an independent researcher with 30 years' experience of providing legal linguistic services to law firms, institutions and companies of all dimensions. In particular, she works in the fields of international financial crime, complex corporate litigation and legislation. Her PhD thesis entitled *Legal Translation Outsourced* was published by Oxford University Press in autumn 2018. Her research draws from a range of intersecting disciplines such as corporate agency theory, functionalism, comparative law, genre theory, interdiscursivity, and the concept of fitness-for-purpose, to inform the various aspects of legal translators' textual agency and the constraints under which they operate. Scott has worked extensively towards legal translators' professionalisation and attempts to reinforce links between academia and practice.

Vilelmini Sosoni is Assistant Professor at the Ionian University, Greece. She teaches legal and economic translation as well as other branches of specialised translation. She has participated in a number of internationally and nationally funded research projects on legal translation and translation technology. Her research interests lie in the areas of legal and institutional translation, corpus linguistics, intercultural communication and translation technology. She has published widely on these topics, including articles in journals such as *Perspectives*, *JoSTrans*, *mTm*, *Journal of Language and Law*, etc. and in volumes by Routledge, John Benjamins, Springer, etc. She is a member of the editorial board of *JoSTrans* and *Intercultural and Intersemiotic Translation*. She has been a practising translator since 1997.

Anja Krogsgaard Vesterager, PhD is Research Assistant at the School of Communication and Culture, Aarhus University, Denmark, where she teaches translation of specialised texts between Danish and Spanish, among other things. Her main areas of research interests are the study of translation strategies in legal translation, explicitation and implicitation techniques in legal translation, the use of student peer feedback in translation training, and post-editing of Google translations as a learning tool in translation classes. Her current research focuses on the translation of judgments from Spanish into Danish. She has published articles in international journals and edited volumes.

Introduction to research methods in legal translation and interpreting

Crossing methodological boundaries

Łucja Biel, Jan Engberg, M. Rosario Martín Ruano, Vilelmini Sosoni

1 Recent developments in legal translation studies

There is no doubt that legal translation and interpreting is a strongly expanding field both as an area of practice and as an area of research. At the level of practice, the volumes of legal translated texts have increased exponentially at international organisations, in public services and the private sector in recent years. Legal translation is currently immersed in an ever-growing range of institutional, social and communicative situations with new and diverse needs, often also merging and overlapping with related activities like interpreting or other text-processing operations.

In parallel, at the level of research, studies on legal translation have not merely proliferated during the last three decades but have also increasingly widened their focus and scope and gradually problematised the object of study of what has emerged as a burgeoning field of inquiry. Indeed, Legal Translation, also known as Legal Translation and Interpreting (LTI) or Legal Translation Studies (LTS), has gradually gained autonomy and recognition as a distinctive area of Translation Studies (TS), even to the point of claiming to be a "discipline" or "interdiscipline" in its own right, committed to contributing to a better understanding of all aspects converging in this complex and multifaceted phenomenon, including its processes, products and agents (Prieto Ramos 2014, p. 261). Considering its phases of development, LTS – as argued by Prieto Ramos – currently experiences a phase of expansion and consolidation (2014, pp. 271–272).

Sharing both a growing awareness of the complexity of legal translation as a phenomenon and the goal to contribute to comprehensive explanations of its workings in different contexts, a growing number of authors have recently expressed the need to diversify, fine-tune and enrich existing theoretical models and research methods in the field both in order to get a better understanding of the role that legal translation plays in our contemporary world and in order to contribute to a more responsible and "reflexive" practice (Koskinen 2008, p. 152). Certainly, as an indication of the growing maturity of the field, research approaches to legal translation have diversified in recent years, paralleling the evolution seen in the general discipline of TS (cf. Saldanha and O'Brien 2013; Angelelli and Baer 2015; Mellinger and Hanson 2016; Sutter *et al.* 2017). In this regard, Cao (2013, p. 422) observes that "[t]he source text and the source language are not the only concern of translators and researchers". Linguistic and textual perspectives on legal translation have been enriched by research which has increasingly incorporated larger social, historical, ideological, political and ethical considerations. At the same time, qualitative research has progressively been informed and supplemented by empirical studies using quantitative methods, resulting in increased methodological rigour and eclectism (Biel and Engberg 2013, p. 1). The discipline has been gradually taking on board an ever-growing variety of quantitative, qualitative and mixed-methods approaches, including corpus-based, corpus-driven and corpus-assisted approaches, process research and experimental methods, workplace studies, practitioner research, critical discourse analysis (CDA), sociological and ethnographic studies, perspectives based on knowledge communication theories and post-structuralist and critical approaches applied to legal translation.

The significant growth in research and the diversification of research angles and perspectives has certainly contributed to broadening our understanding of this activity which has recently been defined as "a norm-governed human and social behaviour, a text producing act of legal communication" (Cao 2013, p. 422). In any event, as part of its development into an independent branch of TS, LTS needs a more substantiated discussion over methods and methodology, as well as knowledge about the variety of approaches actually applied in its field. Complex and multifaceted as it is, legal translation calls for further "methodological eclectism and triangulation, as well as further integration along the interdisciplinary lines" (Biel and Engberg 2013, p. 1), i.e., for research that might cross boundaries across research approaches and disciplines in order to shed light on the many facets of this social practice.

One important area which requires integration is the field of legal interpreting, in particular court interpreting, which has developed separately as part of Interpreting Studies. Much of the focus has been on norms, ethics, working conditions and training, with a solid grounding in empirical data (Berk-Seligson 1990; Hale 2004; Blasco Mayor and del Pozo Triviño 2015; Monteoliva-García 2018). What legal translation and legal interpreting have in common is the cross-systemic and cross-cultural mediation of legal discourse; nevertheless, they seem to be researched in two distinct parallel worlds. Interestingly, the internal boundary is more pronounced in research than in professional practice where court translators and interpreters have joint qualifications in a number of countries.

This edited volume precisely addresses the challenge of consolidation, triangulation and methodological refinement. The contributions to the volume both stand as examples of the variety of theoretical approaches which have been developed in the discipline and of the methodological sophistication which is currently being called for. Thus, the volume maps and explores a range of complex methodological approaches integrating diverse theories and viewpoints. By crossing boundaries between complementary approaches – for instance, between quantitative methods and qualitative analysis – and by linking linguistic and textual aspects to larger macrostructural and sociological factors on the one hand and to legal factors on the other hand, the chapters in the volume build complex methodological models which contribute to a better understanding of the phenomenon of legal translation and interpreting and of its implications, and which thus allow for critical reflection on the future of research and of the profession. Combining different perspectives, they enlarge our understanding of the role(s) played by legal translators and interpreters, who emerge as linguistic and intercultural mediators dealing with a high variety of legal texts; as knowledge communicators and as builders of specialised knowledge; as social agents performing a socially situated activity; as decision-makers and agents subject to and redefining power relations; and as political actors shaping (legal) cultures and negotiating cultural identities, as well as their own professional identity. In this regard, the volume makes the discipline of Legal Translation and Interpreting Studies move forward. By combining different research methods and perspectives, this collection both identifies and opens up new avenues for researching and practicing these multidimensional social activities departing from an enlarged, comprehensive vision of LTI.

2 Contributions to the volume

This volume consists of an introduction by the editors and 11 contributions which draw on different perspectives in order to present traditional methods and construct new, inspiring methodological models for research in legal translation and interpreting.

A concise description of the contributions to the volume makes it possible to perceive both the level of theoretical integration in the methodological approaches used and the broad scope of the findings presented. Departing from **corpus linguistics**, a number of contributions explore the possibilities of research on legal translation both for a more accurate description of the activity of legal translators and for a more effective and conscious praxis.

Quantitative methods are mainly represented by various applications of **corpora** which have gained significant popularity and productivity in LTS in the last decade and have contributed to a major methodological advancement in the field. The mainstream position of corpus methods is corroborated by the fact that nearly half of the chapters apply corpora, to a varied degree, to study some aspects of legal translation (see Pontrandolfo, Orozco-Jutorán, Prieto Ramos, Santalahti and Mikhailov, Giczela-Pastwa). Corpora are typically defined as large representative collections of texts in electronic form analysable with dedicated software (cf. McEnery *et al.* 2006, pp. 4–5). Their popularity has been triggered by the revival of interest in linguistics-related methods in TS combined with technological progress and improved functionalities of software which have allowed scholars to work with big data and test their hypotheses more systematically and objectively (Biel 2010). Following the emergence of corpus linguistics in the

1980s and the postulates to apply it to TS since the early 1990s (cf. Baker 1993), it was not until the late 2000s when we can observe a growing use of corpus methods in LTS (Biel 2018). The chapter by **Gianluca Pontrandolfo** entitled "Corpus Methods in Legal Translation Studies" is an excellent overview of how corpora are applied to explore legal translation and what is trending in such applications. Pontrandolfo synthesises various avenues of corpus research into a range of useful dichotomies, such as local versus global levels of analysis, qualitative (manual) versus quantitative (semi-automatic) analysis, corpus-based versus corpus-driven approaches, monolingual versus multilingual corpus data, comparable versus parallel corpus data and, finally, translated versus non-translated language. These dichotomies are not rigid, Pontrandolfo argues, and should be situated along the cline. The author illustrates the discussion with relevant research projects, showing how corpus methods can uncover diverse facets of legal translation by approaching it from mostly quantitatively oriented perspectives. These facets include formulaicity and various types of patterns in legal discourse, features of translated legal language, functional equivalents of terms and other types of units, translation techniques and strategies. In conclusion, Pontrandolfo highlights the need for methodological triangulation by an eclectic combination of various strands of corpus research and a combination of different methods, that is within-method and between-method triangulation, respectively (cf. Malamatidou 2017). The final section of Pontrandolfo's chapter contains a list of most popular concordancers, e.g. Wordsmith, Antconc, and Sketch Engine, which may be of use to novices to corpus methods.

A quintessential example of methodological triangulation can be found in **Fernando Prieto Ramos**'s chapter entitled "Implications of text categorisation for corpus-based legal translation research: the case of international institutional settings", which combines corpus methods with genre analysis. Prieto Ramos discusses theoretical and methodological aspects of legal text categorisation in relation to translation practice in three international institutions (the European Union, the United Nations, the World Trade Organisation). He demonstrates how the corpus compilation phase made it necessary, first, to identify institutional genres among a mass of corpus files and, secondly, to group them into higher-level functional categories representing the common ground among the institutions. Based on actual text production practices, the adjusted categorisation matrix was structured around the following categories: (1) law-making and policy-making, (2) implementation and compliance monitoring, (3) adjudication, and (4) administrative functions. The functional categories were further divided into key and secondary genres to better contextualise each genre and its position in the system of genres. This internal organisation of a large corpus into an elaborate constellation of genres has profound methodological implications for further phases of corpus creation and enables a better calibration of the corpus in terms of representativeness, balance and stratified sampling. Overall, Prieto Ramos's chapter foregrounds the importance of careful and rigorous corpus design to guard against biases and to ensure the validity of empirical data and subsequent generalisations. By situating genres within the institutional system of genres, Prieto Ramos also shows how corpus methods can improve our understanding of the context of translation production, one of Saldanha and O'Brien's key dimensions of translation (2013, p. 205).

The next chapter by **Justyna Giczela-Pastwa,** "Inverse legal translation: a corpus-driven study of multi-word units related to the structure of translated statutory provisions", shifts the perspective from the macrostructure to the microstructure. Giczela-Pastwa tests the applicability of corpus-driven methods to studying inverse legal translation, that is translation rendered by non-native speakers into their non-mother tongues. Despite being a common market practice in many countries, inverse translation has hardly been studied, in particular with regard to legal translation. For this purpose, Giczela-Pastwa triangulates data gathering by combining comparable and parallel corpora of Polish legislation translated inversely by three major publishing houses, as well as a reference corpus of non-translated English statutes. This complex corpus architecture has been designed, first, to identify differences between inversely translated and non-translated legislation (contrasting the comparable corpus and the reference corpus) and, second, to explain such differences by detecting through the parallel corpus which source language patterns trigger them. Giczela-Pastwa explores selected multi-word units connected with the structure of statutory content, which were identified through shared keywords strongly overrepresented in translations. By closely reading concordances, she analyses collocational patterns of keywords through the lens of the "untypical collocation hypothesis" (cf. Mauranen 2007). The study confirms that legal translations develop their own distinctive phraseological patterns triggered mainly by source language interference. On the other hand, legal translations show a considerable degree of resemblance between them, which supports the levelling-out hypothesis (cf. Baker 1993). This method offers some pedagogical potential by pinpointing patterns which are distorted or overused in legal translation by non-native speakers of English. Such findings may contribute to increasing the functionality of not-so-infrequent inverse translation.

Whereas Giczela-Pastwa pays attention to the consequences of the magnetising effect of the source language in translated texts in terms of natural and fluent language use, **Miia Santalahti and Mikhail Mikhailov** ("Language of treaties – language of power relations?") use corpus-based analysis in order to determine to what extent the presence of uncommon elements in a given language may be indicative of other extralinguistic factors, for instance of power relations which might be reflected and negotiated or updated in certain texts. In this regard, as part of a broader research project relying on the PEST corpus, a collection of aligned bitexts consisting of bilateral treaties signed between Finland and Russia/ Soviet Union and between Finland and Sweden, as well as a number of treaties between Sweden and Russia and international treaties used as a control corpus, the authors analyse in depth the treaties concluded between Finland and Russia/ USSR from 1945 to 1991 in order to explore the correlation of linguistic features (e.g., unusual words and expressions, elements of polarised narratives, etc.) and the political circumstances under which the signatory countries interacted.

In this regard, in addition to determining that the Soviet party had a leading role in the texts studied, in more general terms, the article clearly shows the potential of methodological synergies for the investigation of legal translation. In this particular case, quantitative methods (multidimensional and collostructional analysis, statistical scrutiny) are combined with the qualitative analysis of discursive, semantic and conceptual features in such a way that associations may be established between linguistic behaviour and larger issues involving relations of power and authority. Complex research designs enable the further discovery of legal translation as a social practice (Monzó Nebot 2015; Way 2016, p. 1018) influenced by larger contextual factors, and replete with ideological implications and ethical challenges.

Inspired by a similar goal, other contributions to this volume which also integrate theories and methodologies and which draw more clearly on **qualitative analysis** show further interconnections between linguistic performance and extratextual factors. Based on an experiment analysing the performance of experts and non-experts, **Anja Krogsgaard Vesterager** highlights the importance of the background of individual translators in legal translations as actual products in an article which links the use of explicitation techniques to the degree of expertise of practitioners. The article reports on a study based upon an experiment, in which five expert translators and five non-experts translated a Spanish legal source text into Danish. All of the translators were professionals. Expertise was set to be equivalent with more than 10 years of professional practice, combined with a specialisation in legal translation. The central method applied was contrastive text analysis, assessing on a qualitative basis whether strategies of explicitation may be found in the target text. The results were filtered in order to exclude such explicitations that were due to contrastive linguistic differences between Spanish and Danish at the system level. The qualitative analytical step is followed by a quantification step in order to find out whether links may be established between expertise in the sense investigated here and applying strategies of explicitation. The tendency is that a link may be established: experts use considerably more explicitations. However, the results indicate that two translators without specialisation in legal translation, but with long professional experience, perform almost as many explicitations as experts. Hence, the choice of explicitation may be more related to general long-term experience.

Whereas Krogsgaard Vesterager's contribution emphasises the individual in legal translation as an act of knowledge communication, a fact that has been highlighted by post-structuralist approaches (Engberg 2016), complex research architectures can also help underscore another dimension of legal translation and interpreting – their embeddedness in institutional settings where all participants, including translators and interpreters, occupy and constantly negotiate their particular positions vis-à-vis other agents. Close examination reveals that these positions are conditioned by prevailing expectations and power relations which, nevertheless, may in turn be redefined in context. In this regard, by combining the analysis of a case study from the point of view of critical discourse analysis with interviews, **Karolina Nartowska** reflects on the influence that the subject positions adopted by legal interpreters in the courtroom might exert on the power relations established during the triadic exchange. The contrast between the views on the interpreter's role as declared by the agents taking part in the interaction and the actual performance of the interpreter in the courtroom exposes clear divergences between foreseeable conduct and authentic practice. What is more, the fact that, in the case study analysed, the deviations both from these preconceptions and from professional standards do not meet the opposition of other co-agents contribute to a more nuanced understanding of legal translation and interpreting as activities in which power plays a very important role, both as a coercive force shaping behaviour and as agency to be executed and realised by practitioners in context, in line with what has been underlined by the so-called "power turn" in Translation Studies (Gentzler and Tymoczko 2002; Strowe 2013; Vidal Claramonte 2018).

All these contributions certainly show how systematic research on legal translation allows for improvement by shedding light both on the problems that practitioners face and on the challenges that lie ahead both for the profession and for research. In addition to identifying new avenues for research on legal translation and interpreting, the conclusions of these case studies certainly foster a more effective and conscious praxis, as well as a much-needed debate on the potentialities and limits of professional standards and ethics.

With the clear purpose of improving legal translation practice and research models, some articles draw on relevant disciplines in order to build a more solid interdisciplinary basis which might inform translators' decisions and researchers' conclusions. In this regard, **Sylvie Monjean-Decaudin** and **Joëlle Popineau-Lauvray** explore how Comparative Law might be integrated in a systematic methodological approach to legal texts taking into account the juridical cultures involved. In their chapter, they introduce a specific French variant of Legal Translation Studies called Juritraductology (*Juritraductologie*), developed with a special view to the context of legal studies. It draws specifically upon perspectives of translation rooted in views of law in general and comparative law in particular. On this basis, the authors establish four translational contexts of specific interest for the approach (international public law, international private law, judicial contexts, and scientific contexts). Furthermore, a scale for measuring the level of legal complexity (*degré de juridicité*) is established, based on the criteria of how much legal knowledge is necessary in order to understand and translate concepts and on the force of the legal consequences of the text. Within this framework, the authors suggest a three-step methodology based upon Comparative Law to guide legal translators to be systematic in their quest for translation equivalents. The methodology consists of three steps: (1) a semasiological step, in which the details of the source concept are established; (2) a comparative-law step, in which potential renderings in the target culture are scrutinised in order to establish overlaps and differences between concepts; and (3) an ontological step, in which the translator decides on which term to choose for translation in the respective situations on linguistic and legal grounds.

Carmen Bestué also demonstrates the relevance of the applicability of Comparative Law as a solid foundation for legal translation and court interpreting. In a contribution which stresses the importance of integrating a systematic methodological approach to terms and concepts in a decision-making process which is subject to differing acceptability expectations depending on context, Bestué emphasises both the need to strive for quality and conceptual rigour in legal translation and interpreting and the "intervening" role of translators and interpreters, a point that has also been made in research drawing on sociological and post-structuralist approaches to legal translation (Monzó 2005; Monzó Nebot 2015; Way 2016; Vidal Claramonte 2005; Martín Ruano 2014, 2015) and which can also be seen to be linked to specific calls for an integrative, multi-perspectivist approach to translation-relevant comparisons of legal concepts (Engberg 2017). In this regard, Bestué argues that in-depth research applying comparative law principles needs to be coupled with critical attention to the communicative purpose of the TT and to additional factors including diatopic variation, legal field and applicable law. All these aspects prove to be decisive for the selection of adequate and acceptable translation strategies, which need to be attuned to contexts. In an attempt to provide tools to deal with legal terms that, as Bestué underlines, are not static, the author proposes the "translation-oriented terminological entry" as a model in which to integrate comparative analysis of legal terms and actual translation solutions in order to facilitate the decision-making of legal translators and interpreters. Certainly, any measure for improvement needs to depart from a clear image of the actual reality of the profession and the profile of practitioners. The entry, indeed, has been developed in the framework of two research projects (Law10n and TIPp) presented in the article which precisely depart from a descriptive analysis of existing practices in particular contexts as a stepping stone to the proposal of methodological tools that may assist legal translators and interpreters in adopting translation choices in different scenarios.

The chapter entitled "A mixed-methods approach in Corpus-Based Interpreting Studies: quality of interpreting in criminal proceedings in Spain" by **Mariana Orozco-Jutorán** also reports on the methodological aspects of the TIPp project attempting to operationalise and measure the quality of legal interpreting during criminal trials. The project used an eclectic mix of quantitative and qualitative methods, starting with a compilation of a corpus of transcribed video-recorded criminal proceedings involving interpreters in three language combinations. Although corpus methods have become mainstream in legal translation research, they are seldom applied to study interpreting, where sociological approaches seem to be dominant. One of the key reasons for this status quo is the time-consuming and tedious nature of transcribing interpreting; yet Orozco-Jutorán's ambitious project proves it is feasible and demonstrates how corpus methods may be adjusted for interpreting purposes. Adopting Wadensjö's (1998) dialogic approach to interpreting as "talk as activity" (in addition to "talk as text"), Orozco-Jutorán introduces two dependent variables: text-related problems and interaction-related problems, and assigns quantifiable indicators to them. The interpreting corpus was annotated manually for solutions adopted by interpreters when facing these two groups of problems and next analysed quantitatively. What is worth stressing is the collection of corpus data in three language combinations which show a different intensity of problems and allow for more valid generalisations. The project brings some alarming empirical findings on the low quality of court interpreting, in particular as regards non-renditions and meaning distortions, which ultimately might adversely affect defendants' right of information safeguarded under Directive 2012/13/EU.

In the last two contributions, the emphasis turns to surveys and interviews as tools for conducting research and gathering empirical data in LTS. In particular, in her chapter entitled "An online survey as a means to research the 'outstitutional' legal translation market", **Juliette Scott** reports on a survey consisting of online questionnaires to collect both quantitative and qualitative data regarding the commissioning and performance of legal translation that is being carried out outside institutions. Scott triangulates input from those outsourcing, i.e. in the case at hand mostly lawyers, and those to whom work is outsourced, i.e. legal translators, in order to investigate the area of outsourced legal translation in a comprehensive way. Yet, she does not report on the findings of the study (see Scott 2016 for a detailed discussion of the survey results); instead, she focuses on the use of online questionnaires for the collection and extraction of data. After providing a list of surveys from the past 20 years, she turns her attention to the strengths of online questionnaires, i.e. the fact that they allow data subjects to engage with the questions at their leisure, to retain their anonymity and to participate remotely, as well as the fact that they allow a quick turnaround for data collection and a more streamlined data analysis. More importantly, the author goes on to address the challenges which emerge when researching corporate and legal communication through online questionnaires, ethical as well as epistemological, i.e. accessing respondents, deciding on the nature and order of questions, selecting the online platform (e.g. SurveyMonkey.com, Wufoo), using data analysis sofware (e.g. NVivo, Dedoose), piloting and coding, and analysing the responses. The author's own study reveals that online questionnaires allow researchers to access a wide audience, both geographically and in terms of respondent profiles, and to gain insights into a wide range of language pairs, genres, jurisdictions and areas of law.

Esther Monzó-Nebot's contribution, based on the sociology of the professions, starts with a review of the sociological approaches to Translation and Interpreting (TIS) and to legal TIS which aim to describe and explain how translators and interpreters individually and collectively construct and interact with social structures and are characterised by a broad scope (e.g. focus on interactions, attitudes and perceptions, power construction, ideological conflicts, etc.). She then analyses a research study that aims at defining the factors impacting translators' and interpreters' interactional and structural power through the use of in-depth interviews conducted among translators working for international organisations and court interpreters. The study is part of a wider project on legal interpreters' and translators' *habiti*, where they are interviewed about their socialisations, relations to others in professional settings, their subjective well-being and their perceptions on different issues related to their translation-related *doxas* and *illusios*

(Bourdieu 1972). Two data analysis techniques are used, i.e. content analysis (Berelson 1971; Neuendorf 2002; Krippendorff 2013; Mayring 2014) and narrative analysis (Mishler 1995), and the findings of the study suggest that, by framing themselves as high-status or low-status translators, the subjects created a projected social reality which they enacted in interaction. They also reveal differences both in the perception and in the enactment of status, prestige and power. More importantly, the study affirms that in-depth interviews can be of particular importance to legal TIS as they enable insights into a complex network of interactions that resists simplification. The conclusions of both these studies which cross boundaries among theoretical approaches to build complex methodological models certainly provide a solid foundation on which to base new research initiatives, as well as to promote new professional attitudes, discourses and praxis.

All the contributions to this volume show that legal translation and interpreting are certainly very complex and challenging tasks in which many factors are involved and need to be taken into account, and, which, for the same reason, thus require the construction of similarly complex and challenging models. Making advances in the directions outlined in a special issue on *Research Models and Methods in Legal Translation* edited by Biel and Engberg (2013), this volume discusses methodological issues in researching legal translation and interpreting, overviewing varied methods and approaches and ways to triangulate them, with the goal of contributing to mapping and stimulating new models which cross and move theoretical and disciplinary boundaries in order to better grasp the many-sidedness of legal translation and interpreting as social activities; and models which, hopefully, might also help researchers and practitioners to continue crossing and moving boundaries, either by engaging in further research aiming at identifying the challenges that lie ahead for legal translation and interpreting and attempting to provide answers to its requirements, either by taking informed decisions in their daily practice, perhaps inspired by the findings of studies conducted with ever more complex research models.

LTI is an expanding area of interest, with an increasing community of researchers and expert practitioners interested in the progress of the discipline. With its focus on research methods and its commitment to crossing boundaries with the aim of shedding light on the workings of legal translation and interpreting as complex social activities influenced by a myriad of textual, contextual and sociopolitical factors, we hope the volume is of special interest to researchers on legal translation and interpreting, to practicing legal translators and interpreters, and to translation and interpreting trainers.

References

Angelelli, C.V. and Baer, B.J., eds. (2015). *Researching translation and interpreting.* London: Routledge.

Baker, M. (1993). Corpus linguistics and translation studies – implications and applications. *In*: M. Baker, *et al.*, eds. *Text and technology: In honour of John Sinclair.* Amsterdam: John Benjamins, pp. 233–250.

Berelson, B. (1971). *Content analysis in communication research*. New York: Glencoe.

Berk-Seligson, S. (1990). *The bilingual courtroom: Court interpreters in the judicial process*. Chicago: University of Chicago Press.

Biel, Ł. (2010). Corpus-based studies of legal language for translation purposes: methodological and practical potential [online]. *In*: C. Heine and J. Engberg, eds. *Reconceptualising LSP. Online proceedings of the XVII European LSP symposium 2009*. Available at: www.asb.dk/fileadmin/www.asb.dk/isek/biel.pdf [Accessed 29 Aug. 2018].

Biel, Ł. (2018). Corpora in institutional legal translation: Small steps and the big picture. *In*: F. Prieto Ramos, ed. *Institutional translation for international governance. Enhancing quality in multilingual legal communication*. London: Bloomsbury, pp. 25–36.

Biel, Ł. and Engberg, J. (2013). Research models and methods in legal translation. *Linguistica Antverpiensia. New Series – Themes in Translation Studies*, 12, pp. 1–11.

Blasco Mayor, M.J. and del Pozo Triviño, M., eds. (2015). Legal interpreting and a turning point/La interpretación en el ámbito judicial en un momento de cambio. *MonTI*, 28.

Bourdieu, P. (1972). *Esquisse d'une théorie de la pratique, précédée de trois études d'ethnographie kabyle*. Geneva: Librairie Droz.

Cao, D. (2013). Legal translation studies. *In*: C. Millán-Varela and F. Bartrina, eds. *The Routledge handbook of translation studies*. London: Routledge, pp. 415–424.

Engberg, J. (2016). Emphasising the individual in legal translation: Consequences of knowledge communication and post-structuralist approaches. *In*: G. Garzone, *et al.*, eds. *Language for specific purposes. Research and translation across cultures and media*. Newcastle upon Tyne: Cambridge Scholars Publishing, pp. 41–61.

Engberg, J. (2017). Developing an integrative approach for accessing comparative legal knowledge for translation. *Revista de Llengua i Dret/Journal of Language and Law*, 68, pp. 5–18.

Gentzler, E. and Tymoczko, M. (2002). Introduction. *In:* E. Gentzler and M. Tymoczko, eds. *Translation and power*. Amherst: University of Massachussetts Press, xi–xxviii.

Hale, S.B. (2004). *The discourse of court interpreting: Discourse practices of the law, the witness, and the interpreter*. Amsterdam: John Benjamins.

Koskinen, K. (2008). *Translating institutions: An ethnographic study of EU translation*. Manchester: St. Jerome Publishing.

Krippendorff, K. (2013). *Content analysis. An introduction to its methodology*. Los Angeles: Sage.

Malamatidou, S. (2017). *Corpus triangulation. Combining data and methods in corpus-based translation studies*. London: Routledge.

Martín Ruano, M.R. (2014). From suspicion to collaboration: Defining new epistemologies of reflexive practice for legal translation and interpreting. *The Journal of Specialised Translation*, 22, pp. 1–20.

Martín Ruano, M.R. (2015). (Trans)formative theorising in legal translation and/or interpreting: A critical approach to deontological principles. *The Interpreter and Translator Trainer*, 9 (1) (special issue: *Training legal translators and interpreters: Theory, research and practice*, edited by E. Monzó), pp. 141–155.

Mauranen, A. (2007). Universal tendencies in translation. *In:* G. Anderman and M. Rogers, eds. *Incorporating corpora. The linguist and the translator*. Clevedon: Multilingual Matters, pp. 32–48.

Mayring, P. (2014). *Qualitative content analysis. Theoretical foundation, basic procedures and software solution.* Klagenfurt. Available at: http://nbn-resolving.de/urn:nbn:de:0168-ssoar-395173 [Accessed 10 Oct. 2018].

McEnery, T., Xiao, R. and Tono, Y. (2006). *Corpus-based language studies. An advanced resource book.* London: Routledge.

Mellinger, C.D. and Hanson, T.A. (2016). *Quantitative research methods in translation and interpreting studies.* London: Routledge.

Mishler, E.G. (1995). Models of narrative analysis: A typology. *Journal of Narrative and Life History*, 5, pp. 87–123.

Monteoliva García, E. (2018). The last ten years of legal interpreting research. *Language and Law/Linguagem e Direito*, 5 (1), pp. 38–61.

Monzó Nebot, E. (2005). Being ACTIVE in legal translation and interpreting: Researching and acting on the Spanish field. *Meta: Translators' Journal*, 50 (4), doi:10.7202/019922ar.

Monzó Nebot, E. (2015). Understanding legal interpreter and translator training in times of change. *The Interpreter and Translator Trainer*, 9 (2), pp. 129–140.

Neuendorf, K. (2002). *The content analysis guidebook.* Thousand Oaks: Sage.

Prieto Ramos, F. (2014). Legal Translation Studies as interdiscipline: Scope and evolution. *Meta: Translators' Journal*, 59 (2), pp. 260–277, doi:10.7202/1027475ar.

Saldanha, G. and O'Brien, S. (2013). *Research methodologies in translation studies.* London: Routledge.

Scott, J.R. (2016). *Optimising the performance of outsourced legal translation.* Thesis (PhD). Bristol: University of Bristol. [publication Oxford University Press Oct. 2018 as *Legal Translation Outsourced*].

Strowe, A. (2013). Power and translation. *In*: Y. Gambier and L. van Doorslaer, eds. *Handbook of translation studies*, Vol. 4. Amsterdam: John Benjamins, pp. 134–141.

Sutter, G. de, *et al.*, eds. (2017). *Empirical translation studies: New methodological and theoretical traditions.* Berlin: de Gruyter Mouton.

Vidal Claramonte, M.C.Á. (2005). Re-presenting the "real": Pierre Bourdieu and legal translation. *The Translator*, 11 (2), pp. 259–275.

Vidal Claramonte, M.C.Á. (2018). Power. *In*: O. Carbonell and S-A. Harding, eds. *The Routledge handbook of translation and culture.* London: Routledge, pp. 79–96.

Wadensjö, C. (1998). *Interpreting as interaction.* New York: Longman.

Way, C. (2016). The challenges and opportunities of legal translation and translator training in the 21st century. *International Journal of Communication*, 10, pp. 1009–1029.

1 Corpus methods in legal translation studies

Gianluca Pontrandolfo

1 The perspective: key concepts

The present chapter[1] aims at studying the interaction among three conceptual areas: corpora, methods and Legal Translation Studies. More specifically, it aims at highlighting the contribution of corpus linguistics to research methods in legal translation (Biel and Engberg 2013) within the empirical and 'technological turn' (Cronin 2010) in Translation Studies and in line with the subfield which has been recently defined as 'Computer-Assisted Legal Linguistics' (CAL^2) (Vogel *et al.* 2017).

Before delving into the analysis, some preliminary definitions of the key concepts underpinning the investigation are necessary. Firstly, within the branch of corpus linguistics, a **corpus** is "a collection of texts in electronic format which are processed and analysed using software specifically created for linguistic research" (Zanettin 2012, p. 7). Irrespective of its typology – monolingual or multilingual, comparable or parallel, etc. (see Zanettin 2012, pp. 10–11 for a classification applied to Translation Studies) – the common feature of a legal corpus is its "textual territory" (Prieto Ramos 2014a, p. 264), i.e. the specialised nature of its texts (see section 2). Indeed, legal corpora focus on aspects related to the macro-area of law governing public or private legal relationships, applying legal instruments in specific scenarios, conveying specialised knowledge on sources of law and legal relationships (Prieto Ramos 2014a, pp. 264–265). Secondly, a **method** is understood here as a systematic procedure, technique, or mode of inquiry employed by or proper to a particular discipline or art. Corpus linguistics, which may be conceived as a strongly empirical methodology in itself, allows for an application of various kinds of methods that focus on specific aspects of legal language or translation (see section 3). Finally, **Legal Translation Studies** (LTS) is conceived as an interdisciplinary field that focuses on all the factors involved in the translation of legal texts, e.g. processes, products, agents, texts (Prieto Ramos 2014a, p. 261).

The objective of this chapter is to analyse the ways legal corpora have been used so far and can be used in the future to study legal translation. The angle of analysis is the research method, in line with the overall goal of this volume. The chapter will problematise and exemplify some of the most important methodological issues underlying the use of corpora in LTS. It will also review major trends of research using legal corpora. The focus will be placed specifically on studies on legal translation, rather than on legal language (e.g. Goźdź-Roszkowski 2011) or translator training (e.g. Monzó Nebot 2008), even though corpora are suitable for linguistic and training purposes as well. The pros and cons of respective methods and some examples of empirical applications will also be presented.

From a methodological point of view, it is worth underlying that the chapter is conceived as an overview of methods (various corpus approaches to legal translation) rather than an overview of the existing studies (literature review) on corpus and legal translation, which would go beyond the scope of this contribution. In fact, it would be difficult to carry out a comprehensive and up-to-date review of all corpus methods that have been and are being applied to study legal translation due to the increasing popularity they have enjoyed so far (Biel 2018a, pp. 27–28).

2 The substance: legal corpora

Attempts at classifying legal corpora may be found in the literature (see Pontrandolfo 2012; Marín Pérez and Rea Rizzo 2012; Vogel *et al.* 2017; Biel 2018a). The picture shows that legal corpora are increasingly growing and are used in LTS, although not all legal corpora have been explored for translation purposes.

As far as the "textual territory" is concerned, the notion of 'legal texts' has been widely and diversely applied in LTS. Texts pertaining to the legal sphere have been generally categorised according to different criteria, such as a nature, function or dominant text types. One of the common classifications adopted for translation purposes considers three types of texts: normative (e.g. legislative texts), interpretative (legal scholarly writings) and applied (private, administrative, judicial texts) ones (among the various classifications, see Mortara Garavelli 2001, pp. 25–34; Borja Albi 2007, p. 161; Šarčević 1997, pp. 11–12 based on Bocquet 1994, p. 2; Cao 2007, pp. 9–10; Prieto Ramos 2014a, p. 265 and Prieto Ramos, this volume).

Legal corpora may incorporate any type of these genres, but, on the practical side, LTS scholars usually face a key methodological problem, which is the question of availability and accessibility of legal texts. As pointed out by Vigier and Sánchez Ramos, despite the widespread use in other fields within Translation Studies, the development of corpora has been rather slower in the field of Legal Translation, probably due to the confidential and private nature of many legal documents (2017, p. 261). This is what Biel calls "legicentrism", which is the tendency of existing corpora to be mainly composed of legislation (2018a, p. 29), which results in an underrepresentation of other genres.

The reality is that the majority of legal corpora are institutional ones[2] (see Biel 2018a, pp. 19–33): collections of texts produced, for example, at the EU, UN, or WTO,[3] such as legislative or judicial texts available in many languages, often because they are supranational official versions of the same legal instrument, collected mainly with the purpose of training machine translation systems.

Moreover, as pointed out by Vogel *et al.* (2017, p. 12), most corpora are compiled in the context of a specific research project[4] to serve its research questions and are thus rather small and not always publicly available.

3 The avenues: corpus methods in descriptive legal translation studies

Analysing corpus methods in LTS means exploring the different paths chosen by scholars to approach translation. Corpora are obviously just one of the methodologies allowing for the study of legal translation, the others being, for example, genre analysis (Bhatia 1997), discourse analysis (Pontrandolfo 2019, forthcoming), comparative law (Engberg 2013), sociology of profession (Koskinen 2000; Lambert 2009), and functionalism (Garzone 2000) (see the Editors' Introduction to this volume).

There are several advantages of using corpus methods in LTS. Firstly, scholars who adopt data-driven approaches have an increased methodological awareness and rigour; secondly, empirical methodologies allow for a significant shift from a prescriptive to a descriptive view on legal translation: describing "what translations actually are, rather than simply prescribing how they should be" (Pym 2014, p. 63) proves to be a key perspective in Legal Translation Studies and practice. Finally, corpus methodologies allow for methodological eclecticism (i.e. the possibility to triangulate different methods) and reduced speculation, as well as offer the potential to verify hypotheses more systematically (Biel and Engberg 2013, p. 5).

In the following sections, corpus methods in legal translation research will be analysed through the lens of typical methodological dichotomies. These methodological oppositions are a means of providing a clear picture of the trends in action in legal translation studies based on corpora, since, as it will be seen, many of them can be combined and adopted simultaneously in a single study.

3.1 Local versus global

One of the first dichotomies is the local versus global opposition. As a matter of fact, legal corpora can be used to study microstructural linguistic phenomena (local), such as terms, phrasemes, syntactic patterns, discourse markers, pragmatic features, cohesive devices, etc., or macrostructural phenomena (global), that is aspects related to, say, the genre of legal texts, such as rhetorical moves, performative macro-utterances producing legal effects, stylistic features, etc. (see Pontrandolfo 2019, forthcoming).

From a legal translation point of view, this opposition needs to be taken into consideration when choosing a method of analysis. Emphasis is often put on microstructural traits rather than on global characteristics of legal texts, which is the reason why analysing genre-related features in LTS may be problematic. The opposite situation may occur when the risk is missing the trees (single texts or local features) for the forest (the collection of texts or the global traits) (Egbert and Schnur 2018).

3.2 Quality versus quantity

One of the key debates around corpus linguistics relates to the quality versus quantity dichotomy. The quantitative dimension focuses on the importance of empirical data in confirming or rejecting hypotheses on legal translation, whereas qualitative approaches tend to privilege the centrality of discursive examples rather than (co)occurrences.

This dichotomy can also be associated with the manual versus (semi-)automatic opposition in corpus studies in that quality research seems to rely on the manual reading of legal texts whereas quantitative research tends to explore data semi-automatically with the help of a wide range of software for the analysis of linguistic data (AntConc, ParaConc, WordSmith Tools, Sketch Engine, etc.).

Corpus research is sometimes criticised due to the difficulties scholars may experience when studying more qualitative aspects of legal translation, thus limiting the results to the product rather than giving insights into the process. Indeed, quantitative results may often excessively rely on the 'pattern' rather than on the 'text as a whole' (see Egbert and Schnur 2018, pp. 159–161). This is particularly important in the legal field and in legal translation where the complexity of texts requires a macroanalysis of its context of production.

As it will be demonstrated in the next sections, the recent trend in LTS is to combine the quality and quantity dimensions in corpus methods, triangulating research methods and thus looking at the data from different perspectives.

3.3 Corpus-based versus corpus-driven

The distinction between a corpus-based and corpus-driven language study was introduced by Tognini-Bonelli (2001). Corpus-based studies typically use corpus data in order to explore a theory or hypothesis, aiming to validate, refute or refine it. Thus, they privilege an inferential approach to the analysis of data. Corpus-driven approaches are based on the idea that the corpus itself should be the sole source of our hypotheses about language (they tend to adopt an exploratory perspective on empirical data) (2001, pp. 65, 84–85). Although critical voices were raised after the distinction was established (see, for example, McEnery *et al.* (2006, p. 8), who consider the distinction overstated), keeping the dichotomy is useful from a methodological point of view since most of the studies inevitably combine the two approaches.

In respect of legal translation, this dichotomy proves to be an important parameter to consider when choosing the method. Corpus-based studies are particularly effective when investigating features of legal language in translation since its traits have been clearly identified in the literature (e.g. nominalisations, passive voices, lexical doublets and triplets) and can be used by researchers to test their presence in the texts with empirical data. Corpus-driven research is effective when there are no previous pre-construed ideas or expected results from the corpus analysis. Obviously, there are no pure corpus-based or -driven studies: a combination of both methods proves to be a feasible and productive perspective in LTS.

3.4 *Monolingual versus multilingual*

The monolingual versus multilingual dichotomy lies at the heart of all the oppositions mentioned in this section. As suggested by McEnery and Hardie, many corpora are monolingual in the sense that, while they may represent a range of varieties and genres of a particular language, they are nonetheless limited to that one language (2012, p. 18). Bilingual and multilingual corpora can use different criteria as well, such as the number of languages involved and the content or form of the corpus (2012, p. 19).

Monolingual corpora, which are frequently used in legal language studies to draw comparisons among legal genres (see, among others, Goźdź-Roszkowski 2011; Breeze 2013), are almost exclusively used in LTS to study regularities of translated language. An example would be exploring the differences between original versus translated legal texts (see section 3.6). Multilingual corpora are instead of great help when studying the translation product across languages (e.g. how a legal text is translated into a different language).

This dichotomy is closely related to the following ones: comparable versus parallel (section 3.5) and translated versus non-translated (section 3.6).

3.5 *Comparable versus parallel*

The comparable versus parallel dichotomy may be framed within contrastive linguistics. As Zanettin puts it, "contrastive descriptions are important to translation studies in that they provide the touchstone for assessing the extent to which typical features of translated texts and behavioural patterns of translators are determined by the source language" (2012, p. 25).

Comparable corpora can be defined as collections of original texts in more than one language or variety (the similarity may lie in the genre, proportion of text, domain, sampling period, etc.). Parallel corpora are instead collections of source texts and their translations into one or more languages.

If comparable corpora are generally the basis of translation-oriented studies aimed at searching for 'parallel routines' (functional equivalents) in original texts, parallel corpora are usually used to explore how a specific linguistic feature (term, verb, phraseologism, etc.) of legal language A is translated into legal language B (see also Johansson 2007; Zanettin 2012, pp. 181–182; McEnery and Hardie 2012, p. 20).

Scholars working with comparable corpora of legal texts usually use texts originally written in languages A and B (although a consistent number of studies are being conducted with comparable corpora of translated and non-translated language A, see section 3.6). Comparable corpora provide the opportunity to investigate a variety of linguistic and discursive features, from terminology and phraseology, to pragmatic and textual elements, thus allowing researchers to delve into the regularities of languages.

An application of comparable corpora for lexicographic or terminographic purposes is the JuriGenT termbase (Vanden Bulcke and de Groote 2016), which relies on a bilingual corpus of original Dutch and Spanish developed to study the national terminology used in Belgium and Spain (2016, p. 17) in corporate law. The cross-linguistic methodological approach used to compile around 1,300 terminographic records consists in the analysis of non-translated texts in each legal culture and the proposal of translation equivalents, among other important fields included in the entry (hyponyms, synonyms, phraseology, etc.).

Comparable corpora may also be used to extract legal phraseology, as in the case of the work carried out by Pontrandolfo (2016). Based on a trilingual – Spanish, Italian, English – corpus (around 6 million words) of criminal judgments (COSPE), the author semi-automatically extracted a significant number of phraseological units, ranging from lexical doublets and triplets to complex prepositions, lexical collocations and routine formulae. As far as the method of extracting legal phraseologisms is concerned, it derived from a mixed approach, that is to say, the combination of corpus-based and corpus-driven methods (section 3.3), bottom-up and top-down analyses. As a way of example, complex prepositions were selected in the English unannotated subcorpus semi-automatically by searching for patterns like 'in + * + with' (e.g. *in accordance with, in compliance with, in agreement with, in accordance with*), which proved to be a very efficient method to detect the most relevant patterns. Similarly, doublets and triplets were found by searching for patterns like '* + or + *', '* + and + *' (e.g. *noble and learned, nature and extent*). Lexical collocations were found by studying the environment of some terms playing a pivotal role in criminal judgments of appeal (therefore adopting a more qualitative and 'manual' approach, see section 3.2), whereas routine formulae were detected almost automatically using ConcGram (2016, pp. 86–98). More specifically, due to the nature of these stereotyped formulae, a cutoff frequency and dispersion threshold of five hits in five different judgments was established. The focus was on formulae that constituted entire sentences. Concgrams were automatically extracted by the program, e.g. *For these reasons, I would allow the appeal and quash the appellant's conviction on* . . . or *I agree that the appeal should be allowed* (Pontrandolfo 2016, p. 144).

The idea behind the study is that it is possible to search for functional equivalents without working with translated texts: by looking at the context and function of each phraseologism in the three legal and judicial cultures, translators may discover similar patterns. Therefore, comparable corpora are key tools to comply with 'generic integrity' (Bhatia 1997, pp. 360–362) and conventionalism in legal genres since they allow to search – cross-linguistically – for 'parallel' expressions.

Research into the regularities of languages through translation can be carried out by means of parallel corpora of legal texts, which represent a key source to explore how a specific linguistic element has been translated from language A into language B. The lack of parallel corpora of legal texts produced outside the institutional contexts represents a methodological problem. This is the reason why scholars usually resort to collections of texts produced at a supranational level (the EU, the UN, etc.).

In her PhD thesis, Seracini (2017) investigated the recurrent translation patterns in EU laws translated from English into Italian with a specific focus on expressions of modality. For the purposes of the study, she compiled a bilingual parallel corpus of EU law in English and in Italian and two reference corpora of British and Italian national laws, respectively. The corpus gave her quantitative and qualitative insights which show an oscillation between various tendencies, namely translators' tendency to reproduce patterns of source texts in translations, tendency to comply with target culture conventions and tendency to introduce changes that improve the readability and clarity of translations.

Another example of how parallel corpora may be used to investigate translations is the study by Vigier and Sánchez Ramos (2017). With a view to analysing how the names of some English and Spanish courts[5] were translated in EU texts, they compiled a parallel bilingual corpus (made of two subcorpora, one referring to English courts and the other to Spanish ones) of judgments delivered by the Court of Justice of the European Union (CJEU). By aligning the texts at the sentence level, they investigated translation strategies and techniques adopted to render legal system-bound terms, ranging from foreignising (source language and culture-oriented equivalents) to domesticating (target language and culture-oriented equivalents) solutions. Their study confirms – empirically – what scholars (among others, Rega 1997, p. 123) have been theorising about since the pre-corpus era: the CJEU tends not to translate culture-bound terms resorting to the borrowing technique as a way to preserve the inner specificity and culture-bound nature of some bodies (in this case, courts). By means of the corpus-based study, they confirm that in over 95% of cases the CJEU transcribes court names in the source language, thus opting for a foreignising approach.

From a methodological point of view, one of the advantages of this approach lies in the ease with which one may identify translation equivalents when working with the parallel corpus, which is segmented at the sentence level and aligned to speed up the searches. However, a limitation of this study lies in the inner difficulty of working with supranational judicial texts in that there is no explicit language A and language B (Wright 2018), "no original version" of EU texts (Prieto Ramos and Guzmán 2018, p. 83) and directionality plays a pivotal role in legal translation.

Parallel corpora may also be used for lexicographic or teminographic purposes, as demonstrated by the Law10n corpus (see Bestué, this volume), which is a bilingual parallel corpus (English-Spanish) made of licence software contracts translated from English into Spanish. The corpus was used to compile terminological records that provide key information when translating this genre in the English-Spanish combination as well as examples of real contexts in which the terms occur.

Another interesting example of eclecticism in the use of parallel corpora is the study carried out by Prieto Ramos and Guzmán (2018) within the LETRINT project. With a view to analysing the consistency and adequacy of legal terminology as quality indicators in institutional translation, they built three parallel subcorpora of texts translated from English into Spanish and published in institutional repositories of the UN, the EU and the WTO in 2005, 2010 and 2015. In their 2018 paper, the authors exemplified the methodology with a case study into the term *due process*. By combining the lexicometric (quantitative) analysis, i.e. the measurement of the frequency with which words occur in text, with the acceptability (quality) analysis, they focused on the translations of this illustrative term into Spanish. In particular, they studied translation consistency (in terms of intertextual and intratextual variability) and adequacy in the three organisations using XBench, a quality assurance and terminology management tool (2018, pp. 85–86). The main advantage of the analysis is the triangulation of quantitative and qualitative insights at micro- and macrotextual levels.

The studies discussed in this section are just some of the existing projects carried out with comparable and parallel corpora. In terms of methods, most of them usually combine both kinds of corpora (see the notion of 'multilingually comparable corpus' in Hansen-Schirra and Teich (2009, p. 1162), re-defined as 'comparable-parallel corpus' by Biel (2016, p. 203)), especially when dealing with translated versus non-translated texts, which is the topic of the next section.

3.6 *Translated versus non-translated*

One of the most promising avenues in LTS is research into the regularities of translated language (see Zanettin 2012, pp. 11–31) by means of corpus linguistics. Although Baker's seminal work on what she refers to as "translation universals" was published in 1993, research into the regularities of translation common to translated texts (e.g. simplification, explicitation, normalisation, levelling-out, etc. see Baker 1996, pp. 176–184; Zanettin 2012, pp. 12–25) has only recently been applied to LTS, probably due to the absence of large legal corpora that could be used as test beds to confirm or disconfirm such properties of translated texts.

Most of the studies conducted so far are based on monolingual comparable collections of texts, generally used to compare a corpus of translations with a similar corpus of comparable texts originally written in the target language in order to isolate descriptive features of translations. As far as the material is concerned, the majority of projects usually compare EU legal texts with national ones, which is for practical reasons as well; that is to say, the availability of texts produced at the supra- and national level.

One of the first scholars who studied the regularities of legal translation was Biel, who in many studies tested the 'textual fit' (naturalness, acceptability) between translations (at the EU level) and non-translations (at the national level) (2014a, p. 98), with a specific focus on phraseology and on the 'untypical collocation hypothesis' (Mauranen 2007; Biel 2014a, pp. 105–106).

Working with the Polish-English combination, Biel's research, tested on a number of linguistic elements – such as lexical collocations (2014b), complex prepositions (2015), lexical bundles or n-grams (2018b) – significantly contributed to the understanding of features that supranational language shares with national language or which are different from the latter. From a methodological point of view, the author combines a corpus-based and corpus-driven approach with a view to having a clear picture of the trends in action in these language varieties.

In her 2018b paper on lexical bundles, she obtained two important results. On the one hand, she found that EU translated texts have an increased level of formulaicity in respect to types, tokens and a percentage of words in bundles, which seem to disconfirm the hypothesis according to which translations are less patterned and less formulaic than non-translations. The results are partially in line with a study carried out by Pontrandolfo on a monolingual comparable corpus of original versus translated Italian (2011, p. 223) and fully in line with a recent study carried out on phraseological units in national versus EU Spanish judgments (Pontrandolfo 2018). On the other hand, she found that EU translated texts share few bundles with original domestic legal texts, which points to the existence of 'formulaic profiles' typical of translation, a result which is in line with what she found through the investigation of a different pattern (complex prepositions, Biel 2015).

Another study that integrates a corpus-based analysis of lexical bundles with statistical significance tests is Trklja's research on formulaicity and hybridity in CJEU judgments (2018), which relies – as in the previous studies – on an intralingual comparison of supra- and national language. As far as the method of investigation is concerned, the author anchors a corpus-based analysis of lexical bundles and keyword analysis with theoretical insights from the theory of information distribution in texts and the local grammar approach. The results show a high degree of formulaicity in CJEU judgments, a limited number of argumentative textual devices used in CJEU judgments and the existence of hybrid expressions created through translation (2018, p. 105).

The comparison between EU 'translationese' and national language lies at the very heart of some international projects, such as the project "Law and Language at the European Court of Justice" based on the EUCLCORP corpus (McAuliffe and Trklja 2018) or the "Eurolect Observatory. Interlingual and intralingual analysis of EU legal varieties" that aims at analysing corpora containing EU directives and national implementing measures in a number of languages (Dutch, Finnish, French, English, German, Greek, Italian, Latvian, Maltese, Polish and Spanish) (Mori 2018).

Another interesting project is the one coordinated by Montolío Durán (see endnote 1), which investigates differences between national and EU judicial Spanish. The analysis is based on the JustClar monolingual comparable corpus: the first subcorpus, the national one, contains judgments delivered by the Spanish Tribunal Supremo while the EU one collects judgments delivered by the CJEU. The two corpora can also be seen as representatives of original (non-translated) and translated texts. In line with the main objectives of the project, Pontrandolfo (2018) studies if and how the distribution of phraseological units (e.g. collocations, phrases, routine formulae, etc.) changes between national and EU Spanish and if phraseology affects the quality and readability of texts. In spite of the initial hypothesis, according to which a higher percentage of phraseological units was expected to be found in national texts – due to the long discursive tradition of 'legalese' characterising judges' opinions – preliminary results of the analysis show that EU judgments contain a higher percentage of phraseological units, in line with the results obtained by Biel on a number of legal genres.

These studies demonstrated the key role of monolingual comparable corpora in detecting regularities in translations and they represent first attempts to investigate translation universals, usually studied on literary translations. However, one of the methodological limitations of these studies conducted with EU materials lies in what Biel calls 'text aboutness' in corpus design (2018b, p. 23): EU law and domestic law have very different scopes of regulation which means that there is no complete thematic convergence between the two areas, resulting in an unbalanced comparison among texts. Another aspect which is difficult to weight is the impact of Computer-Assisted Translation tools in the translation process and product. The higher formulaicity of translated texts might depend on the use of translation memories by EU professional translators or lawyer-linguists.

Apart from the research carried out on monolingual comparable corpora, translation universals are also being tested on bilingual parallel corpora, which is corpora of original (source) and translated (target) texts. There are few studies conducted so far in the legal field: a remarkable exception is the study conducted by Simonnæs on the explicitation hypothesis in legal translations from Norwegian into German and English (2011), which confirms that this area still needs further developments. By combining qualitative (contrastive text analysis) and quantitative observations, such studies may efficiently link typical features of judicial language (such as nominalisations, passives, system-bound terms, and elliptical phrases) to translation techniques and therefore to translation universals, thus offering new insights in LTS.

Empirical research on this topic is extremely needed both in training and professional settings. The use of legal corpora effectively helps scholars to isolate descriptive features of translations that actually give insights into the complex dynamics of legal translation.

4 The picture: challenges and new perspectives

While it is now unquestionable that there is a great and productive variety of methods researchers can use when analysing legal translation, it is nevertheless true that "[u]ntil recently, relatively little corpus-based and corpus-driven research has been done in the area of legal translation" (Biel 2018a, p. 34). There is still a lot of research to be carried out in the future.

The studies mentioned in the chapter and analysed through the lens of methodological dichotomies have foregrounded the importance of eclecticism in the selection of method in LTS. These are just some of the oppositions that can be found in the literature on LTS, other important dichotomies being, for example, synchronic versus diachronic or native versus non-native.[6] Triangulating research methodologies proves to be an effective way to overcome binary dichotomies (see Marchi and Taylor 2018, pp. 6–8), which is one of the advantages of corpus linguistics: it allows for a combination of angles (quality versus quantity, corpus-based versus corpus-driven, local versus global, etc.) confirming the importance of positioning those oppositions along a continuum, characterised by fuzzy boundaries.

Scholars adopting corpus methods have to be aware that their collections of texts have their own limitations and cannot be considered as totally representative of the language area they are investigating, notwithstanding their efforts in the design and their constant search for representativeness. One of the disadvantages of current research on LTS based on corpora is, for example, the challenge of studying absences (see Partington 2014), since corpus analyses tend to focus on what corpora contain rather than what is missing in them (see also Duguid and Partington 2018).

As far as the challenges for the future of LTS in terms of methods are concerned, it is important to mention the intersection between Nature Language Processing (NLP) and corpora for the automatic processing of legal texts, in terms of extraction of legal terms, phrasemes or translation equivalents, which is slowly gaining weight in legal studies (see for example the MIREL project).[7]

The years to come will definitely experience a surge in corpus studies that will (hopefully) contribute to a better understanding of the complex interdiscipline of legal translation.

Notes

1 The chapter is partially framed within the project entitled "Legal discourse and clarity. Comparative analysis of national Spanish judgments and judgments in Spanish by the Court of Justice of the European Union", reference: FFI2015–70332-P, Principal Investigator: Estrella Montolío Durán, www.ub.edu/edap/?page_id=316 [Accessed 11 Mar. 2018].

2 Institutional translation has been extensively studied, especially from the quality perspective (see, among others, Svoboda *et al.* 2017), due to the availability of textual resources.

3 E.g. the United Nations Parallel Corpus v. 1.0, the JRC-Acquis parallel corpus; the DGT-Acquis translation memories corpus; the Digital Corpus of the European Parliament (DCEP), the Europarl and the EUR-Lex corpus on Sketch Engine (see Baisa *et al.* 2016; Biel 2018a, pp. 29–33).

4 To this day, there are several research projects involving the compilation and exploration of legal corpora for translation purposes. To mention a few: the LLECJ project (https://llecj.karenmcauliffe.com/); the LETRINT project (http://p3.snf.ch/project-157797); the QUALETRA project (http://eulita.eu/qualetra/); the Eurolect Observatory (www.unint.eu/en/research/research-groups/39-higher-education/490-eurolect-observatory-interlingual-and-intralingual-analysis-of-legal-varieties-in-the-eu-setting.html); the JudGENTT project (www.gentt.uji.es/); the LAW10n project (http://lawcalisation.com/) [Accessed 11 Mar. 2018].

5 The translation of national court names at different international organisations (as well as the assessment of legal entries in terminological databases) has also been studied by Prieto Ramos (2013, 2014b).

6 See the study by Scarpa (2013a, 2013b) on the use of English as a native language versus English as a lingua franca in commercial and legal settings. The author analyses a small monolingual corpus of terms of use translated into English from

the international websites of three car manufacturers from three different countries of origin and legislation based in civil law (Fiat, Renault and Volkswagen) with the overall aim of finding similarities and differences in layout/content and terminology/phraseology.

7 www.mirelproject.eu/publications/D2.1.pdf [Accessed 11 Mar. 2018].

References

Baisa, V., *et al.* (2016). European Union language resources in sketch engine. *The proceedings of the tenth international conference on language resources and evaluation (LREC'16)* [online]. Available at: www.sketchengine.eu/wp-content/uploads/eur_lex_2016.pdf [Accessed 11 Mar. 2018].

Baker, M. (1993). Corpus linguistics and translation studies – implications and applications. *In*: M. Baker, *et al.*, eds. *Text and technology: In honour of John Sinclair*. Amsterdam: John Benjamins, pp. 233–250.

Baker, M. (1996). Corpus-based translation studies: The challenges that lie ahead. *In*: H.L. Somers, ed. *Terminology, LSP and translation. Studies in language engineering in honour of Juan C. Sager*. Amsterdam: John Benjamins, pp. 175–186.

Bhatia, V.K. (1997). The power and politics of genre. *World Englishes*, 16, pp. 359–371.

Biel, Ł. (2010). Corpus-based studies of legal language for translation purposes: Methodological and practical potential [online]. *In*: C. Heine and J. Engberg, eds. *Reconceptualising LSP. Online proceedings of the XVII European LSP symposium 2009*. Available at: www.asb.dk/fileadmin/www.asb.dk/isek/biel.pdf [Accessed 29 Aug. 2018].

Biel, Ł. (2014a). *Lost in the Eurofog: The textual fit of translated law*. Frankfurt am Main: Peter Lang.

Biel, Ł. (2014b). Phraseology in legal translation. A corpus-based analysis of textual mapping in EU law. *In*: L. Cheng, K. Kui Sin and A. Wagner, eds. *The Ashgate handbook of legal translation*. Farnham: Ashgate, pp. 177–192.

Biel, Ł. (2015). Phraseological profiles of legislative genres: Complex prepositions as a special case of legal phrasemes in EU law and national law. *Fachsprache – International Journal of Specialized Communication*, 37 (3–4), pp. 139–160.

Biel, Ł. (2016). Mixed corpus design for researching the Eurolect: A genre-based comparable-parallel corpus in the PL EUROLECT project. *In*: E. Gruszczyńska and A. Leńko-Szymańska, eds. *Polskojęzyczne korpusy równoległe. [Polish-language parallel corpora]*. Warsaw: Instytut Lingwistyki Stosowanej, pp. 197–208. Available at: https://eurolekt.ils.uw.edu.pl/files/2016/09/Mixed-corpus-design-for-researching-the-Eurolect-a-genre-based-comparable-parallel-corpus-in-the-PL-EUROLECT-project.pdf [Accessed 27 Sept. 2018].

Biel, Ł. (2018a). Corpora in institutional legal translation: Small steps and the big picture. *In*: F. Prieto Ramos, ed. *Institutional translation for international governance. Enhancing quality in multilingual legal communication*. London: Bloomsbury, pp. 25–36.

Biel, Ł. (2018b). Lexical bundles in EU law: The impact of translation process on the patterning of legal language. *In*: S. Goźdź-Roszkowski and G. Pontrandolfo, eds. *Phraseology in legal and institutional settings. A corpus-based interdisciplinary perspective*. London: Routledge, pp. 11–26.

Biel, Ł. and Engberg, J., eds. (2013). Research models and methods in legal translation. *Linguistica Antverpiensia. New Series – Themes in Translation Studies*, 12, pp. 1–11.

Bocquet, C. (1994). *Pour une méthode de traduction juridique*. Prilly-Lausanne: Éditions CB.

Borja Albi, A. (2007). Los géneros jurídicos. *In*: E. Alcaraz Varó and J. Yuste, eds. *Las lenguas profesionales y académicas*. Barcelona: Ariel, pp. 141–153.

Breeze, R. (2013). Lexical bundles across four legal genres. *International Journal of Corpus Linguistics*, 18 (2), pp. 229–253.

Cao, D. (2007). *Translating law*. Clevedon: Multilingual Matters.

Cronin, M. (2010). The translation crowd. *Revista Tradumàtica*, 8, pp. 1–7.

Duguid, A. and Partington, A. (2018). Using corpus linguistics to investigate absence/s: you don't know what you're missing. Or do you? *In:* A. Marchi and C. Taylor, eds. *Corpus approaches to discourse: A critical review*. London: Routledge, pp. 38–59.

Egbert, J. and Schnur, E. (2018). The role of the text in corpus and discourse analysis. Missing the trees for the forest. *In*: A. Marchi and C. Taylor, eds. *Corpus approaches to discourse: A critical review*. London: Routledge, pp. 159–173.

Engberg, J. (2013). Comparative law for translation: The key to successful mediation between legal systems. *In*: A. Borja Albi and F. Prieto Ramos, eds. *Legal translation in context: Professional issues and prospects*. Frankfurt am Main: Peter Lang, pp. 9–25.

Garzone, G. (2000). Legal translation and functional approaches: A contradiction in terms? *In: Actes du Colloque International 'La traduction juridique. Histoire, théorie(s) et pratique'*. Genève: École de Traduction et d'Interprétation – Université de Genève, pp. 395–414.

Goźdź-Roszkowski, S. (2011). *Patterns of linguistic variation in American legal English. A corpus-based study*. Frankfurt am Main: Peter Lang.

Hansen-Schirra, S. and Teich, E. (2009). Corpora in human translation. *In*: A. Lüdeling and M. Kytö, eds. *Corpus linguistics. An international handbook*. Berlin: de Gruyter Mouton (1159)–1175.

Johansson, S. (2007). *Seeing through multilingual corpora. On the use of corpora in contrastive studies*. Amsterdam: John Benjamins.

Koskinen, K. (2000). Institutional illusions. Translating in the EU Commission. *The Translator*, 6 (1), pp. 49–65.

Lambert, J. (2009). The status and position of legal translation: A chapter in the discursive construction of societies. *In*: F. Olsen *et al*., eds. *Translation issues in language and law*. Basingstoke: Palgrave Macmillan, pp. 76–95.

Marchi, A. and Taylor, C. (2018). Introduction. Partiality and reflexivity. *In*: A. Marchi and C. Taylor, eds. *Corpus approaches to discourse: A critical review*. London: Routledge, pp. 1–15.

Marín Pérez, M. and Rea Rizzo, C. (2012). Structure and design of the British Law Report Corpus (BLRC): A legal corpus of judicial decisions from the UK. *Journal of English Studies*, 10, pp. 131–145.

Mauranen, A. (2007). Universal tendencies in translation. *In*: G.M. Anderman and M. Rogers, eds. *Incorporating corpora. The linguist and the translator*. Clevedon: Multilingual Matters, pp. 32–48.

McAuliffe, K. and Trklja, A. (2018). The European Union Case Law Corpus (EUCLCORP): A multilingual parallel and comparative corpus of EU court judgments. *In*: F. Andrew, *et al.*, eds. *Proceedings of the second workshop on Corpus-Based Research in the Humanities (CRH-2).* Vienna, Austria, Gerastree Proceedings, TU Wien, Vienna, Vol. 1, pp. 217–226.

McEnery, T. and Hardie, T. (2012). *Corpus linguistics. Method, theory and practice.* Cambridge: Cambridge University Press.

McEnery, T., *et al.* (2006). *Corpus-based language studies: An advanced resource book.* London: Routledge.

Monzó Nebot, E. (2008). Corpus-based activities in legal translator training. *The Interpreter and Translator Trainer*, 2 (2), pp. 221–251.

Mori, L., ed. (2018). *Observing Eurolects: Corpus analysis of linguistic variation in EU law.* Amsterdam: John Benjamins.

Mortara Garavelli, B. (2001). *Le parole e la giustizia. Divagazioni retoriche e grammaticali su testi giuridici.* Torino: Einaudi.

Partington, A. (2014). Mind the gaps: The role of corpus linguistics in researching absences. *International Journal of Corpus Linguistics*, 19 (1), pp. 118–146.

Pontrandolfo, G. (2011). Phraseology in criminal judgments: A corpus study of original vs. translated Italian. *Sendebar*, 22, pp. 209–234.

Pontrandolfo, G. (2012). Legal corpora: An overview. *RITT (Rivista Internazionale di Tecnica della Traduzione)*, 14, pp. 121–136.

Pontrandolfo, G. (2016). *Fraseología y lenguaje judicial. Las sentencias penales desde una perspectiva contrastiva.* Roma: Aracne.

Pontrandolfo, G. (2018), June 18–20. *National and EU judicial phraseology under the magnifying glass: A corpus-assisted discourse study.* Paper delivered at the 2018 TRANSIUS Conference, University of Geneva.

Pontrandolfo, G. (2019, forthcoming). Discursive constraints in legal translation: A genre-based analytical framework. *In*: M. Kristiansen and I. Simonnaes, eds. *Legal translation studies as a challenge/Herausforderungen an das Rechtsübersetzen.* Berlin: Frank & Timme.

Prieto Ramos, F. (2013). ¿Qué estrategias para qué traducción jurídica? por una metodología integral para la práctica profesional. *In*: I. Alonso Araguás, *et al.*, eds. *Translating the law. Theoretical and methodological issues/Traducir el derecho. Cuestiones teóricas y metodológicas.* Granada: Comares, pp. 87–106.

Prieto Ramos, F. (2014a). Legal Translation Studies as interdisciplinary: Scope and evolution. *Meta: Translators' Journal*, 59 (2), pp. 260–277.

Prieto Ramos, F. (2014b). Parameters for problem-solving in legal translation: Implications for legal lexicography and institutional terminology management. *In*: L. Cheng, K. Kui Sin and A. Wagner, eds. *The Ashgate handbook of legal translation.* Farnham: Ashgate, pp. 121–134.

Prieto Ramos, F. and Guzmán, D. (2018). Legal terminology consistency and adequacy as quality indicators in institutional translation: A mixed-method comparative study. *In*: F. Prieto Ramos, ed. *Institutional translation for international governance. Enhancing quality in multilingual legal communication.* London: Bloomsbury, pp. 81–101.

Pym, A. (2014). *Exploring translation theories.* 2nd ed. London: Routledge.

Rega, L. (1997). La sentenza italiana e tedesca nell'ottica della traduzione. *In*: L. Schena, ed. *La lingua del diritto. Difficoltà traduttive. Applicazioni didattiche. Atti del primo convegno internazionale*, Milano, 5–6 ottobre 1995, Centro Linguistico dell'Università Bocconi. Roma: CISU, pp. 117–126.

Šarčević, S. (1997). *New approach to legal translation*. The Hague: Kluwer Law International.

Scarpa, F. (2013a). Investigating legal information in commercial websites: The terms and conditions of use in different varieties of English. *Linguistica Antverpiensia. New Series – Themes in Translation Studies*, 12, pp. 71–93.

Scarpa, F. (2013b). Similar yet different. ELF variation in international website terms and conditions of use. *Cultus, the Journal of Intercultural Mediation and Communication*, V (6), pp. 69–94.

Seracini, F. (2017). *A corpus-based descriptive translation studies analysis of European Union legislation*. Unpublished Thesis (PhD). Università Cattolica del Sacro Cuore.

Simonnæs, I. (2011). Das multilinguale fachsprachliche Korpus TK-NHH – Eine korpusbasierte Fallstudie über die explicitation hypothesis anhand von ins Deutsche und Englische übersetzten Rechtstexten. *Hermes – Journal of Language and Communication in Business*, 46, pp. 103–117.

Svoboda, T., Biel, Ł. and Łoboda, K., eds. (2017). *Quality aspects in institutional translation*. Berlin: Language Science Press.

Tognini-Bonelli, E. (2001). *Corpus linguistics at work*. Amsterdam: John Benjamins.

Trklja, A. (2018). A corpus investigation of formulaicity and hybridity in legal language: A case of EU case law texts. *In*: S. Goźdź-Roszkowski and G. Pontrandolfo, eds. *Phraseology in legal and institutional settings. A corpus-based interdisciplinary perspective*. London: Routledge, pp. 89–108.

Vanden Bulcke, P. and de Groote, C. (2016). JuriGenT, un banco de datos jurídico neerlandés/español diferente. *CLINA*, 2 (2), pp. 15–38.

Vigier, F.J. and Sánchez Ramos, M.D.M. (2017). Using parallel corpora to study the translation of legal system-bound terms: The case of names of English and Spanish courts. *In*: R. Mitkov, ed. *Computational and corpus-based phraseology*, Second International Conference, Europhras 2017, London, proceedings. Cham: Springer, pp. 260–273.

Vogel, F., Hamann, H. and Gauer, I. (2017). Computer-assisted legal linguistics: Corpus analysis as a new tool for legal studies. *Law & Social Inquiry*, 42, pp. 1–24.

Wright, S. (2018). The impact of multilingualism on the judgments of the EU Court of Justice. *In*: F. Prieto Ramos, ed. *Institutional translation for international governance: Enhancing quality in multilingual legal communication*. London: Bloomsbury, pp. 141–155.

Zanettin, F. (2012). *Translation-driven corpora. Corpus resources for descriptive and applied translation studies*. Manchester: St. Jerome Publishing.

List of software for the analysis of linguistic data

AntConc:

Anthony, L. *AntConc* [computer software]. Tokyo: Waseda University. Available at: www.laurenceanthony.net/software [Accessed 31 Aug. 2018].

ConcGram:

Greaves, C. (2009). *ConcGram 1.0. A phraseological search engine*. Amsterdam: John Benjamins. [Accessed 31 Aug. 2018].

ParaConc:

Barlow, M. (2009). *ParaConc* [computer software]. Available at: www.paraconc.com/index.html [Accessed 31 Aug. 2018].

Sketch Engine:
Kilgarriff, A., *et al. The sketch engine* [computer software]. Available at: www.sketchengine.eu/ [Accessed 31 Aug. 2018].
WordSmith Tools:
Scott, M. *WordSmith tools* [computer software]. Available at: https://lexically.net/wordsmith/ [Accessed 31 Aug. 2018].
Xbench:
Terminology and QA for professional translators. Available at: www.xbench.net/ [Accessed 31 Aug. 2018].

2 Implications of text categorisation for corpus-based legal translation research

The case of international institutional settings

Fernando Prieto Ramos

1 Introduction: why does text categorisation matter?

Text categorisation is a key aspect of research into discourse features and translation patterns, and an essential methodological consideration in corpus design and analysis. Systematic categorisation of text is pivotal in delineating the scope of research questions, producing valid datasets and deriving findings accordingly. In fact, the comparability, representativeness and balance of corpus components depend on the boundaries and hierarchical organisation of the target population (e.g. Biber 1993; Halverson 1998). Since "different ways of classifying and characterizing texts can produce different text typologies" (McEnery *et al.* 2006, p. 16), the criteria applied for text classification and category definitions must be made explicit (e.g. Biber *et al.* 1998; Halverson 1998; Lee 2001), particularly when a corpus encompasses a large amount of texts from various categories and the boundaries between these categories cannot be presupposed.

Genre stands out as a widely accepted operational concept for categorising texts. As highlighted by Lee (2001, p. 37), genre is "the level of text categorisation which is theoretically and pedagogically most useful and most practical to work with". This is associated with the idea that genre conventions are recognisable, as reflected in Bhatia's classic definition (1993, p. 13):

> Genre is a recognizable communicative event, characterized by a set of communicative purpose(s) identified and mutually understood by the members of the professional or academic community in which it regularly occurs. Most often it is highly structured and conventionalized with constraints or allowable contributions in terms of their intent, positioning, form and functional value.

The link between communicative purposes and discourse conventions is virtually uncontested in genre-based text categorisations, especially since Biber's (1988) multidimensional analysis of register variation. This work has influenced subsequent approaches to the study of similarities between texts through both manual annotation and automated measurements of functional attributes (see e.g. Forsyth and Sharoff 2014; Melissourgou and Frantzi 2017). However, there is no consensus about these genre attributes or the method for identifying them, let alone for establishing genre ontologies that reflect inter-genre connections and further subdivisions.

In the case of legal texts, this is compounded by the overwhelming diversity of legal discourses, as they fulfil multiple functions and address all kinds of themes within countless legal frameworks (both national and supranational), branches and communicative settings. The high levels of variability and hybridity of legal language, as "a set of related legal discourses" (Maley 1994, p. 13), make it difficult to build universally valid classifications of legal texts. The hierarchy and boundaries of categorisations ultimately depend on research priorities and perspectives (e.g. Biel 2014, p. 19; Prieto Ramos 2014a, p. 263).

Corpus-based legal linguistic and legal translation studies are crucially contributing to characterise legal genres across languages and jurisdictions (see e.g. Goźdź-Roszkowski 2011a; Borja Albi 2013; Biel 2014; Pontrandolfo 2016). Yet, definitions of "legal text" and the scope of legal translation remain contested. This is not only an academic debate on the nature of a discipline; it also reflects the many textual facets of law itself as a matter of language use, and it is of significance for translation practice. In fact, categorising texts is a critical step in situating and conducting translation-oriented text mining and analysis. As pointed out by Alcaraz Varó and Hughes (2002, p. 103), "the translator who has taken the trouble to recognise the formal and stylistic conventions of a particular original has already done much to translate the text successfully". This is notably the case in the field of law, since legal writing is most often shaped by the "normative force of genre bias", as contended by Rappaport (2014, p. 199). For this legal scholar, lawyers who "understand legal writing as, at least partially, a function of genre bias will better comprehend how legal texts are conceived, received, and perceived, and will be better lawyers as a consequence", as all legal professionals, including judges and legal scholars, have "an audience with expectations precast by genre" (2014, p. 203).

This chapter highlights the relevance of text categorisation for research in legal translation by focusing on institutional translation settings, namely: the European Union (EU), the United Nations (UN) and the World Trade Organization (WTO), and their corresponding adjudicative bodies.[1] After briefly reviewing recurrent issues and models of legal text classification (section 2), a multidimensional approach is applied to the multilingual text production of the three representative institutional translation settings during three years over the span of a decade (2005, 2010 and 2015), as part of the project "Legal Translation in International Institutional Settings: Scope, Strategies and Quality Markers" (LETRINT) (section 3). The resulting subdivisions are integrated into a categorisation matrix and discussed as a way of illustrating the relative nature and implications of text classifications. The fine-grained description of corpus design and representativeness, technical aspects of corpus compilation and full taxonomies of genres are not addressed in this chapter.

2 Classifying legal texts: beyond legal genres?

2.1 Commonalities and diverging views

In corpus building, "the conception of the object which a discipline more or less agrees on provides the motivation for defining a target population" (Halverson 1998, p. 495). This entails defining category boundaries and internal structure "on the basis of theoretical notions pertaining to the relevance of various types of text, and the relative significance of the different types" (1998, p. 499). In Legal Translation Studies (LTS), scholars tend to converge on the relevance of genres to study legal discourse conventions in translation, but diverge on the classification of these genres into broader categories or text types, and on their boundaries based on the notion of "legal text".

The metalanguage applied to these categories also differs between authors. "Text type" and "genre" are sometimes used as interchangeable (see e.g. Berūkštienė 2016, pp. 92–94, on scholarly distinctions between these concepts), while notions such as "genre system" (Bazerman 1994, p. 97) and "genre network" (Fairclough 2006, p. 34) emphasise the idea of interconnection.[2] Regardless of supra-genre level denominations, most approaches include legislative, contractual, judicial and scholarly texts by focusing on key legal functions and associated types of legal discourse (e.g. Bocquet 1994; Šarčević 1997; Tiersma 1999; Kjær 2000). Some authors add considerations on specific branches of legal practice, such as administrative or business law (e.g. Gémar 1995; Mattila 2013). A comparison of approaches suggests that functional and domain elements tend to be embedded in classifications by situation of use or discursive situation parameters, including setting, purposes, addressor and addressee (e.g. Trosborg 1997; Borja Albi 2000; Bhatia 2006; Cao 2007).

As illustrated by Table 2.1, parallels can be drawn between approaches. The link between legal discourse features and legal function or theme emerges as their common ground, and explains the inclusion of legal subcategories of macro-genres as legal texts, e.g. legal academic articles as a subcategory of academic articles. Variations are found, among other details, in the way legislative and contractual texts are grouped together or not, considering their normative value; and also, particularly, in the fuzzier realm of private legal texts written by non-lawyers and other texts that are not "intrinsically" legal (by function or theme) but are used in legal settings (see e.g. differences in Trosborg 1997; Cao 2007). While the fundamental link between legal purpose or theme and discourse features can be found in the first group, the same link seems totally absent in the second group (e.g. personal correspondence or technical reports used in court proceedings).

Scholars disagree on whether the texts of this second group can be classified as legal texts. Abdel Hadi (1992, p. 47) and Harvey (2002, p. 178), for example, consider them legal texts as long as they are used in legal settings. Likewise, Cao (2007, p. 9) defines legal texts as "texts produced or used for legal purposes in legal settings", regardless of the original purpose for which they were produced, whereas she perceives legal language as "the language of and related

Table 2.1 Legal text classifications based on situational parameters

Trosborg (1997, p. 20): "types of texts or genres" by situation of use	Borja Albi (2000, pp. 84–134): "text categories" by discursive situation	Bhatia (2006, pp. 6–7): "system of legal genres" by communicative purposes	Cao (2007, pp. 9–10): "variants or sub-varieties of legal texts" by situation of use
Language of the law (legal documents): • legislation • common law (contracts, deeds)	Prescriptive texts (e.g. acts, statutes, bills, regulations)	Primary genre (legislation)	Legislative texts (e.g. statutes and subordinate laws, international treaties)
Language of the courtroom: • judge declaring the law • judge/counsel exchanges • counsel/witness exchanges	Judicial texts (claim forms, judgments, appeals, writs, orders, etc.) Case-law (decisions of higher courts)	Derived secondary genres (e.g. judgments, cases)	Judicial texts (produced by judicial officers and other legal authorities in judicial processes)
Language in textbooks	Reference works (dictionaries, repositories, encyclopaedias) Scholarly texts (articles, textbooks, manuals, casebooks, manuals, etc.)	Derived enabling (pedagogic) genres: • academic (e.g. textbooks, moots) • professional (e.g. legal memoranda, pleadings)	Legal scholarly texts (scholarly works and commentaries)
Lawyers' communication: • to other lawyers • to laymen	Law application texts (contracts, deeds, wills, legal briefs, etc.)	Target genres (property conveyance documents, client consultation documents, affidavits, agreements and contracts)	Private legal texts • texts written by lawyers (e.g. contracts, leases, wills and litigation documents) • texts written by non-lawyers (e.g. private agreements, witness statements and other documents used in litigation and other legal situations)
People talking about the law			

to law and legal process", including "language of the law, language about law, and language used in other legal communicative situations". She problematises Šarčević's (1997) focus on legal texts for specialists as restrictive (1997, p. 9), and claims that "ordinary texts that are not written in legal language by legal professionals" constitute "a major part of the translation work of the legal translator in real life" (1997, p. 12). It is difficult to accept that personal letters or technical reports that contain no sign of legal language are legal texts. Taken in isolation, rather than through the lens of the translation context, such texts would hardly be considered legal texts in their own right. It can be understood, however, that these texts might be translated in legal settings and play an instrumental role in legal processes. In other words, from a translation perspective, the categorisation of texts without any legal discourse as "legal texts" is only possible in an expansive (or inclusive) classification of texts based on translation settings rather than discourse features.

In this kind of expansive approach, one may claim not only that legal texts encompass multiple combinations of legal and non-legal discourse, but also that legal translation may include more than just legal texts. The preceding triggers at least two related questions for research purposes: where should the boundary be drawn between legal and non-legal texts when mapping a setting or branch of legal translation comprising a variety of text types? To what extent should the link between legal functions or themes and discourse features be a determining factor in the definition and classification of legal text types in a corpus? This brings us back to the question of legal genre conventions and legal discourses.

2.2 *The crucible of legal discourses*

Extensive work has been conducted on the distinctive lexical, syntactic and structural features of legal discourses. Tiersma (2003) summarises some of the most common ones associated with "legalese", including: archaic, formal and unusual or difficult vocabulary, technical terminology, impersonal constructions, nominalisations, passive constructions, long and complex sentences, wordiness and redundancy (see also e.g. Galdia 2009; Mattila 2013). These features are found, in varying degrees and clusters, in what is traditionally perceived as the core of legal discourses or styles: the language of legal experts, particularly legislators, judges and lawyers (as well as notaries in many jurisdictions). They constitute conventions inherited through precedents in law-making and implementation, and are sometimes described as "fossilized language" (Alcaraz Varó and Hughes 2002, p. 9), which calls for investigation into discourse patterns and variations.

These legal discourse feature clusters are highly interdependent. Legislative discourse, as primary expression of the law, occupies a central position and permeates the other legal discourses that apply or describe the law (see e.g. Kjær 2000, pp. 138–140; Bhatia 2006, pp. 6–7). In a similar vein, Monjean-Decaudin (2013, p. 24) couples the "degree of juridicity" with the legal effect of texts (i.e. more legal force and consequences imply a higher degree of juridicity) and the level of legal knowledge required to understand and translate them. However, generalisations on legal discourses are difficult to establish because of their vast scope and variability through space and time, not only across jurisdictions and legal traditions, but also within them, e.g. through deliberate simplification, legal reform or harmonisation processes. As rightly expressed by Goźdź-Roszkowski (2011b, p. 3281), far from being uniform, legal language "represents an extremely complex type of discourse embedded in the highly varied institutional space of different legal systems and cultures", and "should be viewed as an umbrella term referring to a universe of remarkably diverse texts, both written and spoken", including "statements on law reproduced in the media" and "any fictional representation" of legal genres.

Legal discourses are also commonly characterised as hybrid, not only as a result of contact between legal systems and drafters with different backgrounds (see e.g. Robinson 2005 on EU legislative drafting), but also in terms of interdisciplinarity, due to the diversity of subjects and specialised knowledge covered by law. This means that non-legal specialised language may often be as prominent as legal language in legal texts. For instance, it is not striking that a financial regulation may be viewed simultaneously as a matter of legal and financial translation, even if the text belongs to a legal genre, i.e. it may typically adhere to specific structural and phraseological conventions to establish legal obligations, but the content may use more financial than legal terminology, thus reflecting the interdisciplinary reality of financial law. Similar patterns of hybridity occur with other technical discourses embedded in legal texts (see e.g. Fontanet 2018).

2.3 *Fuzzy boundaries and layers*

Since legal texts may be seen as frames and carriers of all kinds of knowledge related to law in many different degrees and forms, corpus analysis emerges as a very useful tool to provide granularity. To answer the methodological questions formulated previously, researchers must acknowledge that any text classification of multiple genres must be flexible and sensitive to ambiguities and overlaps that may be a natural consequence of the complex reality of law. A pragmatic method of legal text categorisation should be: (1) grounded on solid legal conceptualisations of the object of study; (2) explicit about the expansive or restrictive approach adopted with regard to legal text definitions, and aware of their relative nature and limitations; and (3) permeable to redefinitions of category boundaries and connections during the process of text analysis and classification. In other words, a balance must be struck between what is presupposed and what the corpus "tells" the researcher in order to refine classifications.

In the classification of multi-genre legal corpus components, multi-layered approaches can be helpful to test existing definitions of text types, and tailor their boundaries to the area of scrutiny and specific research needs. One of these approaches, the multidimensional model represented in Table 2.2, attempts to encapsulate the complementary nature of previous LTS approaches by connecting legal functions, text types (by discursive situation) and genres (according to more specific textual functions and conventions), from more general to more

Table 2.2 Multidimensional approach to legal text classification (Prieto Ramos 2014a, p. 265)

1 Main functions	• Govern public or private legal relations • Apply legal instruments in specific scenarios • Convey specialised knowledge on sources of law and legal relations
2 Text types	• Legislative (including treaties) • Judicial (including court and litigation documents) • Other public legal instruments or texts of legal implementation (issued by institutional bodies, public servants or registries; subtypes to be identified by legal system*) • Private legal instruments • Legal scholarly writings [*Notarial instruments can be considered as a specific category in civil law countries]
3 Genres	Textual realisations of specific legal functions following culture-bound discursive conventions (e.g. different kinds of court orders or contracts)

specific, and trying to avoid legal system bias. Similarly, from the field of Law, Rappaport (2014, pp. 222–223), inspired by Sinding (2002), proposes a multi-layered approach comparable to Russian nesting dolls: (1) sociocognitive action or "thinking as a lawyer" as "the outermost generic frame" to situate texts; (2) rhetorical situation or "type of law –patent, divorce, criminal, etc.–" as "the middle doll"; and (3) discourse structure, i.e. "the most specific genre, being the actual document, such as application, divorce decree, or jury waiver". These approaches will set the scene for the investigation of legal translation in international institutional settings.

3 The case of international organisations: surveying institutional legal translation

3.1. Research needs as a determining factor

The challenges outlined in the previous sections clearly apply to corpus building and text classification in the LETRINT project, which aims to shed light on the scope, features and quality indicators of legal translation at international organisations. With a view to situating and surveying legal translation within each representative institutional setting (EU, UN and WTO), three massive parallel corpora were compiled from institutional repositories,[3] including all publicly accessible textual production of three years (2005, 2010 and 2015) in the three common languages of these institutions: English, French and Spanish (with the exception of the ICJ, whose official languages are English and French). Each parallel sub-corpus therefore includes a high volume of translated texts (amounting to several million words per institution) and a wide variety of institutional genres.

Given the ambitious mapping objective of the first phase of the project, a comprehensive approach to text compilation and classification was mandatory. Corpus boundary and internal structure definition is thus not only instrumental to other phases of the project, but also a goal in itself. This inclusive approach differs from other translation-driven corpus studies as regards its large-scale comparative dimension between institutions, and also, crucially, in that text categorisation is not restricted to a fixed number of genres that are isolated for scrutiny from the outset. Among recent examples of such studies, in the Polish Eurolect project, Biel (2016) concentrates on four genres for corpus analysis "as most prototypical and hence representative of EU communication" (2016, p. 199): (1) legislation (including regulations and directives); (2) judgments and other decisions of the EU's Court of Justice (CJEU) and the General Court; (3) administrative reports prepared by EU institutions; and (4) EU official websites (2016, pp. 202–203). She contrasts these genres with comparable monolingual corpora in Polish to study variation between genres and the Europeanisation of administrative Polish.

Also centred on EU discourses, the EU Case Law Corpus (EUCLCORP) includes judgments by the CJEU and several constitutional and/or supreme courts with a view to comparing their language (Trklja and McAuliffe 2018), while the European Parliament Translation and Interpreting Corpus (EPTIC) is an intermodal bi-directional (English-Italian) corpus of speeches primarily compiled to examine lexical simplification patterns (Bernardini *et al.* 2016). Among resources developed by institutions, the United Nations Parallel Corpus v1.0, created as a parallel corpus mostly for computer-aided translation purposes, is organised by language, publication year and document symbol, and also includes UN duty station and keywords as metadata, but provides no additional information on text type classification (Ziemski *et al.* 2016).

A further-reaching proposal of institutional text categorisation, albeit not strictly based on corpus analysis, is that of Koskinen (2014). In conceptualising institutional translation in terms of governing functions, Koskinen identifies four "regimes of practices" corresponding to "distinct areas of text production and translation" (2014, pp. 487–488): maintenance, regulation, implementation and image building. She places regulation at the centre of the model as "a core activity in governing, and core genres include legislation and other juridical and administrative texts, as well as secondary documents required by law or needed for legal processes" (see Figure 2.1). Maintenance features as "the most introverted layer", and "image-building and persuasive genres" as "the most extroverted one" in what she describes as an "overview of text types, or regimes of textual and translation practices, involved in governing" (2014, p. 488).

This classification seems to mix different text-extrinsic and intrinsic criteria, including systemic, linguistic, symbolic and pragmatic parameters, without referring to corpus-supported methodological considerations. It calls for further elaboration and explicitation, particularly with regard to the rationale of labels and subdivisions. For example, the author associates the "implementation of regulations and norms" with "a need for various informative and instructive modes of communication", but excludes these modes from image-building "persuasive,

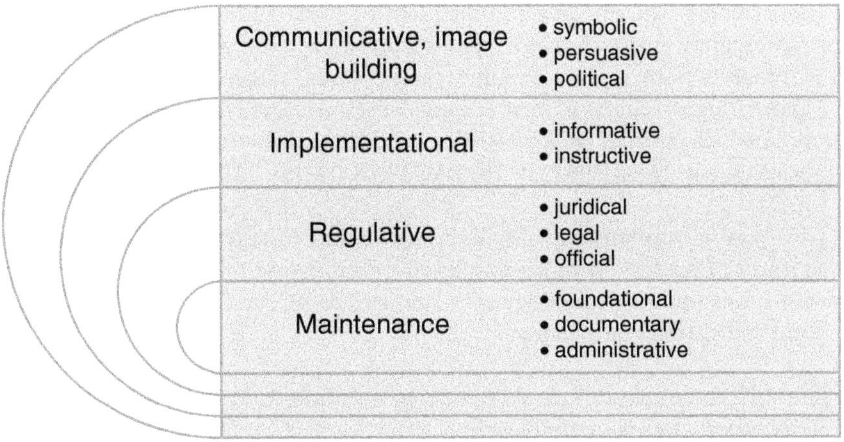

Figure 2.1 Text types in institutional translation (Koskinen 2014, p. 488)

political and symbolic genres"; she refers to "administrative texts" under regulative and maintenance categories, and seems to equate the first of these categories with "regulative" purposes. Yet, she includes "secondary documents required by law or needed for legal processes" (2014, p. 488) in this category, which would include non-regulatory texts. It is not clear whether judicial processes and adjudicative functions have been considered, why foundational documents (typically legal) are classified as "maintenance", why "official" genres or "modes of communication" are reserved for the "regulative" category, or in which way legislation is less "extroverted" than other categories.

The preceding approaches clearly illustrate how the level of detail in text categorisation is very much determined by research aims and concomitant data representativeness requirements. The broader the area of investigation and the more numerous and interrelated the textual varieties, the higher the risk of overlaps and categorisation problems. Our brief review of previous studies also suggests that more empirical data are needed to define the scope of institutional legal translation, especially at inter-governmental organisations.

3.2 The LETRINT approach

Mapping the confines of institutional translation and situating legal texts from a comparative diachronic perspective, involving three organisations and periods, could only start by defining the common denominators of institutional missions, i.e. the key functions fulfilled through comparable processes of text production. This would be the foundation for subsequent:

- selection of genres that are representative of those key institutional functions and corresponding text production processes;

- stratified (systematic) sampling (see e.g. Mellinger and Hanson 2017, p. 12), according to quantitative and qualitative criteria, in order to ensure optimal representativeness of subgroups or further strata (e.g. treaty bodies under UN treaty body reports or subcategories of EU directives);
- annotation of legal discourse features of selected genres and translation "rich points" (as defined by Agar 1991, p. 168,[4] and drawn upon in Translation Studies, e.g. Nord 1997, p. 25; PACTE 2009, pp. 212–216; Munday 2012, p. 2);
- analyses of translation quality indicators and their perception among various groups of readers (with varying levels of translation or subject matter expertise), including terminology as a key marker of both specialised discourses and translation competence.

In line with the methodological considerations outlined in section 2.3, the LETRINT approach goes from more general to more specific layers or strata of categorisation, proceeding in a "cyclical fashion" (Biber 1993, p. 256); it applies theoretically grounded conceptualisations to identify the primary categories and then refines and adds granularity according to the insights gained through text analysis.

Based on the legal contextualisation of institutional functions and the purposes of their text production processes (Prieto Ramos 2014b, 2017), three primary categories held in common were identified: (1) law-making, including hard and soft law; (2) monitoring of Member States' compliance; and (3) adjudication, including contentious and advisory proceedings (although the latter do not apply to the WTO's dispute settlement bodies). This preliminary legal contextualisation confirmed that the wide range of genres produced by the three institutions shared the same legal core as the foundation of all institutional work. Unsurprisingly, it also elicited a prototypical global hierarchy in which international legal instruments feature at the top of each institutional system and frame the other processes of application in recognisable ways.

In turn, all these processes rely on instrumental or subsidiary text categories, and are themselves the subject of other texts that describe institutional activities. As a caveat on the level of dissemination of texts, it is worth mentioning that webpages were deliberately excluded from the project because it would be materially impossible to trace them reliably for all periods and websites. Additionally, it soon became apparent that a high proportion of their web content is based on other texts considered in the project such as reports, memoranda or press releases. The exclusion of webpages would therefore have no impact on the adequacy of the compiled corpora for LETRINT's research needs.

The classification of all corpus components according to these categories entailed a dual process of: (1) identifying genres, i.e. verification of document titles, metadata and discourse features such as structural conventions and lexical markers of key legal functions; (2) situating their role with regard to the major categories and determining inter-genre connections within and between categories and subcategories. Throughout this process, it was essential to remain permeable to nuances and unexpected data, especially texts that would not easily fit into any of the main categories. Institutional document symbols often facilitated the task of situating entire document series (e.g. WTO dispute settlement reports or EU directives). However, in other cases, document symbols or titles were of little help, and demanded closer analysis by textual unit (e.g. groups of miscellaneous communications). The manual verification of large volumes of texts by several validators (at least two LETRINT researchers per organisation, including the project supervisor) was time-consuming but yielded dividends. Given the comparative approach, the delineation of boundaries applicable to the three organisations called for a regular examination of classification issues and gradual modulation of definitions. The more advanced the categorisation work, the fewer adjustments proved necessary, until the categorisation matrix became stable.

3.3 An evolving categorisation matrix

The cyclical categorisation process confirmed the applicability of the three primary categories and shed light on their interwoven subcategories and an additional category of administrative texts, as represented in Table 2.3.

Within **major categories**, relevant subdivisions included the distinction between hard law and soft law, which was merged with other policy formulation as part of a single "law- and policy-making" macro-category. The distinction between the binding and non-binding nature of instruments was generally straightforward. However, the degree of legal force that a particular non-binding instrument or policy document may attain to be considered "soft law" (or "informal international law-making") is not always easy to establish, as it may ultimately depend on their influence on binding instruments or case-law (see e.g. Pauwelyn *et al.* 2012; Ştefan 2013). While all law-making can be understood as a prescriptive form of policy-making (see e.g. Plein 2016), policy formulation might adopt a variety of other shapes in the pursuit of institutional objectives, and they constitute a fuzzy area for categorisation purposes from a legal perspective. Accordingly, in the case of monitoring, a distinction is made between: (1) mandatory compliance monitoring procedures (e.g. universal periodic review at the UN or infringement procedures at the European Commission, which in fact may resemble judicial procedures (see Prieto Ramos 2017, pp. 199–206)); (2) pre-accession monitoring (more prevalent at the WTO); and (3) other monitoring and implementation matters, i.e. coordination and follow-up of States' policies in the framework of cooperation mechanisms. Finally, the added category of "administrative functions", i.e. devoted to the functioning of the institution itself, included two large subgroups in connection with human resources, finance and procurement procedures, and other coordination and internal matters. This category may be considered as globally instrumental and gravitates around the others, as administrative housekeeping is necessary for the smooth running of all activities.

Typically "administrative" texts such as meeting agendas or procedural notes are also found as "instrumental" types within **subordinated categories**, i.e. within the second level of classification based on the relevance of texts to the main functional category. The key genres are those that perform the main functions (e.g. judgments in adjudication or regulations in law-making), while secondary

Table 2.3 LETRINT text categorisation matrix

MAIN FUNCTIONAL CATEGORIES	*SUBCATEGORIES BASED ON RELEVANCE TO MAIN FUNCTION (ILLUSTRATIVE GENRES)*
1 LAW- AND POLICY-MAKING	
1.1 HARD LAW	**a** Key (e.g. treaties, agreements, regulations, directives) **b** Secondary (input, instrumental or derived) (e.g. technical reports, proposals, minutes)
1.2 SOFT LAW AND OTHER POLICY FORMULATION	**a** Key (e.g. declarations, resolutions, guidelines, model laws) **b** Secondary (input, instrumental or derived) (e.g. records, technical reports, letters)
2 MONITORING	
2.1 MANDATORY COMPLIANCE MONITORING	**a** Key (e.g. States' reports, monitoring bodies' reports) **b** Secondary (input, instrumental or derived) (e.g. procedural notes, letters)
2.2 PRE-ACCESSION MONITORING	**a** Key (e.g. communications, questions and replies) **b** Secondary (input, instrumental or derived) (e.g. statements, minutes)
2.3 OTHER MONITORING AND IMPLEMENTATION MATTERS	**a** Key (e.g. progress reports, working papers, notes) **b** Secondary (input, instrumental or derived) (e.g. checklists, letters)
3 ADJUDICATION	**a** Key (primary case documents, e.g. requests, appeals, judgments) **b** Secondary (input, instrumental or derived) (e.g. activity reports, summaries, press releases)
4 ADMINISTRATIVE FUNCTIONS (not included in other categories)	
4.1 ORGANISATION'S HUMAN RESOURCES, FINANCE AND PROCUREMENT	(e.g. budgets, recruitment notices, calls for tenders, staff notices)
4.2 OTHER COORDINATION AND INTERNAL MATTERS	(e.g. minutes, notes, presentations, reports)

genres: (1) address **preparatory work** or provide **input** for the production of the key genres (e.g. treaty negotiation documents or technical reports); (2) play a purely **instrumental** role (e.g. meeting agendas or checklists); or (3) are **derived** genres that describe the main institutional functions for institutional follow-up or general dissemination purposes (e.g. activity reports or press releases). A high proportion of these secondary genres are found across categories, but not all of them are equally relevant to the four main categories. For instance, in the case of the administrative category, primary and secondary relevance often blurred, so genres within this category were not further classified on that basis.

At the level of **text**, each unit belongs to only one category and subcategory. According to this principle, secondary administrative texts (typically minutes) that take stock of more than one primary institutional function had to be classified as a miscellaneous subgroup of the administrative category rather than as secondary units of various other primary categories. This would avoid duplications or fragmentations of textual units for the sake of methodological consistency.

Overall, each institutional setting can be viewed as a constellation formed of **systems of genres** that are gravitationally bound and orbit around the key genres (see Figure 2.2), i.e. "interrelated genres that interact with each other in specific settings" (Bazerman 1994, p. 97). They are all interdependent within the legal framework of each organisation, and have internal (intra-institutional) and external (inter-governmental, inter-institutional and general dissemination) interfaces.

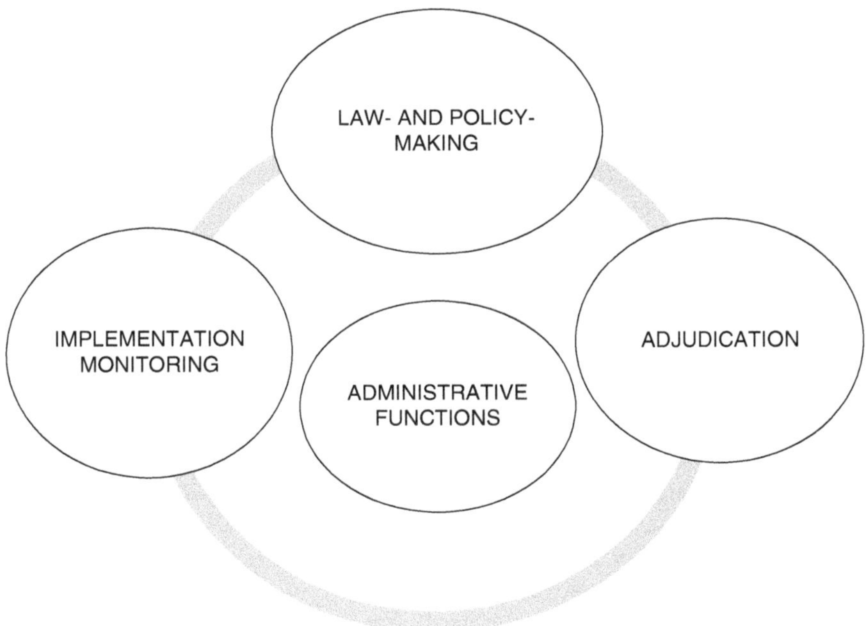

Figure 2.2 LETRINT primary functional categories

Their internal hierarchy (with legal instruments at the top) is comparable, as mentioned in section 3.2, but the size and focus of each system differ between organisations. For example, adjudicative functions are much more prominent at the WTO than at the UN. A closer examination reveals that specific bundles or chains of genres also exist within these systems (e.g. trade policy reviews systematically generate government reports, Secretariat reports, minutes and press releases), and that further **strata** can be identified within genres for sampling purposes according to quantitative and qualitative criteria (e.g. procedural, authorship or thematic considerations).

Text producers with very diverse profiles contribute in varying degrees to the circulation and perpetuation of *sui generis* discourse conventions within each institutional setting, including specialist legal drafters (particularly international lawyers and, where relevant, international judges and court staff), political representatives and technical experts. The closer to the core of key legal functions, the more recognisable legal discourse conventions are to be expected. The text mapping so far reveals the link between main functions and legal discourse features, particularly lexical markers, as well as the intermingling with other specialised discourses, not only in secondary preparatory genres but also in key ones (e.g. long technical annexes in EU legislation and dispute settlement body reports). These aspects will be further examined by the LETRINT project.

For the methodological purposes addressed here, the categorisation results may support at least three approaches to defining the scope of institutional legal translation as the first objective of LETRINT:

1 A more restrictive approach including representative key genres of hard law, mandatory compliance monitoring and adjudication, i.e. focusing on the creation and enforcement of legal obligations and the related case-law.
2 A less restrictive approach also including genres of soft law and other implementation monitoring, but excluding the administrative macro-category and all secondary genres.
3 A more inclusive approach that would consider all genres, i.e. adopting an expansive definition of institutional legal translation determined by setting, including legal and administrative text types.

In terms of research design, this decision has a number of implications for the subsequent analysis of representativeness, stratified sampling and balancing of corpus components in the next phases of the project. In all scenarios, for the sake of research validity, generalisations must be explicit about the legal contextualisation of selected categories and subcategories within the constellation of institutional functions, and they must take account of the insights provided by further corpus analysis. In other words, adjustments to the matrix and selected strata are possible as the research progresses, and definitions may be fine-tuned according to new findings. For instance, in the third scenario, the scope might be described as "institutional legal and administrative translation" or simply acknowledge that "institutional legal translation" (as a *sui generis* area of practice) integrates policy, technical and administrative dimensions of public law. This does not imply that texts which do not belong to a legal genre or deal with legal matters should be considered as legal texts in their own right.

4 Concluding remarks

The categorisation of texts lies at the heart of research design in Translation Studies, as it draws on the boundaries and underlying conceptions of the object of study, and conditions data representativeness and findings validity. In LTS, the definition of boundaries remains a seminal debate about the nature of legal texts and the scope of the field. Šarčević's (1997, p. 55) well-known definition of legal translation as "an act of communication *within* the mechanism of the law" (our emphasis) can be interpreted in a restrictive or expansive way, as law frames all aspects of life, while texts *about* the law, such as legal scholarly texts, are also generally regarded as legal texts. In fact, legal translation and legal genres, like law itself, embraces all kinds of technical discourses and covers as broad a scope as legal function and legal settings can reach. The more expansive and setting-oriented the categorisation approach, the more text types and internal subdivisions might be elicited. In classifying them as interrelated sets of genres, taxonomies based on discursive situation parameters tend to agree on the link between legal functions or themes and legal discourse features. Discourse-oriented categorisations may accordingly include texts of non-legal genres that deal with legal subjects, and exclude other non-legal texts that contain no legal discourse but might be used in legal settings.

Multidimensional approaches combining legal context of text production, legal functions and genre conventions have been advocated for as particularly suited to illuminating the different layers of text types, their central or ancillary positions in relationship to each other, and hence the boundaries and internal structure of the object of study. They may vary depending on research aims, theoretical grounds and legal system-bound factors. The researcher must be rigorous and explicit about these considerations, their constraints and their impact on research design. Permeability to new data and regular testing is required to provide granularity on the variations and fuzzy areas of hybrid discourses. The fabric of a corpus itself may lead the researcher to reconsider pre-conceived ideas about legal texts and language, or to redefine the scope of the research. In the case of international institutional translation settings, a short review of corpus-based categorisations confirms that classification granularity levels are very much determined by the breadth and depth of the research goals.

The first phase of the LETRINT project has served to illustrate the preceding considerations. Since it seeks to situate and characterise legal translation in international institutional contexts, a comprehensive mapping was necessary to dissect layers of primary and secondary institutional functions from a legal comparative perspective. A cyclical multi-layered categorisation of three parallel corpora reaffirmed the applicability of three major functional categories composed of interconnected networks of key and secondary genres. It also confirmed, among other aspects, the instrumental role of an additional administrative category, as well as the fuzzy area between soft law instruments and policy documents. The resulting categorisation matrix may be viewed as a dynamic constellation of genres that may further evolve as new insights emerge from corpus analysis. More importantly, this analysis must be sensitive to the implications of more expansive or restrictive approaches to institutional text genres for subsequent research stages, such as the selection and stratified sampling of representative genres for further analysis. All definitions and labels can ultimately be justified in light of the lens of observation, but only those supported by consistent methodological choices can be empirically sound.

Acknowledgements

I would like to thank Giorgina Cerutti, Diego Guzmán and Albert Morales for their contributions to the categorisation work referred to in this paper, as well as the Swiss National Science Foundation for its support through a Consolidator Grant.

Notes

1 More precisely, for the purposes of the project, the main EU institutions include the European Commission, the Council of the EU, the European Parliament and the Court of Justice of the EU. In the case of the UN, the International Court of Justice (ICJ) is considered as the main judicial body of the organisation, while the WTO's adjudicative bodies include dispute settlement panels and the Appellate Body.
2 "Text type" will be considered here as an umbrella term to refer to supra-genre categories of texts according to a definition or set of distinctive characteristics, while "text typology" will be understood as the overall classification of texts, including subdivisions at genre or supra-genre level.
3 As indicated in the introduction, given the focus of this paper, technical details of corpus compilation will not be addressed here.
4 This anthropologist described "rich points" as "things –lexical items through speech acts up to extensive stretches of discourse–" that "strike you with their difficulty, their inability to fit into the resources you use to make sense of the world".

References

Abdel Hadi, M. (1992). Géographie politique et traduction juridique, le problème de la terminologie. *Terminologie et traduction*, 2/3, pp. 43–57.

Agar, M. (1991). The biculture in bilingual. *Language in Society*, 20, pp. 167–181.

Alcaraz Varó, E. and Hughes, B. (2002). *Legal translation explained*. Manchester: St. Jerome Publishing.

Bazerman, C. (1994). Systems of genres and the enactment of social intentions. *In*: A. Freedman and P. Medway, eds. *Genre and the new rhetoric*. London: Taylor & Francis, pp. 79–101.

Bernardini, S., *et al.* (2016). From EPIC to EPTIC: Exploring simplification in interpreting and translation from an intermodal perspective. *Target*, 28 (1), pp. 58–83.

Berūkštienė, D. (2016). Legal discourse reconsidered: Genres of legal texts. *Comparative Legilinguistics*, 28, pp. 89–117.
Bhatia, V.K. (1993). *Analysing genre: Language use in professional settings*. London: Longman.
Bhatia, V.K. (2006). Legal genres. *In*: K. Brown, ed. *Encyclopedia of language and linguistics*. 2nd ed. Oxford: Elsevier, pp. 1–7.
Biber, D. (1988). *Variation across speech and writing*. Cambridge: Cambridge University Press.
Biber, D. (1993). Representativeness in corpus design. *Literary and Linguistic Computing*, 8 (4), pp. 243–257.
Biber, D., *et al.* (1998). *Corpus linguistics: Investigating language structure and use*. Cambridge: Cambridge University Press.
Biel, Ł. (2014). *Lost in the Eurofog: The textual fit of translated law*. Frankfurt am Main: Peter Lang.
Biel, Ł. (2016). Mixed corpus design for researching the Eurolect: A genre-based comparable-parallel corpus in the PL EUROLECT project. *In*: E. Gruszczyńska and A. Leńko-Szymańska, eds. *Polskojęzyczne korpusy równoległe. Polish-language parallel corpora*. Warsaw: Instytut Lingwistyki Stosowanej, pp. 197–208.
Bocquet, C. (1994). *Pour une méthode de traduction juridique*. Prilly and Lausanne: Éditions C. B.
Borja Albi, A. (2000). *El texto jurídico inglés y su traducción al español*. Barcelona: Ariel.
Borja Albi, A. (2013). A genre analysis approach to the study of the translation of court documents. *Linguistica Antverpiensia, New Series – Themes in Translation Studies*, 12, pp. 33–53.
Cao, D. (2007). *Translating law*. Clevedon: Multilingual Matters.
Fairclough, N. (2006). Genres in political discourse. *In*: K. Brown, ed. *Encyclopedia of language and linguistics*. 2nd ed. Oxford: Elsevier, pp. 32–38.
Fontanet, M. (2018). Translating hybrid legal texts for science and technology institutions: The case of CERN. *In*: F. Prieto Ramos, ed. *Institutional translation for international governance: Enhancing quality in multilingual legal communication*. London: Bloomsbury, pp. 126–138.
Forsyth, R.S. and Sharoff, S. (2014). Document dissimilarity within and across languages: A benchmarking study. *Literary and Linguistic Computing*, 29, pp. 6–22.
Galdia, M. (2009). *Legal linguistics*. Frankfurt am Main: Peter Lang.
Gémar, J-C. (1995). *Traduire ou l'art d'interpréter. Tome I: Principes. Fonctions, statut et esthétique de la traduction. Tome II: Application. Langue, droit et société: Éléments de jurilinguistique*. Sainte-Foy: Presses de l'Université du Québec.
Goźdź-Roszkowski, S. (2011a). *Patterns of linguistic variation in American legal English. A corpus-based study*. Frankfurt am Main: Peter Lang.
Goźdź-Roszkowski, S. (2011b). Legal language. *In*: C.A. Chapelle, ed. *The encyclopedia of applied linguistics*. Chichester: Wiley-Blackwell, pp. 3281–3289.
Halverson, S. (1998). Translation studies and representative corpora: Establishing links between translation corpora, theoretical/descriptive categories and a conception of the object of study. *Meta: Translators' Journal*, 43 (4), pp. 494–514.
Harvey, M. (2002). What is so special about legal translation? *Meta: Translators' Journal*, 47 (2), pp. 177–185.
Kjær, A.L. (2000). On the structure of legal knowledge: The importance of knowing legal rules for understanding legal texts. *In*: L. Lundquist and R.J. Jarvella, eds.

Language, text and knowledge. Mental models of expert communication. Berlin: de Gruyter Mouton, pp. 127–161.

Koskinen, K. (2014). Institutional translation: The art of government by translation. *Perspectives*, 22 (4), pp. 479–492.

Lee, D. (2001). Genres, registers, text types, domains, and styles: Clarifying the concepts and navigating a path through the BNC jungle. *Language Learning and Technology*, 5 (3), pp. 37–72.

Maley, Y. (1994). The language of the law. *In*: J. Gibbons, ed. *Language and the law.* London: Longman, pp. 11–50.

Mattila, H.E.S. (2013). *Comparative legal linguistics.* 2nd ed. Aldershot: Ashgate.

McEnery, A.M., *et al.* (2006). *Corpus-based language studies: An advanced resource book.* London: Routledge.

Melissourgou, M.N. and Frantzi, K.T. (2017). Genre identification based on SFL principles: The representation of text types and genres in English language teaching material. *Corpus Pragmatics*, 1 (4), pp. 373–392.

Mellinger, C.D. and Hanson, T.A. (2017). *Quantitative research methods in translation and interpreting studies.* New York: Routledge.

Monjean-Decaudin, S. (2013). Réflexion sur l'inflexion du signifié dans la traduction juridique de Claude Bocquet. *Parallèles*, 25, pp. 19–29.

Munday, J. (2012). *Evaluation in translation: Critical points of translator decision-making.* London: Routledge.

Nord, C. (1997). *Translating as a purposeful activity.* Manchester: St. Jerome Publishing.

PACTE (2009). Results of the validation of the PACTE translation competence model: Acceptability and decision making. *Across Languages and Cultures*, 10 (2), pp. 207–230.

Pauwelyn, J., *et al.*, eds. (2012). *Informal international lawmaking.* Oxford: Oxford University Press.

Plein, C. (2016). A Policymaking checklist for the legislative process. *West Virginia Law Review Online* [online], 6 (15). Available at: http://wvlawreview.wvu.edu/west-virginia-law-review-online/2016/01/20/a-policymaking-checklist-for-the-legislative-process [Accessed 20 May 2007].

Pontrandolfo, G. (2016). *Fraseología y lenguaje judicial. Las sentencias penales desde una perspectiva contrastiva.* Roma: Aracne.

Prieto Ramos, F. (2014a). Legal Translation Studies as interdiscipline: Scope and evolution. *Meta: Translators' Journal*, 59 (2), pp. 260–277.

Prieto Ramos, F. (2014b). International and supranational law in translation: From multilingual lawmaking to adjudication. *The Translator*, 20 (3), pp. 313–331.

Prieto Ramos, F. (2017). Global law as translated text: Mapping institutional legal translation. *Tilburg Law Review*, 22 (1–2), pp. 185–214.

Rappaport, B. (2014). A lawyer's hidden persuader: Genre bias and how it shapes legal texts by constraining writers' choices and influencing readers' perception. *Brooklyn Journal of Law and Policy*, 21 (1), pp. 197–263.

Robinson, W. (2005). How the European Commission drafts legislation in 20 languages. *Clarity*, 53, pp. 4–10.

Šarčević, S. (1997). *New approach to legal translation.* The Hague: Kluwer Law International.

Sinding, M. (2002). After definitions: Genre, categories, and cognitive science. *Genre*, 35 (2), pp. 181–219.

Ştefan, O. (2013). *Soft law in court: Competition law, State aid and the Court of Justice of the European Union*. The Hague: Kluwer.

Tiersma, P.M. (1999). *Legal language*. Chicago: University of Chicago Press.

Tiersma, P.M. (2003). *The creation, structure, and interpretation of the legal text* [online]. Available at: www.languageandlaw.org/LEGALTEXT.HTM [Accessed 15 Oct. 2017].

Trklja, A. and McAuliffe, K. (2018). The European Union Case Law Corpus (EUCLCORP): A multilingual parallel and comparative corpus of EU Court judgments. *In*: A.U. Frank, *et al.*, eds. *Gerastree Proceedings*, 1, pp. 217–226.

Trosborg, A. (1997). *Rhetorical strategies in legal language: Discourse analysis of statutes and contracts*. Tübingen: Gunter Narr Verlag.

Ziemski, M., *et al.* (2016). The United Nations parallel corpus v1.0. *In*: *Language resources and evaluation (LREC'16)* [online]. Available at: http://conferences.unite.un.org/UNCorpus/Content/Doc/un.pdf [Accessed 20 May 2017].

3 Inverse legal translation

A corpus-driven study of multi-word units related to the structure of translated statutory provisions

Justyna Giczela-Pastwa

1 Introduction

Inverse translation[1] takes place when translators render texts from their mother tongue into a foreign language. It is often assumed that no matter how perfect their command of the target language (TL) is, patterns typical of their native source language (SL) may become unconsciously transferred into the translated texts, therefore "expert (and no doubt public) opinion favours translation into the first language" (Campbell 1998, p. 57). Nevertheless, it should be remembered that the unpreventable influence of the SL on the TL is likely to occur in every translation act, no matter the direction. In fact, this phenomenon is so common that it was encapsulated by Toury (2012, p. 310) in his seminal law of interference: "in translation, phenomena pertaining to the make-up of the source text tend to force themselves on the translators and be transferred to the target text".

Notwithstanding, inverse translation has been marginalised in Translation Studies. In accordance with what Pokorn (2005, p. 37) and Pavlović (2007, p. 81) call the traditional, post-Romantic view of translation theorists, translators should only translate into their mother tongue, because the language competence of a native speaker is the best guarantee of quality. As Pokorn (2005, p. IX) observes,

> [t]ranslation into a non-mother tongue or inverse translation, especially of literary texts, has always been frowned upon within Translation Studies in Western cultures with a dominant language, and regarded as an action doomed to failure by both literary scholars and linguists.

As a result, little research on the subject has been done to date, with Pokorn (2005) being one of the notable exceptions. Her project focuses on the translation of literary texts and aims to determine possible shared characteristics of inverse translations that would distinguish them from the translations performed by native speakers of the TL (2005, p. 41). From a methodological point of view, Pokorn's research is qualitative (a limited number of the STs, all written by the same author) and is based on subjects' answers to a questionnaire. In the conclusions, Pokorn makes several important statements concerning: (1) the vagueness and subjectiveness of the concepts of *mother tongue* and *native speaker*; (2) the frequent acceptability of inversely translated texts, reflected in native speakers' inability to identify them as such; and (3) the lack of dependence between the quality of translation and the translator's mother tongue. Pokorn calls for further research into the subject, in particular carried out with reference to non-literary texts, "created in a different linguistic environment" (2005, p. 122).

In addition to this, inverse translation and directionality were the focal point of the research conducted by Pavlović (2007) in reference to Croatian, and by Wang (2011) in the Chinese context. The relation between directionality in translation and cognitive load was researched into by Marmaridou (1996), Malkiel (2004) and Chang (2011). So far directionality has been mainly studied using process research methods, such as eye-tracking (Pavlović and Jensen 2009; Chang 2011).

However, inverse translation has been widely practised and in the case of languages of limited diffusion, such as Polish, it is often unavoidable. There is still a significant shortage of native speakers of dominant languages who would be able to translate from peripheral languages as their foreign languages into their mother tongues. As noted by Weatherby (1998, p. 21) in reference to Spain, even in the case of major languages, inverse translation is frequently practised: "more than half of many professional translators' work is done into their L2". Similar observations may be made on the basis of a thorough report prepared by the International Association of Professional Translators and Interpreters (IAPTI's Ethics Committee 2015). Therefore, it seems justified to consider inverse translation as a valuable research direction within Translation Studies, and to develop an appropriate methodology that would enable researchers to better understand this linguistic phenomenon, especially through the prism of legal translation. The relation which seems particularly crucial for the evaluation of inverse translation functionality is the one of textual fit (i.e. the naturalness of target texts (TTs) analysed against non-translated TL texts), discerned by Koller (1988), fully described by Chesterman (2004) and revisited and operationalised by Biel (2014a).

It is impossible to underestimate the importance of phraseology in the context of inverse legal translation. In this chapter phraseology is understood as redefined by Sinclair (1991), whose conclusions were aptly summarised by Hunston (2013, p. 5): "(a) more language occurs in 'fixed phrases' than might otherwise be thought and, furthermore, that (b) 'fixed phrases' are more varied than might otherwise be thought". It follows that as in the case of any other language use, non-native translators construct their translations using prefabricated chunks, and that these chunks may vary considerably, also from the chunks prevalent in the TL. What seems particularly appropriate as regards specialised inverse translation is evaluating the degree to which the phraseology in the translations diverges from the word combinations in non-translated TL, especially in terms of: (1) the frequency with which particular chunks are used; and (2) the structure of the chunks and their lexico-grammatical environment. Next, it would be most revealing to discover what triggers the mechanism of the observed untypical collocation, understood in this chapter as a non-standard variant of the established phraseological unit, or an untypical pattern of its use, including a considerably higher frequency of use (cf. Mauranen 2007, p. 44). Importantly, phraseology in translation – not only inverse – is prone to distortions. This is due to the fact that translation is a bilingual processing situation and as such cannot resemble "ideally monolingual processing of a native speaker" (Mauranen 2007, p. 44). Therefore, what may distinguish inverse translation from the translation into one's mother tongue is the intensity and extent of the phenomenon.

Even though research into phraseology in legal translation has until recently been rather scarce, the studies undertaken in the field have yielded interesting and informative results. In her study on EU legislation translated into Polish, Biel (2014a) reveals, *inter alia*, that the translations use untypical collocational patterns as regards collocational ranges and strength, and are less consistent and careful than the non-translations, e.g., use collocations that are typical of a different register of Polish, or suppress collocations that are not prompted in translation. Biel's analysis clearly shows that "translated law has developed its own patterns at the phrase level" (2014a, p. 285). In the follow-up study concerning legal phrasemes with complex preposition, Biel (2015) demonstrates how the translator-mediated EU variants of Polish and English differ from the non-translated legal languages in terms of their phraseological profiles. A related finding is reported by Trklja (2018), who identifies hybrid expressions created through translation in judgments of the Court of Justice of the European Union. Focusing on criminal judgments in Italian, Spanish and English, Pontrandolfo (2015, p. 153) detects "the comparability of phraseologisms", or "parallel phraseologisms", which enables the functional translation of the MWUs typical of judicial discourse.

This chapter reports on the methodology applied in the ongoing InLeTra (Inverse Legal Translation) research project. As already suggested, most often it is phraseology that bears the mark of (inverse) translation. Therefore, the main focus of the proposed methodology is on discovering the discrepancies between the English patterns inversely translated from Polish, and the phraseology observable in non-translated legal English. The main aim is to identify and examine multiword units (MWUs) typical of the analysed translations. Multiword units are understood in this chapter as constructs with a high frequency of occurrence, used "to express concepts or fulfil discoursal functions that cannot be carried out by means of a single word" (Goźdź-Roszkowski 2011, p. 40). Once the MWUs are identified, an effort is made to compare their visibility and patterns of use (if any) in non-translated UK legislation, and to evaluate the adequacy (textual fit) of the solutions adopted by non-native translators.

2 Methodology

The research procedure is inspired by the multilingually comparable corpus method (Hansen-Schirra and Teich 2008), more explicitly referred to as the comparable-parallel corpus method (Biel 2016). In addition to the monolingual comparable corpora, a parallel corpus of the Polish legal acts is used for consultation purposes. This is in line with the suggestion that only by observing the realisation of a feature in the underlying ST are we able to detect differences between translations and non-translations (Evert and Neumann 2017, p. 49). The investigation focuses on proportionalities and frequencies. It is assumed that a different frequency of use of typical lexical or grammatical units results in markedness. In this chapter, markedness is understood as unexpected, non-standard, yet meaningful linguistic behaviour (Baker 2018, pp. 129–130). Untypical frequency of a particular linguistic unit or structure may make the target reader perceive the translation as awkward, with no obvious reason. This is the case described by Steiner (2012, p. 10), who indicates that borrowing or interference may result in a different 'feel' of apparently good translations.

The search for potential untypical collocations is conducted in the following manner:

1 Keyword lists are produced for the translational subcorpora, with non-translated legislation compiled in the reference corpus (RC); next, a set of the most salient keywords is excerpted.

   A keyword list produced by Wordsmith Tools contains words that are unusually frequent in a given corpus, compared with an RC. The lists are compiled on the basis of three statistical significance tests: log likelihood, log ratio and BIC score, using Wordsmith's default settings. Words are listed as key only when they pass all of the tests (Scott 2017, p. 274). The statistical test of choice that determines the order of keywords is log likelihood.

2 Clusters are identified in the translational subcorpora; clusters that contain the most salient keywords are singled out for further analysis.

   As observed by Wray (2002, p. 9), the linguistic phenomenon of clusters has been referred to using a plethora of terms, with *n-grams* and *lexical bundles* appearing to be the most popular. Clusters are frequently recurring sequences of words, which are not necessarily structurally complete or idiomatic (Biber and Barbieri 2007, p. 264), although many of them constitute "important textual building blocks" (Tracy-Ventura *et al.* 2007, p. 217). In the analysis of clusters, the following constraints are suggested: (a) due to the nature of the texts and the high frequency of legal references, the cluster lists should not include clusters containing numbers; (b) to be included in the lists, with regard to the nature of the corpus used in the analysis, clusters have to occur with the minimal NF of 40 per 1m words, in at least three texts. The frequent threshold of five texts (cf. Biber and Barbieri 2007, p. 268) has been modified due to the InLeTra corpus design: each of the three translational subcorpora consists of nine texts only. The otherwise high dispersion threshold of three texts is meant to exclude idiosyncrasies of individual translators who in some cases translated two acts included in the corpus. The recurrence threshold of 40 occurrences is relatively high in order to exclude clusters that reflect the aboutness of particular texts.

3 The lexico-grammatical environment of clusters is studied and compared in both the translational subcorpora and the reference corpus, by analysing concordances.
4 The parallel Polish-English corpus is consulted, in an attempt to determine a possible SL textual stimulus for untypical collocations.

3 Material

The multilingually comparable corpus used in the InLeTra project consists of a translational corpus (English translations of selected legal acts, aligned with the source texts in Polish with the aid of the free-text alignment software LF Aligner)[2] and a monolingual comparable corpus of non-translated legal English texts.

The translations analysed in the project were downloaded from the online databases offered by each of the publishers (*Legalis Translator* by C.H. Beck – CHB; *Polish Law Collection* by Translegis – PLC; *LEX Tłumaczenia* by Wolters Kluwer – WK) and are referred to throughout the paper using the previously mentioned abbreviations. Team translation by native speakers of the SL is interpreted, after Pokorn (2005), as a valid example of inverse translation. Likewise, a note on linguistic consultancy (found in three out of 27 translations) does not automatically exclude this translation from the analysis.

The English subcorpus of the InLeTra translational corpus, with the exclusion of the Polish source texts, has almost 1.8m tokens[3] and 11,668 types (different words). It is divided into several subcorpora, according to two criteria: (1) the legal act and (2) the publisher (see Figure 3.1). In this way, it is possible to: (1) analyse an act in three parallel translations, concentrating on, for example, its inherent terminology and phraseology in alternative renderings (horizontally); or (2) focus on a set of translations published by the same publisher, e.g. in search for translation strategies preferred by particular publishers (if any), by comparing and contrasting three subcorpora consisting of nine files each (vertically). The first option is more instance-based and has to take account of the idiosyncrasies of individual translators. In the second option, the grounds for generalising seem more valid, as there were 29 translators involved in the preparation of the translations.

The monolingual comparable corpus of non-translated English texts was compiled from selected UK public general acts, downloaded from the legislation database (www.legislation.gov.uk) – the LEN-UK Corpus of 70 legal acts (LEN-UK). Even though "representativeness is a fluid concept" (McEnery *et al.* 2006, p. 18), efforts were made to ensure LEN-UK is well-balanced. The acts included in the corpus regulate a wide range of issues, starting from banking and childcare, through contracts and property, to pension and wills. LEN-UK has 3,606,780 tokens and 11,336 types. The main limitation of the study is its

SOURCE TEXT IN POLISH [parallel corpus]	ENGLISH TRANSLATIONS (SORTED BY PUBLISHER) [study corpus]			NON-TRANSLATED UK LEGISLATION [reference corpus]
	CHB	PLC	WK	LEN-UK
Ustawa o rachunkowości	The Accounting Act	Act on Accounting	Accounting	70 UK public general acts
Prawo bankowe	The Banking Act	Banking Law	Banking Law	
Kodeks cywilny	The Civil Code	The Civil Code	Civil Code	
Kodeks spółek handlowych	The Commercial Companies Code	The Code of Commercial Partnerships and Companies	Code of Commercial Companies	
Ustawa o podatku od towarów i usług	The Goods and Services Tax Act	Act on Goods and Services Tax	Act on Goods and Services Tax	
Kodeks pracy	The Labour Code	The Labour Code	Labour Code	
Ustawa o podatku dochodowym od osób fizycznych	Personal Income Tax Act	Act on Natural Persons' Income Tax	Act on Personal Income Tax	
Prawo zamówień publicznych	Public Procurement Law	Public Procurement Law	Public Procurement Law	
Ordynacja podatkowa	The Tax Ordinance Act	Tax Ordinance	Tax Ordinance	
	510,425 tokens 8,099 types	658,955 tokens 8,666 types	596,078 tokens 8,580 types	3,606,780 tokens 11,336 types

Figure 3.1 InLeTra corpus design

reference to only one variety of non-translated English, i.e. UK legal English. Future research within the InLeTra project will incorporate reference corpora covering other jurisdictions.

In order to compare corpora of different sizes, normalised frequencies have to be calculated by converting raw frequencies into a value per a common base. In this chapter, the abbreviations NF and nf are used; NF denotes the normalised frequency and nf denotes the normalisation factor, calculated by dividing the base by the number of tokens. The frequencies are normalised to 1m words. The NF values are rounded to whole numbers.

4 Application of the methodology

In a first step, three keyword lists were produced, one for each subcorpus of the InLeTra translational corpus (CHB, PLC and WK). The top 50 keywords were compared in order to separate out the units present in each of the lists. As much as 50% of the top 50 keywords were identical (in alphabetical order: *article*, *bank*, *board*, *contract*, *due*, *economic*, *entities*, *entity*, *financial*, *goods*, *obliged*, *performance*, *Poland*, *provisions*, *referred*, *Republic*, *scope*, *shall*, *shareholders*, *supervision*, *taxpayer*, *territory*, *their*, *thing*, *well*). Out of these 25 keywords, five words with the highest scores were selected to be further described in this chapter (see Table 3.1).

Subsequently, the lists of clusters (3- to 8-grams) in each of the translational subcorpora were generated. The previously mentioned constraints were then applied, i.e. the clusters with fewer than 40 occurrences in at least three texts were excluded. In the remaining sets, the clusters containing the previously mentioned keywords were singled out. As shorter clusters are frequently part of longer ones (Biber *et al.* 1999, p. 990), the procedure began from the longest clusters, i.e. 8-grams, in an attempt to effectively identify the longest MWUs. Once all the clusters containing the five keywords were studied, the following patterns of use observable in each of the translational subcorpora were discerned, as shown in Table 3.2.

The majority of the MWUs listed in Table 3.2 function as routine intertextual and intratextual referencing patterns and create the structure of a typical statutory provision in Polish law. The analysis presented in this chapter covers only the most frequent and hence more salient MWUs.

Table 3.1 Keywords to be analysed: the position on the keyword lists

	CHB	*PLC*	*WK*
article	2	1	1
referred	3	3	2
shall	4	2	3
provisions	9	7	12
obliged	7	9	19

Table 3.2 Top MWUs typical of the InLeTra translational subcorpora

article	*the information referred to in article*
	the conditions referred to in article
	as referred to in article
	within the meaning of article
	the provision of article
	in the case/cases referred to in article
referred	*other than those referred to in*
	hereinafter referred to as the
	the documents referred to in
	the circumstances referred to in
	the notification referred to in
	the amount referred to in
	the act referred to in
	the exemption referred to in
	the decision referred to in
shall	*shall not apply to*
	shall apply accordingly
provisions	*in accordance with the provisions of*
	within the meaning of the provisions
	the provisions of this act
	the provisions of this chapter
obliged	*shall be obliged to*
	obliged to notify the

4.1 *article/referred*

The keyness of *article* in the translational subcorpora (Table 3.3) stems from the structure of Polish legislation: *artykuł* (abbreviated to *art.* whenever it precedes a provision and functions as a subheading) is the basic editing unit of Polish statutes.

The occurrences of *article* in the RC are significantly less frequent – they account for approximately two percent of the use of the word in each of the translational subcorpora. Whenever it denotes an editing unit in LEN-UK, *article* refers to a different type of statutory instruments, namely UK secondary legislation (orders) or EU legislation. The intertextual references to particular secondary legislation or EU legislation instruments usually occur in definitions and in schedules that contain amendments, repeals and revocations. The corresponding editing unit in UK public general acts is *section*. This is confirmed by the positions on the frequency lists: *section* is the first content word, following such grammar words as *the*, *of*, *a*, *to*, *in*, *or*, on the LEN-UK list. Similarly, *article* occurs as the first content word on the PLC and WK lists. In the case of CHB, this has not been observed due to the fact that *artykuł* and *art.* are translated with the full and abbreviated forms preserved, as *article* and *art.*

Subsequently, the appropriate searches for the MWUs containing *section* as the functional equivalent of *article* were conducted in LEN-UK. As shown in Table 3.4, the MWUs with the basic editing unit prevalent in the translational

Table 3.3 The distribution of *article* (NFs)

	Translational subcorpora			*RC*
	CHB (nf 1.96)	*PLC (nf 1.52)*	*WK (nf 1.68)*	*LEN-UK (nf 0.3)*
article	6,221	13,007	13,546	230
art.	7,720	2	12	2

Table 3.4 Most frequent MWUs with the basic editing unit in the translational subcorpora (NFs)

	Translational subcorpora				*RC*
	CHB	*PLC*	*WK*		*LEN-UK*
referred to in article	2413	2503	2812	*referred to in section*	49
as referred to in article	76	65	289	*as referred to in section*	1
within the meaning of article	108	138	119	*within the meaning of section*	98
the provision of article	104	217	126	*the provision of section*	–
in the case(s) referred to in article	94	150	131	*in the case(s) referred to in section*	–

subcorpora (*referred to in*, *as referred to in*, *within the meaning of*, *the provision of*, *in the case(s) referred to in*) are absent from the non-translated corpus, or much less salient and occurring in just a few texts. The only exception is the MWU *within the meaning of*, with similar frequencies in the translational subcorpora and the RC. Its occurrence in the former is prompted by the Polish *w rozumieniu (przepisów/ustawy)* [lit., as understood under the provisions of law/the act].

On the other hand, the most frequent MWUs containing *section* are absent from or much less visible in the translational subcorpora (Table 3.5).

To sum up, not only is the salience of *article* in the non-translated English much lower than in the translational subcorpora, which is due to a different system-bound textual organisation of legislation, but also, whenever the term is used, the collocational patterns in the non-translated legal language diverge. What is more, as shown in Table 3.5, the MWUs with an equivalent editing unit, i.e. *section*, typical of the non-translated language, are mostly absent from the translational subcorpora.

The clusters *referred to in* and *referred to in article* are top 3- and 4-grams in the translational subcorpora (vs *in relation to* and *for the purposes of* in LEN-UK, respectively). The overall salience of *referred to in* remains much greater in the

Table 3.5 Most frequent MWUs with the basic editing unit in the reference corpora (NFs)

	Translational subcorpora				*RC*
	CHB	*PLC*	*WK*		*LEN-UK*
under this article	–	–	–	*under this section*	1001
in this article	–	9	–	*in this section*	782
this article applies	–	–	–	*this section applies*	772
the purposes of this article	–	–	–	*the purposes of this section*	372
for the purposes of article	–	12	–	*for the purposes of section*	320
the meaning given by article	–	–	–	*the meaning given by section*	310
in accordance with article	267	102	186	*in accordance with section*	240
by virtue of article	12	17	–	*by virtue of section*	212

Table 3.6 The distribution of *referred to in* (NFs)

	Translational subcorpora			*RC*
	CHB	*PLC*	*WK*	*LEN-UK*
referred to in	6,166	6,025	6,782	279

translational subcorpora than in the RC (Table 3.6). The cluster is found in 100% of the texts in each of the translational subcorpora, whereas in the RC, it is found in only 79% of the texts.

As is easily discovered in the next step of the procedure (i.e. the consultation of the Polish-English parallel corpus), the high visibility of *referred to in* in the translational subcorpora is caused by a close rendering of the Polish legal phrase *o którym/której/których mowa w* [which is/are mentioned in], which is the predominant referencing pattern typical of Polish law. Interestingly, as revealed in Biel's study (2014b, p. 188), the high formulaicity of *referred to in (article)* in the translational corpus stands out not only against non-translated UK English, but also against EU English: the NFs in Biel's subcorpora of EU regulations and EU directives are 987 and 685, respectively.

As far as the nouns typically post-modified by *referred to in* in the translational subcorpora are concerned, hardly any of them can be found in identical clusters in non-translated UK legal English (see Table 3.7).

All of the previously mentioned MWUs are close renditions of recurrent Polish phrases that help to navigate the text. The original MWUs in Polish are as follows: *kwota, o której mowa* [the amount referred to]/*okoliczności, o których*

Table 3.7 MWUs with *referred to in* (NFs)

	Translational subcorpora			*RC*
	CHB	*PLC*	*WK*	*LEN-UK*
the amount referred to in	59	47	54	8
the circumstances referred to in	65	50	55	2
the conditions referred to in	47	73	74	5
the documents referred to in	77	55	66	–
the information referred to in	122	120	109	2
the notification referred to in	65	46	55	–

mowa [the circumstances referred to]/*warunki, o których mowa* [the conditions referred to]/*dokumenty, o których mowa* or *dokumentacja, o której mowa* [the documents referred to]/*informacja, o której mowa* or *informacje, o których mowa* [the information referred to]/*powiadomienie, o którym mowa* [the notification referred to] in various grammatical forms. Obviously, the low salience of *referred to in* and of the examined clusters in LEN-UK should not be interpreted as a lack of such features, but rather as a difference in the way they are verbalised. A more detailed analysis of the LEN-UK wordlist revealed a preference for *mentioned* (total NF 989) and *given* (total NF 1508) over *referred* (total NF 383). On the other hand, the translations use *given* much more rarely than *referred to in* (on average eight times less often) and *mentioned in* is used sporadically (NFs 45 / 219 / 25 in CHB, PLC and WK, respectively). This data demonstrates that legal referencing patterns are system-bound, and depending on the legal system, differ in their formulaicity.

4.2 *shall/obliged*

Although *shall* is similarly key in each of the translational subcorpora, they differ as regards its distribution. In two of them (PLC, WK) *shall* occurs in every text, whereas in CHB, it occurs in only five out of the nine texts comprised in the subcorpus. This means that there is no uniform method of expressing deontic modality in the CHB series of translations. Nevertheless, CHB with its lowest NF of *shall* still exceeds the RC: the modal verb is used over four times as often as in LEN-UK (see Table 3.8).

The MWU *shall not apply to*, highly prevalent in the translational subcorpora (NFs 216 / 389 / 207 in CHB, PLC and WK, respectively), is hardly observable in the RC (NF 14 in LEN-UK; moreover, the MWU occurs in only 20% of the corpus). In the translational subcorpora, the expression functions mostly as a predicate of *the provision(s)* followed by a relevant editing unit, whereas in the non-translated UK legislation a relevant editing unit alone forms the subject of the clause (e.g., *Section 5 shall not apply*; *this subsection shall not apply*). The redundant MWUs in the translational subcorpora are calqued on the recurrent

Table 3.8 The distribution of *shall* (NFs)

	Translational subcorpora			*RC*
	CHB	*PLC*	*WK*	*LEN-UK*
shall	8,271	16,974	11,091	1,788

Polish *przepisu/przepisów x nie stosuje się* [the provision of/the provisions of (editing unit) shall not apply]. However, the observed preference for *shall* to denote obligation brings to mind normalisation, i.e. "a tendency to exaggerate features of the target language and to conform to its typical patterns" (Baker 1993, p. 183), especially given that the inspection of the LEN-UK wordlist and clusters suggests that other ways of expressing deontic modality may be more frequent in non-translated legal English. It seems that the infrequent use of *shall* in LEN-UK is balanced by the high salience of *must* (NF 2,623; the modal verb is observable in 89% of the corpus) and of the construction *is/are to* (NFs 1,029 and 458 for the clusters *is to be* and *are to be*, respectively). The empirical observation is mirrored in a prescription: "Office policy is to avoid the use of the legislative 'shall'. There may of course be exceptions. One reason for using 'shall' might be where the text is being inserted into an Act that already uses it" (Office of the Parliamentary Counsel 2017, p. 4). Furthermore, this corresponds to Garzone's findings that "UK legislation has replaced *shall* with *must* and the semi-modal *is/are to*" (2013, pp. 70, 75). The salience of *must*, combined with the decreasing frequency of *shall*, may be a sign of successful efforts to make legislative language more transparent.

The MWU *shall apply accordingly* is rare in LEN-UK: it occurs in less than 10% of the RC, with the NF 2. Its salience in the translational subcorpora results from the literal translation of the Polish *stosuje się odpowiednio.*

Low frequencies of *must* in the translational subcorpora (NFs 527 / 185 / 116 in CHB, PLC and WK, respectively) seem to reflect another quality of legal Polish: the closest Polish equivalent, namely *musieć*, is rare in Polish law (Biel 2014a, p. 162). Therefore, there is little direct motivation for using *must* while translating into English.

The keyness of the MWU *obliged to notify* reflects the overall visibility of the clusters combining *obliged to* with an infinitive. The high ranking of this particular MWU is due to the repetitive Polish legal phrase *obowiązany jest (niezwłocznie) zawiadomić/zawiadamiać* [is required to immediately notify]. The past participles in both the SL (*obowiązany*) and the TL (*obliged to*) stem from the same Latin root. However, apart from phrasemes with *must* and *shall*, typically used to express deontic modality, the synonymous *required to* seems to be preferred in LEN-UK as the MWU with a past participle that expresses obligation (see Table 3.9).

The previously mentioned hypothesis has been tested with the searches for patterns containing *notify* and *pay* (Table 3.10 and Table 3.11):

Table 3.9 The distribution of *obliged* and *required* (NFs)

	Translational subcorpora			*RC*
	CHB	*PLC*	*WK*	*LEN-UK*
obliged	577	747	481	12
required	218	225	269	728

Table 3.10 Selected MWUs with *notify* that express obligation (NFs)

	Translational subcorpora				*RC*
	CHB	*PLC*	*WK*		*LEN-UK*
obliged to notify	49	49	55	*obliged to notify*	–
must notify	–	–	–	*must notify*	51
shall notify	51	150	101	*shall notify*	8
required to notify	–	–	–	*required to notify*	2

Table 3.11 Selected MWUs with *pay* that express obligation (NFs)

	Translational subcorpora				*RC*
	CHB	*PLC*	*WK*		*LEN-UK*
obliged to pay	114	87	62	*obliged to pay*	–
must pay	–	–	–	*must pay*	30
shall pay	20	27	55	*shall pay*	6
required to pay	–	–	–	*required to pay*	16

As can be seen, divergent patterns are used in the inverse translations and the non-translations, which makes it more difficult for the reader to recognise the genre identity of the translated text. Apart from the strong preference for a literal *obliged to* + infinitive, the overrepresentation of the MWUs with *shall* can be observed in the translational subcorpora. Moreover, both in the case of *notify* and *pay*, a number of alternative patterns with the same meaning has been noticed in LEN-UK (e.g., *required to give (a) notice*; *required under* (+ editing unit) *to notify*; *notice required to be served/given*; *obligation under* (+ editing unit) *to notify*; *obligation to pay*; *requirement to pay*). Except for *obligation to pay*, which is even more salient in the translational subcorpora than in the RC (NFs 31, 24 and 47 in CHB, PLC and WK, respectively, vs NF 6 in LEN-UK), due to its being a literal translation of the frequent *obowiązek zapłaty*, the other patterns are absent from the inverse translations. As regards the analysed MWUs, the translational subcorpora seem to be more consistent in using one particular pattern, prompted by the ST, whereas the non-translations show greater phraseological variation.

4.3 provision(s)

As regards the singular form of the noun, the NFs in the translational subcorpora – although varied (723 / 1,196 / 951 in CHB, PLC and WK, respectively) – are on average three times lower than the NF in LEN-UK. The overuse of *provision* in UK public general acts must have been perceived as problematic, because a suggestion has been made: "*Provision* is a useful generic phrase for what legislation does, but can be legalistic and off-putting. It may be worth thinking about what the legislation actually does in the case you are concerned about: does it regulate, authorise, require?" (Office of the Parliamentary Counsel 2017, p. 80). As shown by concordance analysis, the patterns of use in the translations and non-translations differ. In the translational subcorpora *provision* is mostly used in the sense of a legal condition or requirement, because there are recurrent phrases containing the term *przepis*, typical of legal Polish, namely *przepis x stosuje się (odpowiednio)* [the provision of paragraph x shall apply (accordingly)]; *przepisu x nie stosuje się*; [the provision x shall not apply]. This is confirmed by the high salience of the MWU *the provision of article*. In LEN-UK, *provision* is frequently used to describe an action of providing or supplying something, and when it is used in the earlier meaning, it is much less often accompanied with an editing unit and a numerical reference.

The plural form *provisions* is generally overrepresented in the translations (NFs 3,998 / 4,475 / 3,948 in CHB, PLC and WK, respectively), in comparison to its distribution in the non-translations (NF 1,124 in LEN-UK). Again, the overrepresentation results from a close rendering of typical Polish legal phrases built around an appropriate form of *przepisy*, in particular *w rozumieniu przepisów* [within the meaning of the provisions], *zgodnie z przepisami* [in accordance with the provisions of], but also *określone w przepisach wydanych na podstawie* [specified in the provisions issued under], and *stosuje się przepisy* [the provisions shall apply]. The first of the previously mentioned MWUs is absent from LEN-UK, even though the formula *within the meaning of* is almost as frequent as in the translational subcorpora (NF 323 in LEN-UK, as compared with NFs 376 / 483 / 376 in CHB, PLC and WK, respectively). However, as was the case with the MWU *the provisions of* [editing unit] *shall not apply* (see 4.2 above), also in this instance, the pattern observable in LEN-UK is less redundant than the one observed in the translational subcorpora, namely *within the meaning of* is always directly followed by an editing unit. It is clear that the translated MWU is a literal rendition of the SL pattern that results in a marked variant of the TL cluster.

5 Conclusions

The present study has revealed some discrepancies between the phraseology observable in legal English inversely translated from Polish and the non-translated legal English of UK public general acts, and simultaneously, a significant degree of similarity among the three translational subcorpora. The similarity of the translations provides evidence for the levelling-out hypothesis put forward by Baker (1996, p. 184), according to which translations are less idiosyncratic and less lexically divergent than non-translations. The patterns of MWUs in use, discerned in the translational subcorpora, have been recognised as untypical collocations: even though the analysed MWUs consist of lexical units present in the non-translated variety of English, they are used in divergent combinations or with dissimilar frequency. This runs contrary to the common expectation of phraseological conformity in translations (Gouadec 2007, p. 23), i.e. their collocational unmarkedness and resemblance to non-translated TL texts in a given domain. Although there are situations in which unnatural MWUs are acceptable in legal translation (especially in the event of conceptual lacunas between legal systems, cf. Biel 2014b, pp. 182–183), this does not seem to be applicable when it comes to the examined MWUs. In most cases, the untypical collocations identified can easily be explained once the underlying SL structure has been analysed. In almost all of the examples presented in this chapter, the non-standard TL combination directly reflects the SL pattern. This regularity is clear evidence of Toury's law of interference: "in translation, phenomena pertaining to the make-up of the source text tend to force themselves on the translators and be transferred to the target text" (2012, p. 310).

In fact, interference can be observed in translation irrespective of directionality. The findings presented here show that the interference of the translators' mother tongue is pervasive, although the method used is not able to precisely measure the intensity of the phenomenon. Notwithstanding, in consequence of the interference, the textual fit of the MWUs under analysis is rather limited. The reason for the high degree of interference may be a preoccupation with SL formulaicity on the part of the translators, who tend to adopt a source-oriented approach to legal translation. This is not in accord with "the predominant view in the contemporary legal literature that strongly advocates a receiver-oriented approach to both legal translation in general and EU Translation in particular" (Baaij 2018, p. 6). While source-oriented legal translation has its strong proponents (e.g., Baaij 2018; Poon 2005; Schroth 1986), what needs to be considered when applying this strategy in practice is the language pair involved in the process of translation and their mutual power relations. Toury (2012, p. 314) observes that "tolerance of interference (. . .) tends to increase when translation is carried out from a 'major' or highly prestigious language/culture". Considering the position of English as the *lingua franca* of today's globalised world of international business and law, the source-oriented strategy seems better suited to translation *from* English, but not necessarily vice versa. What is more, as noted by Baaij (2018, p. 132), source orientation in legal translation does not involve preservation of general language – in fact, achieving appropriate levels of intelligibility in this respect allows the reader to identify and understand what truly makes the legal text foreign in the target culture. As the MWUs described in the chapter are (1) mainly non-terminological, or contain a term that in Shelov's view (1982, cited in Picht and Draskau 1985) is characterised by a low degree of terminologicality (or termness); and (2) related to the structure of provisions, it seems justified to translate them functionally, in order not to obscure the genuine meaning of the laws coming from a different legal system. Although likely to be perceived as less challenging for the translator than patterns built around terms, the analysed types of MWUs are equally system- and genre-bound, and to a great extent contribute to the naturalness of the translated text. The method presented here makes it possible to identify corresponding MWUs that are more standard in the TL (e.g., *mentioned in* rather than *referred to in*, *must* + infinitive or *required to* rather than *obliged to*), which could be of use for professional and training purposes. Unmarked variants of MWUs would improve the textual fit of inverse translations and could favourably influence their reputation.

Notes

1 Inverse translation is also referred to as 'L2 translation' / 'translation into the second language' or, less frequently, 'prose translation' or 'service translation'. There is no widely accepted terminology to describe the phenomenon. For practical reasons, throughout the paper, only the first term is used, even though I fully acknowledge the justification presented by the AVANTI Research Group, who suggest replacing 'inverse' with 'L2' due to the negative connotations which the first term may carry (cf. Beeby Lonsdale 2009).

2 Farkas, A. (n. d.) LF Aligner. Available at: https://sourceforge.net/projects/aligner/ [Accessed 28 March 2018].

3 Throughout the chapter, the values represent the number of tokens used for the wordlist. The total of the tokens in texts (running words) is higher and covers numbers that are removed by the software.

References

Baaij, C.J.W. (2018). *Legal integration and language diversity. Rethinking translation in EU lawmaking*. New York: Oxford University Press.

Baker, M. (1993). Corpus linguistics and translation studies: Implications and applications. *In:* M. Baker, G. Frances and E. Tognini-Bonelli, eds. *Text and technology: In honour of John Sinclair*. Amsterdam: John Benjamins, pp. 233–250.

Baker, M. (1996). Corpus-based translation studies: The challenges that lie ahead. *In:* H. Somers, ed. *Terminology, LSP and translation: Studies in language engineering in honour of Juan C. Sager*. Amsterdam: John Benjamins, pp. 175–186.

Baker, M. (2018). *In other words. A coursebook on translation*. 3rd ed. Abindgon: Routledge.

Beeby Lonsdale, A. (2009). Directionality. *In:* M. Baker and G. Saldanha, eds. *Routledge encyclopedia of translation studies*. 2nd ed. Abindgon: Routledge, pp. 84–88.

Biber, D., *et al.* (1999). *Longman grammar of spoken and written English*. Harlow: Pearson Education.

Biber, D. and Barbieri, F. (2007). Lexical bundles in university spoken and written registers. *English for Specific Purposes*, 26 (3), pp. 263–286.

Biel, Ł. (2014a). *Lost in the Eurofog: The textual fit of translated law*. Frankfurt am Main: Peter Lang.

Biel, Ł. (2014b). Phraseology in legal translation: A corpus-based analysis of textual mapping in EU law. *In:* L. Cheng, *et al.*, eds. *The Ashgate handbook of legal translation*. Farnham: Ashgate, pp. 177–192.

Biel, Ł. (2015). Phraseological profiles of legislative genres: Complex prepositions as a special case of legal phrasemes in EU law and national law. *Fachsprache: International Journal of Specialized Communication*, 37 (3–4), pp. 139–160.

Biel, Ł. (2016). Mixed corpus design for researching the Eurolect: A genre-based comparable-parallel corpus in the PL EUROLECT project. *In:* E. Gruszczyńska and A. Leńko-Szymańska, eds. *Polskojęzyczne korpusy równoległe. Polish-language parallel corpora*. Warsaw: Instytut Lingwistyki Stosowanej, pp. 197–208.

Campbell, S. (1998). *Translation into the second language*. London: Longman.

Chang, V.C-Y. (2011). Translation directionality and the revised hierarchical model: An eye-tracking study. *In:* S. O'Brien, ed. *Cognitive explorations of translation*. London: Continuum, pp. 154–174.

Chesterman, A. (2004). Hypotheses about translation universals. *In:* G. Hansen, *et al.*, eds. *Claims, changes and challenges in translation studies*. Amsterdam: John Benjamins, pp. 1–13.

Evert, S. and Neumann, S. (2017). The impact of translation direction on characteristics of translated texts. A multivariate analysis for English and German. *In:* G. de Sutter, M-A. Lefer and I. Delaere, eds. *Empirical translation studies. New methodological and theoretical traditions*. Berlin: Walter de Gruyter, pp. 47–80.

Garzone, G. (2013). Variation in the use of modality in legislative texts: Focus on *shall*. *Journal of Pragmatics*, 57, pp. 68–81.

Gouadec, D. (2007). *Translation as a profession*. Amsterdam: John Benjamins.

Goźdź-Roszkowski, S. (2011). *Patterns of linguistic variation in American legal English. A corpus-based study*. Frankfurt am Main: Peter Lang.

Hansen-Schirra, S. and Teich, E. (2008). Corpora in human translation. *In:* A. Lüdeling and M. Kytö, eds. *Corpus linguistics. An international handbook*, Vol. 2. Berlin: Walter de Gruyter, pp. 1159–1175.

Hunston, S. (2013). *Corpus approaches to evaluation*. Abingdon: Routledge.

IAPTI's Ethics Committee. (2015). *Translation into a non-native language* [online]. Available at: www.iapti.org/files/surveys/2/IAPTI_non-native_report.pdf [Accessed 10 Nov. 2015].

Koller, W. (1988). Przekład literacki z perspektywy językoznawstwa [Literary translation from the perspective of linguistics]. Translated by P. Zarychta. *In:* P. Bukowski and M. Heydel, eds. *Współczesne teorie przekładu. Antologia [Contemporary theories of translation. Anthology]*. Kraków: Znak, pp. 145–172.

Malkiel, B. (2004). Directionality and translational difficulty. *Perspectives: Studies in Translatology*, 12 (3), pp. 208–219.

Marmaridou, A.S.S. (1996). Directionality in translation processes and practices. *Target*, 8 (1), pp. 49–73.

Mauranen, A. (2006). Translation universals. *In:* K. Brown, ed. *Encyclopedia of language and linguistics*. 2nd ed., Vol. 13. Oxford: Elsevier, pp. 93–100.

Mauranen, A. (2007). Universal tendencies in translation. *In:* G. Anderman and M. Rogers, eds. *Incorporating corpora. The linguist and the translator*. Clevedon: Multilingual Matters, pp. 32–48.

McEnery, T., *et al.* (2006). *Corpus-based language studies*. London: Routledge.

Office of the Parliamentary Counsel (2017). *Drafting guidance*. [online] Available at: https://assets.publishing.service.gov.uk/government/uploads/system/uploads/

attachment_data/file/666328/drafting_guidance_Dec_2017.pdf [Accessed 4 Apr. 2018].

Pavlović, N. (2007). Directionality in translation and interpreting practice. Report on a questionnaire survey in Croatia. *In:* A. Pym and A. Perekrestenko, eds. *Translation research projects 1*. Tarragona: Intercultural Studies Group, pp. 79–95.

Pavlović, N. and Jensen, K. (2009). Eye tracking translation directionality. *In:* A. Pym and A. Perekrestenko, eds. *Translation research projects 2*. Tarragona: Intercultural Studies Group, pp. 93–109.

Picht, H. and Draskau, J. (1985). *Terminology: An introduction*. Guildford: University of Surrey.

Pokorn, N. (2005). *Challenging the traditional axioms. Translation into a non-mother tongue*. Amsterdam: John Benjamins.

Pontrandolfo, G. (2015). Investigating judicial phraseology with COSPE: A contrastive corpus-based study. *In:* C. Fantinuoli and F. Zanettin, eds. *New directions in corpus-based translation studies*. Berlin: Language Science Press, pp. 119–137.

Poon, W.Y.E. (2005). The cultural transfer in legal translation. *International Journal for the Semiotics of Law*, 18, pp. 307–323.

Schroth, P.W. (1986). Legal translation. *American Journal of Comparative Law*, 34, pp. 47–65.

Scott, M. (2017). *WordSmith tools manual*. Version 7.0. Stroud: Lexical Analysis Software. Available at: http://lexically.net/downloads/version7/HTML/index.html [Accessed 27 July 2018].

Sinclair, J. (1991). *Corpus, concordance, collocation*. Oxford: Oxford University Press.

Steiner, E. (2012). Introduction. *In:* S. Hansen-Schirra, *et al.*, eds. *Cross-linguistic corpora for the study of translations*. Berlin: Walter de Gruyter, pp. 1–17.

Toury, G. (2012). *Descriptive translation studies – and beyond*. Revised ed. Amsterdam: John Benjamins.

Tracy-Ventura, N., *et al.* (2007). Lexical bundles in Spanish speech and writing. *In:* G. Parodi, ed. *Working with Spanish corpora*. London: Continuum, pp. 217–231.

Trklja, A. (2018). A corpus investigation of formulaicity and hybridity in legal language. *In:* S. Goźdź-Roszkowski and G. Pontrandolfo, eds. *Phraseology in legal and institutional settings. A corpus-based interdisciplinary perspective*. Abingdon: Routledge, pp. 89–108.

Wang, B. (2011). Translation practices and the issue of directionality in China. *Meta: Translators' Journal*, 56 (4), pp. 896–914.

Weatherby, J. (1998). Teaching translation into L2. *In:* K. Malmkjær, ed. *Translation and language teaching: Language teaching and translation*. Manchester: St. Jerome Publishing, pp. 21–28.

Wray, A. (2002). *Formulaic language and the lexicon*. Cambridge: Cambridge University Press.

4 Language of treaties – language of power relations?

Miia Santalahti and Mikhail Mikhailov

1 Introduction

This chapter deals with research that taps into the connection between language and political relations through the study of interstate treaties. Treaties have a long history and an established position, so an abundance of research has been conducted on them. However, the majority of this research has taken place in the fields of political or social science and other such disciplines; the genre has not aroused particular interest among language and communication specialists. One reason for this may be that, being a legal, institutional, highly standardised type of text, the treaty has appeared to be an unfruitful topic for language-based research. The COSST (Corpus-based Study of State Treaties) research group at the University of Tampere (Finland), however, has adopted a different approach, based on the notion that analysing the language of treaties can shed light on the roles of treaty-negotiating parties from a novel perspective.

One of the basic starting points for our research is the hypothesis that the language of bilateral treaties is not as neutral and standardised as it is supposed to be, despite the guidelines and criteria defined to govern it, and that the political, cultural and even personal background factors of treaty text writers may be reflected in the text. Another hypothesis is that the influence of translation and other forms of interlingual communication can be detected in the treaty texts. Consequently, our key research questions are the following: by analysing various linguistic features of the treaty texts, can we identify elements produced in each party's language and, correspondingly, elements translated between these languages? If the answer to the former question is affirmative, can we draw conclusions from the results as to whether one of the parties had a dominant position in the treaty negotiations?

These questions are addressed in this chapter. In the following, we will describe the application of corpus-based methods in the study of treaty language, introduce the PEST corpus of treaties, and then present one case study performed on Finnish-Soviet corpus material.

2 The bilateral treaty

According to the Vienna Convention on the Law of Treaties (UN 1969, Article 2), *treaty* means an international agreement concluded between states in written form and governed by international law. As such, a treaty is an important text: it is a binding document whose effect extends over the entire nation that is a party to it. Treaties have long served as one of several sources of international law, and nowadays they have become the preferred vehicle by which states structure their rights and obligations under international law (Hollis *et al.* 2005, pp. 1–2). It can be said that treaties are no longer just contracts between governments; they are instruments of law-making (Bunn-Livingstone 2002, p. vii). Therefore, the study of treaties is of increasing importance.

Language is an essential element in all contract documents: the contents of a contract only obtain meaning through interpretation, and the interpretation is inevitably based on verbal expression. Due to their nature as vehicles of international agreement, treaties often involve more than one language. The Vienna Convention on the Law of Treaties states that when a treaty has been authenticated in two or more languages, the text is equally authoritative in each language, unless the treaty stipulates or the parties agree otherwise (UN 1969, Article 33; see also Schäffner 1997). The language used in treaties is governed by official instructions and guidelines. For example, in Finland, such guidelines are provided in the Legal Writer's Guide (Ministry of Justice of Finland 2016). In Russia, the corresponding guideline is titled Recommendations on the Preparation of Materials Concerning the Concluding and Termination of International Treaties (Ministry of Foreign Affairs of the Russian Federation 2009).

Treaty language belongs to the realm of legal language, which is a language for special purposes (LSP), but it is not a "technolect" in the sense that it would be primarily used among specialists of one profession only; on the contrary, many legal documents – such as treaties – are intended for the larger public (Mattila 2013, p. 1). Therefore, besides the requirement for accuracy, the treaty text should also be comprehensible. As stated in the Finnish Legal Writer's Guide, the treaty should feature fact-oriented, precise, unambiguous and standardised language (Ministry of Justice of Finland 2016, p. 439). However, Heikki E. Mattila points out that linguistic ambiguity may also be a conscious choice in certain negotiating situations; a treaty article on which the negotiators have not reached agreement can be left equivocal deliberately (Mattila 2013, pp. 87–88).

Apart from their general political importance, treaties also constitute an interesting object of research based on linguistic perspectives – Translation Studies in particular – since the bilateral treaty text is practically always a product of interlingual communication (except for cases where the agreeing parties have the same language). Treaties can be drafted in different ways, and translation plays a significant role in all of them. First, treaties can be prepared by means of negotiation, in which case the final texts are of a hybrid nature, outcomes of a long process during which segments of text are written in both parties' languages, translated, updated and back-translated so that ultimately no source or target language can be identified (Probirskaja 2009, p. 47). Another way to conclude a treaty is by the exchange of notes (see e.g. Ministry of Justice of Finland 2017, pp. 13–14), in which case the treaty text is usually written in one party's language and the other language version is a translation. Moreover, treaties can be concluded by using a so-called intermediary language, which means that the treaty text is written in three languages: one international language (in most cases, English or French) and the language of both parties; usually the parties' language versions are translations of the international one. This adds an interesting dimension to the study of treaty language from a Translation Studies point of view: comparing treaty texts that represent different methods of preparation can give us valuable insight regarding the influence of translation, help identify features that are typical of translated texts, and, consequently, possibly allow us to draw conclusions about the roles of different parties in treaty negotiations.

According to the Vienna Convention on the Law of Treaties (UN 1969, Article 33), the terms of a treaty are presumed to have the same meaning in each authentic language version; when a difference of meaning is detected, the meaning which best reconciles the texts shall be adopted. However, from a linguistic point of view, it can be questioned whether it is possible to guarantee that all meanings in texts written in different languages are identical. Nevertheless, it is often taken for granted that different language versions of each treaty are indeed exactly identical. Fernando Prieto Ramos (2011, pp. 204–205) notes that many working groups and other parties using treaties for official purposes quite commonly choose to work with the version whose language is the most familiar to them, without paying any attention to other language versions.

According to Bunn-Livingstone (2002), a basic quality of public international law is universality, or globality. However, there is one underlying difficulty related to this: the undoubted cultural differences between countries (Bunn-Livingstone 2002, p. vii). As mentioned previously, the language of treaties is largely governed by specific conventions, which also contributes to a high level of homogeneity within the genre (Probirskaja 2009, pp. 28–29). However, such conventions and guidelines are culture-specific by nature, while the treaty text is expected to be neutral and refrain from reflecting the culture or legal system of either party. This means that the treaty texts represent a compromise. Analysing this compromise can open up new perspectives regarding the position of the parties: if the outcome is significantly closer to one side than the other, this may point towards the domination of one language and maybe also of one party.

3 Research data and methods

3.1. The PEST corpus

This chapter is based on research conducted using the Finnish-Russian section of the Parallel Electronic Corpus of State Treaties (PEST), which is being compiled by the COSST research group at the University of Tampere. When completed, the corpus will contain official versions of all treaties concluded between Finland and Russia/USSR, Finland and Sweden, and Sweden and Russia/USSR from

1918 until the present day, as well as a collection of international treaties as reference data. This corpus composition enables versatile parallel analyses, for example, by country or chronological period, and provides interesting reference data for the comparison of findings, as the relations between the three states – Finland, Russia/USSR, and Sweden – have been quite different over the 100-year period covered. The Finnish-Russian/Soviet section of the corpus (hereinafter, PEST-FI-RU) has been completed, but the other sections are still being compiled. The estimated size of the whole corpus will be about 2 million running words, with around 200 texts per language pair.

The PEST corpus is a collection of aligned bitexts (FI-RU, SV-FI, SV-RU) for bilateral treaties and multilingual aligned documents (EN-FR-RU-FI-SV) for international conventions. The texts are lemmatised and morphologically and syntactically annotated. Alignment is performed with an Open Source aligner (LF Aligner),[1] and grammatical parsing and lemmatisation are carried out with open universal dependency parsing software for English, Russian, Finnish, French and Swedish.

The corpus is stored on the servers mustikka.uta.fi and puolukka.uta.fi, and a separate user account is required to access it. For the time being, the corpus is mainly intended for the use of the COSST research group, but access can be granted to other researchers upon request. Once completed, the corpus may be opened for larger-scale use within the research community. For corpus queries, the research group has developed its own web-based corpus manager, Text-Hammer,[2] which is specifically designed for working with parallel corpora. The software includes various tools, such as parallel concordances, frequency lists, n-grams, collocations, etc., and new functionalities are continuously developed alongside the corpus compilation and use.

The corpus data can be studied at the lexical, morphological and syntactic levels, both by language and by language pair, using quantitative methods such as multidimensional analysis and collostructional analysis (see e.g. Glynn 2014; Hilpert 2014). In addition, statistical methods such as analysis of variance (ANOVA), logistic regression, cluster analysis, factor analysis, etc., can be used on a large scale. The quantitative methods are complemented by such qualitative methods as discourse analysis, semantic analysis, concept analysis, etc., to identify different phenomena linked to the quantitative findings. One significant strength of corpus-based research is the automated processing of large masses of empirical data, while in this case, the limited size of the corpus allows very comprehensive qualitative analyses as well. The combination of quantitative and qualitative methods is analysed in more detail in Part 3.3.

3.2 The Russian-Finnish section of PEST

The Finnish-Russian section of PEST (PEST-FI-RU) includes all treaties concluded between Finland and Russia/USSR from 1918 to 2018. In total, it comprises 228 pairs of documents, aligned at the sentence level, in Russian and Finnish.

Table 4.1 The structure of PEST-FI-RU

Subsection	*Period*	*Number of text pairs*	*Word count: Finnish*	*Word count: Russian*
A	1918–1944	47	76,394	91,836
B	1945–1991	128	115,187	141,773
C	1992–2017	47	54,594	68,809
Total		**222**	**246,175**	**302,418**

The documents have been divided into three subsections based on chronological periods:

A. 1918–1944: from the year following the Russian Revolution (October 1917) and the independence of Finland (declared in December 1917) to the year of the signing of the Moscow Armistice, which brought the Finnish-Soviet hostilities of World War II to an end.
B. 1945–1991: the period of stable relations between the Soviet Union and Finland, which lasted until the collapse of the Soviet Union.
C. 1992 to the present: the post-Soviet period.

This division seems natural from a historical point of view, and it is also in keeping with the types of bilateral treaties concluded during each of the periods. All three of the previously mentioned periods began with the termination of old treaties and the ratification of new ones, thus reflecting the new realities. Moreover, each period features certain typical activities; for example, peace treaties were concluded during period A only, while treaties on cultural exchange are typical for periods B and C. Naturally, some topics, such as trade and transportation, remain relevant throughout the entire corpus.

As can be seen from Table 4.1, subsections A and C are of comparable size and include the same number of documents, while subsection B is almost twice as large. However, using data sampling for subsection B in order to make the subsections equally sized would have made the total size of the corpus even more modest than it is now without offering any guarantees of achieving balance.

This chapter focuses particularly on subsection B. The analysis presented herein updates, expands and rechecks the findings of a pilot study published earlier in Finnish (Mikhailov and Santalahti 2017).

3.3 The methodology

As pointed out earlier, our research combines quantitative and qualitative methods. In corpus work (and more generally), figures and frequencies are only a starting point; they draw our attention to some features that are likely to be worth investigating in more detail (Baker 2004, p. 183). In other words, various metrics and statistics form a kind of a magnifying glass that brings out such noteworthy features in the data that could not be detected by studying it with the naked eye. Corpus software helps process large amounts of data in order to discover the phenomena the researcher is looking for; it is the researcher's task to work out search routines that serve the given purpose.

This principle is also applied in the case study featured in this chapter: quantitative findings are reviewed with the aim of detecting elements and factors that appear unusual or otherwise interesting and worthy of further qualitative analysis. In order to detect such unusual elements – or to determine an element to be unusual in the first place – the research data must be compared with certain reference data. In the analysis featured herein, the primary research dataset consists of the Russian and Finnish data from PEST-FI-RU subsection B (see Table 4.1), while the other two subsections (A and C) within this corpus section serve as reference datasets. In other words, we compare documents representing the period when relations between the two states were stable and the Soviet Union was at the peak of its power (subsection B) with documents representing a period of hostile relations and war (subsection A), and a period involving a different social and value system for one of the parties (subsection C). Such a twofold comparison adds dimensions to the analysis and increases the reliability of the results. Moreover, reviewing the Russian and Finnish data in parallel complements the analysis from the perspective of Translation Studies in particular.

While the vocabulary of treaties in general is primarily linked to the topics of agreement, differences in lexis can also be attributed to various other factors: the overall development of language, the individual style of the writers, translation/editing activities, ideological issues, etc. Therefore, filtering out the features relevant for the study at hand is an important step in the analysis.

One way to discover lexical differences is to compare word frequencies in the primary research data and the reference datasets to find items that stand out in terms of statistically significant difference in frequency. This method is widely applied; it has been used by different researchers at different times under different names. Anatoly Šajkevič refers to the objects of such comparisons as *lexical markers* (see Šajkevič *et al.* 2003, pp. x–xi), but the term *keywords* is currently more popular, because it is used in the WordSmith Tools utility (see the following). The methods of comparing frequencies and computing the significance of observed deviations may differ. Šajkevič suggests his own formula, which uses the average frequency in a reference corpus as an expected value; other researchers use log-likelihood or chi-square tests (see e.g. Lâševskaâ 2016, pp. 233–234). Keyword search-based analysis started to gain popularity when large amounts of data in electronic form became available and the method was introduced in the KeyWords tool, which is part of the WordSmith Tools software package.[3]

In our research, we use the formula and methodology suggested by Paul Rayson (see http://ucrel.lancs.ac.uk/llwizard.html and Rayson *et al.* 2004). It is important to point out that we work with lemmatised word lists, which is critical for languages with a rich morphology, such as Russian and Finnish. The TextHammer corpus tool creates lemmatised word frequency lists for the two selected subcorpora, consolidates them into one table, and calculates the log-likelihood

Table 4.2 Top ten items from the keyword list obtained by comparing the Russian corpus subsections PEST-FI-RU-B vs PEST-FI-RU-C.

Russian word	*English translation*[4]	*Freq. B*	*Freq. C*	*LL index*
метр	metre	1212	3	1041.59
знак	sign	1387	35	975.63
советский	Soviet	1129	53	679.43
линия	line	913	24	636.99
граничный	demarcation (adj.)	768	6	625.57
сухопутный	terrain (adj.)	690	1	600.49
союз	union	953	46	570.09
граница	border	1157	130	453.48
финляндия	Finland	937	97	388.51

index for each item. The items whose index value is more than +5 (items more frequent in the primary dataset) or less than –5 (items more frequent in the reference dataset) are statistically significant. Table 4.2 shows the top ten items from one of the keyword lists used in this study.

Keyword lists demonstrate lexical differences between the primary research data and reference data; in the study at hand, they contain words that are significantly more common in subsection B than in subsections A or C respectively. However, as we have already mentioned, the lists are simply the basis for a deeper analysis. Once generated, they are read through to search for words indicating the phenomena we are focusing on – in this case, elements of Soviet discourse – and such items are annotated in the lists. Then, the findings from the B vs A and B vs C lists are compared and analysed more thoroughly in the bilingual context.

4 Case study: Soviet discourse in post-war treaties

During the Soviet era, drastic changes were made in the ways of using the Russian language: basically, an entirely new discourse was created. A central aspect of this discourse was the construction and maintenance of a polarised, dualistic worldview: "we" vs "not-we". The polarisation was manifested in terms of referential and temporal quantifiers, and even in terms of modality: the "we" were referred to using words describing unity, continuity and necessity, whereas the "others" were described with words reflecting dispersion, isolation, instability, and uncertainty (Weiss 2005, pp. 254–256). A very typical syntactic feature of this discourse, also related to the aforementioned phenomenon, is the abundant use of modifiers, most typically of an intensifying nature (Weiss 2005, p. 253). Further elements typical of Soviet discourse include the extensive use of metaphors and clichés, the flexible adaptation of vocabulary, and a high degree of expressiveness (see e.g. Borisova 1997).

Of course, the previously mentioned phenomena are primarily related to mass media, public speeches, and texts, and to some extent even to fiction and non fiction literature. We set out to review whether some of these features can be observed in our research data as well. The following analysis focuses on lexical features representing the previously mentioned phenomena in the Russian treaty texts of corpus subsection B. We also review the Finnish counterparts for the discovered elements to see whether they appear to be "foreign" and most likely translated, which would point towards the Soviet party's initiative in the wording of the said parts of the treaty texts.

4.1 Findings: Soviet discourse in the Russian treaty versions

The lexis of treaties consists mainly of contract terminology and vocabulary related to the topics of agreement. Therefore, keyword lists are dominated by topic-related words. For example, subsection B includes many treaties on the demarcation of national borders and, as can be seen from Table 4.2, the keyword list is therefore topped by such words as *метр* (metre), *знак* (sign), *просека* (forest clearing), etc. There are also some words referring to the Soviet reality, such as *социалистический* (socialist, adj.), but words such as this, used in a concrete meaning, are not of interest in this analysis.

Consequently, the list of words clearly reflecting typical Soviet discourse, which was obtained by reviewing keyword lists indicating words that are significantly more common in subsection B than in subsections A or C, is quite short but nevertheless interesting. The most relevant findings are listed in Table 4.3, and some of them are analysed in more detail in the following. The list is limited to words that can be deemed to be atypical of the treaty genre, either as such or in the sense or context in which they have been used in the treaty texts. Some of the words listed below may also have other, more concrete meanings (e.g. *паритетный* is also a specialised financial term that means "parity"), but our analysis focuses on their figurative meanings only. The "textual function" column in the table refers to the typical elements of Soviet discourse that were described previously.

To understand the uncharacteristic nature of these words, they must naturally be reviewed in context. It is worthy of note that apart from their stand-alone usage, many of the listed words are often used together, forming expressions that contribute to an expressive way of denoting facts, and even clichés. In the following

Table 4.3 Words reflecting Soviet discourse in the Russian treaty texts of subsection B.

Russian word	*English translation*	*Textual function*
взаимовыгодный	mutually beneficial	Unity
дальнейший	further	intensifying modifier
добрососедский	neighbourly	Unity
долгосрочный	long-term	continuity
дружба, дружественный	friendship, friendly	Unity
паритетный	equal	fairness
расширение	expansion	intensifying modifier
углубление	deepening	intensifying modifier
укрепление	strengthening	strength
успешный	successful	intensifying modifier

part, we will illustrate some of our most essential findings through examples. We will also address the corresponding expressions in the Finnish treaties.

4.2 *Strength, continuity and unity: further analysis of the study results through examples*

Emphasising the element of strength is a common feature that upholds the polarisation between "the good, strong we" and "the poor, weak not-we". In the treaties in subsection B, the word *укрепление* (strengthening) is typically used in the figurative sense in expressions referring to relations, connections, cooperation, etc.; there is only one case in which the word is used in the concrete meaning of "fortification", and this is in the 1947 peace treaty. Moreover, it is commonly linked with the modifier *дальнейшее* ("further"; as in Example 4.1), or with the phrase *дальнейшее развитие* (further development), in which case the word in itself constitutes an intensifying modifier.

Example 4.1 (Consular treaty 1966)

В целях дальнейшего укрепления дружественных отношений между обоими государствами . . .	. . . lujittaakseen edelleen molempien maiden keskisiä ystävällisiä suhteita. . .
"With the aim of further strengthening the friendly relations between both countries"	"in order to further strengthen the friendly mutual relations between both countries"

The Finnish wording we can see in Example 4.1 gives us reason to believe that this passage has been originally written in Russian and translated into Finnish, because using the word *molempien* (both) in the expression "between the [both] countries" does not observe the rules of proper Finnish language use – it is an excess modifier and, moreover, one that indicates unity, making it quite compatible with the typical features of Soviet discourse described earlier.

As pointed out previously, continuity is also a typical feature implied as a characteristic of "the good, strong we" in Soviet discourse. This can be seen in the use of the word *дальнейший* (further). Overall, it is a very common word in treaties, because it can be used to convey different meanings, both concrete and figurative; for example, in PEST-FI-RU subsection C, i.e., in the latest treaties, it is most commonly used in the standard contract phrase *в дальнейшем* (hereinafter). However, in the treaties in subsection B it predominantly serves the purpose of being an intensifying modifier. It is most typically linked to the word *развитие* (development), and this phrase is used to such an extent that it can be classified as a cliché. The Russian word *дальнейший* is ambiguous: it can be interpreted as referring to time (as more time elapses) or a process (moving on from the current status); both of these interpretations contribute to the goals of Soviet discourse, indicating continuity and/or progress, particularly with the presupposition that things are "going from good to better". In the Finnish treaty texts, this ambiguity is reflected in the use of two different words as the counterparts of *дальнейший*:

edelleen (further), which also allows the previously described twofold interpretation, or *jatkuva* (continuous), which refers to the elapse of time only. Furthermore, emphasising the nature of being an excess attribute, in some contexts the word *дальнейший* has been completely omitted in the Finnish version. Examples 4.2, 4.3, and 4.4 demonstrate each of these cases respectively.

Example 4.2 (Educational protocol 1979)

. . . желая способствовать дальнейшему развитию дружественных финляндско-советских отношений, . . .	. . . haluten edelleen kehittää [–] suomalais-neuvostoliittolaisia ystävyyssuhteita. . .
"wishing to contribute to the further development of friendly Finnish-Soviet relations"	"wishing to further develop the Finnish-Soviet friendly relations"

Example 4.3 (Cooperation in economy and industry 1971)

. . . уверенные в том, что дальнейшее развитие взаимного экономического сотрудничества и товарооборота соответствует интересам обеих стран . . .	. . . vakuuttuneina siitä, että keskinäisen taloudellisen yhteistyön ja tavaranvaihdon jatkuva kehittyminen vastaa molempien maiden etuja. . .
"convinced that the further development of mutual economic collaboration and goods exchange will serve the interests of both parties"	"convinced that the continuous development of mutual economic cooperation and goods exchange will serve the interests of both parties"

Example 4.4 (Cooperation in culture and science 1978)

Стороны будут продолжать активно способствовать дальнейшему развитию дружественных связей [–] между советскими и финскими городами . . .	Osapuolet kehittävät aktiivisesti suomalaisten ja neuvostoliittolaisten kaupunkien välisiä ystävyyssuhteita. . .
"The parties shall continue to actively promote the further development of friendly connections [–] between Soviet and Finnish cities"	"The parties shall actively develop friendly relations between Finnish and Soviet cities"

Example 4.5 is very illustrative for the purposes of this analysis, as it contains several words from our list: *дальнейший* (further), *укрепление* (strengthening), *дружественный* (friendly), and *добрососедский* (neighbourly). This phrasing was originally introduced in the Protocol on the extension of the Friendship, Cooperation, and Mutual Assistance treaty (see the following) in 1955, after which it has been cited, either as such or in slightly modified formats, in many other treaties. This passage is also interesting from the point of view of translation: the Finnish language does not have a single word or idiom corresponding to *добрососедский* (neighbourly), and this concept is usually expressed using the phrase *hyvät naapuruussuhteet* (good neighbour relations). This leads to a slight difference in attribution between the Russian and Finnish versions of the passage in question.

Example 4.5 (Protocol on the extension of the FCMA Treaty 1955)

. . . желая содействовать дальнейшему развитию и укреплению сложившихся дружественных и добрососедских отношений между Финляндией и СССР . . .	. . . haluten edistää Suomen ja Neuvostoliiton välille muodostuneiden ystävällisten ja hyvien naapuruussuhteiden edelleen kehittämistä ja lujittamista. . .
"hoping to contribute to the further development and strengthening of the prevailing friendly and neighbourly relationship between Finland and the USSR"	"hoping to promote the further development and strengthening of the friendly and good neighbour relationship that has formed between Finland and the USSR"

It is noteworthy that many of the listed words mainly appear in one treaty or in references to it: the Agreement of Friendship, Cooperation, and Mutual Assistance (*Договор о дружбе, сотрудничестве и взаимной помощи* in Russian and *Ystävyys-, yhteistyö- ja avunantosopimus* in Finnish; hereinafter, the FCMA Treaty). The first FCMA Treaty was signed in 1948, after which it was renewed in 1950, 1970, and 1983. This treaty was of essential significance as an instrument defining Soviet-Finnish relations. For the Soviet party, its main purpose was to prevent Western or Allied Powers from attacking the Soviet Union through Finnish territory, while the Finnish side's key interest was to increase Finland's political independence from the Soviet Union. The Soviet Union had signed bilateral security pacts with Romania, Bulgaria, Hungary, Yugoslavia, Czechoslovakia and Poland earlier, but the FCMA Treaty signed between the Soviet Union and Finland differed from the parallel treaties signed with the aforementioned Eastern European countries.

While it can be said that the FCMA Treaty is, essentially, a typically Soviet instrument of interstate agreement, we know from history – e.g. from the notes of the Finnish leaders who participated in the negotiations – that the Finnish party made big efforts to influence the contents and wording of the treaty (see e.g. Rainio-Niemi 2014; Vesa 1998). The treaty text has been formulated as the result of negotiations, i.e., it is a hybrid text (cf. Part 2). Therefore, the presence of elements typical of the Soviet discourse cannot be simply explained by assuming that the majority of the text had been dictated by the Soviet party and translated from Russian into Finnish. It is nevertheless interesting that one treaty stands out so clearly in terms of vocabulary and language use. For example, in all of the PEST material, the traditional diplomatic custom of referring to the parties to the treaty as High Agreeing Parties (*высокие договаривающиеся стороны*, *korkeat sopimuspuolet*) can only be found in the FCMA Treaty and two other treaties also related to security: the non-aggression treaty and procedure of conciliation, both from 1932 (i.e., in subsection A). While this expression is not of Soviet origin, it nevertheless fits perfectly in the category of intensifying modifiers. Moreover, the FCMA Treaty is understandably the main source of expressions featuring the word *дружба* (friendship) and its derivative forms.

5 Discussion and conclusions

In the case study presented in this chapter, we set out to see whether elements typical of the Soviet discourse could be found even in bilateral treaties which, being legal and institutional texts, are expected to feature a very neutral style. Our analysis revealed that examples of language use that could be deemed atypical for the genre – such as ideologically loaded elements – were indeed present in our material. This finding supports the view that it is virtually impossible for language to be completely free from the influence of ideology, a position that has been featured as an underlying assumption in the approaches of many translation and discourse scholars (see e.g. Bassnett and Lefevere 1990; van Dijk 1998; Tymoczko 2006, 2014). This case study, for its part, indicates that this is true even in a text type that is considered to be highly standardised – the bilateral treaty. As set forth by Mannheim (1972), no human thought is immune to the ideologising influences of its social context (cited by Meyer 2009, p. 5). Language inevitably reflects social systems and worldviews, and this is one factor that makes the study of treaty language interesting.

Another finding made in conjunction with this study was that treaties, even those concluded between the same two states, do not form an entirely homogeneous group of texts, as certain individual documents (such as the FCMA Treaty in this material) may, for some reason, differ from the general trend in terms of language or style. This also supports our initial hypothesis and encourages further study.

In a review of passages of text in the bilingual context, it was revealed that the typically Soviet style of expression is also present in the Finnish treaty versions. However, in the Finnish context, the "sovietisms" do not have a similar ideological load; they are merely semantic loans, and in some cases they even constitute unidiomatic Finnish, which strongly suggests that these segments of text have been translated from Russian into Finnish. This gives rise to the interesting question as to why such a formulation was chosen and accepted for the Finnish versions – was it a deliberate choice of a "foreignizing" strategy to indicate that those sections were of Soviet origin, or was the strategy simply based on the requirement of identicalness and accuracy?

The conclusions are further supported by the fact that many of the words and expressions dealt with previously – e.g. *lujittaa* (to strengthen), *ystävyys* (friendship), and *yhteistoiminta* (collaboration) – do not occur in the Finnish-Swedish treaties, at least according to our knowledge based on the documents collected so far. In this respect, this small-scale pilot study is an encouraging example of the potential embedded within the corpus structure, enabling comparisons between various reference materials.

While the presence of typical Soviet discourse in the treaty texts and the "foreign", even unidiomatic wordings in Finnish clearly suggest that such passages of text have been initiated by the Soviet party, this does not necessarily affirm the presupposition that the Soviet party occupied the dominant position in negotiating the treaty in question. As pointed out earlier, the treaty text is always a compromise, and it is one also in the sense that one party may agree to accept a wording that is important to the other party in one part of the treaty text in exchange for getting its own preference accepted in another part. Additionally, as was also noted previously, the language of the treaty can even intentionally reflect certain characteristics of the negotiations, such as difficulties in reaching full agreement. Therefore, it is also possible that the FCMA Treaty was written in a slightly different style in order to emphasise its special nature, or its belonging to "the same family" as similar non-aggression treaties co-signed by the Soviet Union and other countries, albeit with certain significant differences.

In terms of methodology, this study was based on quantitative analysis in the form of keyword searches, followed by a qualitative, manual review of the search results. Despite the interesting results obtained, it should be noted that lexical analysis is not the most fruitful approach for studying treaties, because the lexis is primarily linked to the topics of agreement. The same issue has also come up in other pilot studies conducted on this corpus material. Some "off-topic" issues can be traced by means of quantitative methods, but it is difficult to justify the significance of the findings. Even if they are proven to be statistically significant, there remains some doubt, because the treaty texts are short and the overall size of the corpus is relatively small. However, the alternative would be to read the entire material in order to detect the desired elements. Even though the corpus is not extremely large, this would be an inefficient, unproductive method. The lemmatisation and annotation of the corpus material enable quantitative searches focusing on grammar and syntax (cases, parts of speech, sentence length, etc.), which will be explored in our future studies.

Soviet clichés are only one particular case of non-neutrality markers. One possible way to continue our research would be to study all such markers occurring in our data. This would broaden the scope of the research and possibly bring new insights into studying ideology via its reflections in the lexis. After all, texts consist of words, and studying words enables us to understand the texts better.

Notes

1 https://sourceforge.net/projects/aligner/
2 mustikka.uta.fi/texthammer and puolukka.uta.fi/texthammer
3 www.lexically.net/downloads/version7/HTML/keywords.html
4 Back translations have been given in all tables and examples with the aim of depicting the meaning of the words/expressions out of context as accurately as possible for the purposes of this article; they may differ from those used in the possibly released English translations of the treaties.

References

Baker, M. (2004). A corpus-based view of similarity and difference in translation. *International Journal of Corpus Linguistics*, 9 (2), pp. 167–193.

Bassnett, S. and Lefevere, A., eds. (1990). *Translation, history and culture*. London: Pinter.

Borisova, E. (1997). Opposition discourse in Russia: Political pamphlets 1989–1991. *In:* J. Mey, *et al.*, eds. *Political discourse in transition in Europe, 1989–1991*. Amsterdam: John Benjamins.

Bunn-Livingstone, S. (2002). *Juricultural pluralism vis-à-vis treaty law: State practice and attitudes*. Developments in International Law. The Hague: Brill.

Glynn, D. (2014). Techniques and tools: Corpus methods and statistics for semantics. *In:* D. Glynn and J.A. Robinson, eds. *Corpus methods for semantics. Quantitative studies in polysemy and synonymy*. Amsterdam: John Benjamins, pp. 307–342.

Hilpert, M. (2014). Collostructional analysis. Measuring associations between constructions and lexical elements. *In:* D. Glynn and J.A. Robinson, eds. *Corpus methods for semantics. Quantitative studies in polysemy and synonymy*. Amsterdam: John Benjamins, pp. 391–404.

Hollis, D.B., *et al.* (2005). *National treaty law and practice*. Leiden: Brill.

Lâševskaâ, O.N. (2016). *Korpusnye instrumenty v grammatičeskih issledovaniâh russkogo âzyka [Corpus tools for linguistic research of the Russian language]*. Moskva: Âzyki slavânskoj kul'tury.

Mannheim, K. (1972). *Ideology and utopia*. London: Routledge & Kegan Paul.

Mattila, H.E.S. (2013). *Comparative legal linguistics. Language of law, Latin and modern lingua francas*. 2nd ed. Farnham: Ashgate.

Meyer, R.E., *et al.* (2009). *Institutions and ideology*, Vol. 27. Bingly: Emerald Group.

Mikhailov, M. and Santalahti, M. (2017). Mistä kertoo valtiosopimusten kieli? Tapaustutkimus interferenssistä Suomen ja Venäjän välisissä valtiosopimuksissa. [What can we read from the language of treaties? A case study on interference in Finnish-Russian bilateral treaties.] *MikaEL*, 10, pp. 73–87. Available at: www.sktl.fi/liitto/seminaarit/mikael-verkkojulkaisu/mikael-vol-10-2017/ [Accessed 14 Feb. 2018].

Ministry of Foreign Affairs of the Russian Federation. (2009). *Rekomendacii o porâdke podgotovki materialov, otnosâŝihsâ k zaklûčeniû i prekraŝeniû meždunarodnyh dogovorov Rossijskoj Federacii [Recommendations on the preparation of materials concerning the concluding and termination of international treaties of the Russian Federation]*. Pravovoj departament Ministerstva inostrannyh del Rossijskoj Federacii. Available at: www.mid.ru/ru/foreign_policy/international_contracts/international_contracts/-/asset_publisher/kxW4m3muIEqP/content/id/787306 [Accessed 15 Feb. 2018].

Ministry of Justice of Finland. (2016). *Lainkirjoittajan opas. [Legal writer's guide]*. Available at: http://urn.fi/URN:ISBN:978-952-259-318-4 [Accessed 14 Feb. 2018].

MinistryofJusticeofFinland.(2017). *Valtiosopimusopas [Thetreatymanual]*. Ulkoasiainministeriön julkaisuja. Availableat: http://urn.fi/URN:ISBN:978-952-281-321-3 [Accessed 14 Feb. 2018].

Prieto Ramos, F. (2011). El traductor como redactor de instrumentos jurídicos: El caso de los tratados internacionales [The translator as an editor of legal instruments: The case of international treaties]. *The Journal of Specialised Translation*, 15, pp. 200–214.

Probirskaja, S. (2009). *Rajankäyntiä: Suomen ja Venäjän kahdenväliset valtiosopimukset käännöstieteellisen avainsana-analyysin valossa [Getting boundaries: Bilateral treaties between Finland and Russia in light of a translatological keyword analysis]*. Thesis (PhD). Tampere: Tampere University Press.

Rainio-Niemi, J. (2014). *The ideological cold war: The politics of neutrality in Austria and Finland*. New York: Routledge.

Rayson, P., *et al.* (2004). Extending the Cochran rule for the comparison of word frequencies between corpora. *In:* G. Purnelle, *et al.*, eds. *Le poids des mots: Proceedings of the 7th international conference on statistical analysis of textual data* (JADT 2004), Vol. 2. Louvain-la-Neuve, Belgium: Presses universitaires de Louvain, pp. 926–936. Available at: http://ucrel.lancs.ac.uk/people/paul/publications/rbf04_jadt.pdf [Accessed 14 Feb. 2018].

Šajkevič, A.Â., *et al.* (2003). *Statističeskij slovar' âzyka Dostoevskogo [Statistical dictionary of the language of Dostoyevski].* Moskva: Âzyki slavânskoj kul'tury.

Schäffner, C. (1997). Strategies of translating political texts. *In:* A. Trosborg, ed. *Text typology and translation.* Amsterdam: John Benjamins, pp. 119–143.

Tymoczko, M. (2006). Translation: Ethics, ideology, action. *Massachusetts Review*, 47 (3), pp. 442–461.

Tymoczko, M. (2014). Ideology and the position of the translator. In what sense is a translator 'in between'? *In:* M. Calzada Pérez, ed. *Apropos of ideology: Translation studies on ideology – ideologies in translation studies.* London: Routledge.

UN. (1969). *Vienna Convention on the law of treaties.* Vienna: United Nations, Treaty Series, Vol. 1155. Available at: www.refworld.org/docid/3ae6b3a10.html [Accessed 14 Feb. 2018].

van Dijk, T.A. (1998). *Ideology: A multidisciplinary approach.* London: Sage.

Vesa, U., ed. (1998). *YYA. Aika ja sopimus [The FCMA. Time and Treaty].* Rauhan- ja konfliktintutkimuskeskus. Tampere: University of Tampere.

Weiss, D. (2005). Stalinist vs. fascist propaganda. How much do they have in common? *In:* L. de Saussure and P.J. Schulz, eds. *Manipulation and ideologies in the twentieth century: Discourse, language, mind.* Amsterdam: John Benjamins, pp. 251–274.

5 Explicitation in legal translation: a feature of expertise?

A study of Spanish–Danish translation of judgments

Anja Krogsgaard Vesterager

1 Introduction

In Translation Studies, explicitation is generally understood as a translation technique by which implicit information of the source text is rendered explicitly in the target text (e.g. Klaudy 2009, p. 104). Explicitation has been proposed as one of the universals of translation (e.g. by Baker 1996), that is, a linguistic feature which is typical of translations compared to non-translations. Explicitation has been a very fruitful area of translation research, with most studies focusing on providing evidence for Blum Kulka's (1986) explicitation hypothesis, which suggests that explicitation may be an inherent feature of the translation process (e.g. Pápai 2004; Øverås 1998). Other studies have tried to establish a link between explicitation and translation expertise (Krogsgaard Vesterager 2017; Englund Dimitrova 2005; Laviosa-Braithwaite 1996, among others). However, the studies conducted until now offer conflicting evidence.

This study contributes to the research on explicitation and translation expertise by providing empirical evidence of explicitations in Danish professional translations of an excerpt from a Spanish judgment. The study aims to examine whether there are differences between experts and non-experts (as defined according to parameters proposed in previous literature) in terms of the explicitations they perform in their translations (for a definition of expert and non-expert translator, see section 3). The present study follows up on previous research by the same author (Krogsgaard Vesterager 2017). In the previous study, the data consisted of a source text of 221 words (an excerpt from a Spanish judgment) and ten translations into Danish. The analysis focussed on four focal points typical of legal Spanish and legal Danish (and of legal language in general): passives, nominalisations, system-bound terms (see Šarčević 2000, p. 149), and elliptical phrases (Alcaraz Varó and Hughes 2002; Šarčević 2000; Faber *et al.* 1997). The results of the study revealed that experts explicitated more than non-experts did. In addition, the findings revealed clear differences between the two groups in the focal points they explicitated. While experts performed explicitations of all the focal points, non-experts only explicitated system-bound terms and elliptical phrases. Thus, the results suggested that explicitation techniques develop gradually with experience.

This study takes the previous findings a step further by looking at a longer source text consisting of 885 words (of which 221 words constitute the source text of the previous study). In addition, rather than looking at selected focal points, this study examines all explicitation techniques used by the participants (see section 2).

The chapter is structured as follows. Section 2 presents central concepts of the study, section 3 looks at the literature on translation expertise and its link with explicitation, section 4 introduces the study, section 5 presents the results of the qualitative analyses and quantification, and section 6 discusses the results and implications of the study.

2 Central concepts

Following Becher (2010, p. 3), explicitness is defined as the verbalisation of information, which the recipient may be able to infer from the context, his/her world knowledge, etc. Explicitation, then, occurs when implicit information of the source text is verbalised in the target text. Thus, the present chapter is concerned with the product only, not the translation processes.

As in the previous study, explicitations can take two forms: (1) additions of new elements; and (2) specifications, that is, a translation which provides more specific information than the source text. Furthermore, the present study examines language-specific (Spanish to Danish) additions and specifications, which are optional in the sense that the translator may opt for a literal translation, or a translation that is less explicit than the source text, that is, implicitation. Thus, this study is not concerned with obligatory explicitations caused by structural differences between the two languages (e.g. the gerund which does not exist in Danish), nor with translation-inherent explicitations (resulting from the translation situation itself), or with examining the explicitation hypothesis (for a description of explicitation types, see Klaudy 2009, pp. 104–108).

In Translation Studies, the concepts of professionalism and expertise are often used interchangeably. However, in this study, a distinction is made between the two concepts. Thus, *professionalism* concerns the translator's ability to earn a living translating (Enríquez Raído 2014), while *expertise* involves translation processes "that are observed to result in good performance" (Tirkkonen-Condit 2005, p. 406).

3 Translation expertise and its link with explicitation: a review of the literature and main results from previous studies

Translation expertise (often referred to as translation competence) is a central concept in Translation Studies, especially in translator training, as evidenced by the number of publications on this topic. In the literature, there seems to be consensus that translation expertise is a complex concept, consisting of an array of sub-competences, or skills (e.g. Göpferich 2009). Translation scholars generally agree that expert translators are not born, but made through formal instruction and practice (e.g. Chesterman 2000). For instance, Muñoz (2014) has described translation expertise as a dynamic process of life-long practice and improvement. Drawing on expertise studies from cognitive psychology, some scholars suggest that experts be defined as translators with more than ten years' experience (e.g. Shreve 2006; Englund Dimitrova 2005). In addition, and important for the present study, legal translation scholars generally agree that extensive translation expertise alone does not make for expert legal translators, but rather requires practice in legal translation (e.g. Šarčević 2000).

Although translation expertise is generally considered to be derived from practice, empirical studies have shown that extensive experience in translation does not guarantee superior performance (e.g. Tirkkonen-Condit 2005; Jääskeläinen 1990). The individual differences between translators at all expertise levels observed in some studies have caused Bernardini (2001) to caution against measuring translation expertise in terms of number of years' experience in the profession.

While some studies have identified individual differences between translators, a number of studies have found evidence of shared characteristics of translation expertise and non-expertise. In the following, some of these differences are summarised (for an overview, see Tirkkonen-Condit 1996). According to some studies, non-experts operate at a superficial level, translating in a word-for-word manner, also referred to as literal translation (Jääskeläinen 1989). Experts, on the other hand, take a more holistic approach to translation, focusing on the source text as a whole and thus translate in a sense-oriented and iterative manner (e.g. Angelone 2010). Other studies have shown a general tendency towards literal translation. For example, Tirkkonen-Condit (2002) found that both experts and non-experts opted for literal translation as a first solution. Based on the findings of the study, Tirkkonen-Condit (2005) proposed *the literal translation automaton hypothesis*, which suggests that literal translation is a default mechanism in translation interrupted only when conscious decision-making is required. Thus, translators resort to literal translation at all linguistic levels, as long as the translation produced is acceptable. When encountering a problem, the literal translation automaton is interrupted by an internal *monitor* alerting the translator that conscious decision-making is necessary to solve the problem. In other words, the purpose of this monitoring mechanism is to prevent literal translations that are unacceptable in the target language because they result in an unidiomatic translation, also referred to as interference. There is empirical evidence that this internal monitoring function works better in experts than in non-experts. For example, Tirkkonen-Condit *et al.* (2008) found that interference emerged more frequently in translations by non-experts than in those produced by experts, which suggests that the translator's ability to monitor his or her own performance evolves from experience. According to Hansen (2003, p. 26), experts "possess the ability to give feedback to themselves. . . . They feel and know at once if they have done something really well, or not so well".

Another difference between experts and non-experts relates to problem-identification and problem-solution. Studies have found that experts are better at identifying translation problems and at solving them quickly and efficiently (e.g.

Angelone 2010), having access to a greater range of solutions than non-experts do (Shreve 2006). In addition, experts tend to focus their attention on translation problems that are crucial to the task, whereas non-experts often waste effort on "irrelevant details" (Tirkkonen-Condit 2005, p. 407). Furthermore, experts are able to multitask, that is, they constantly search for acceptable alternatives while looking out for translation problems and critically monitoring their translation output at the same time (Göpferich and Jääskeläinen 2009).

Finally, some studies have indicated that there is a link between explicitation and translation expertise, although the studies conducted until now show conflicting evidence. Some scholars suggest that explicitation is a characteristic feature of non-expert translations. In her study of English-to-French and French-to-English translations, Blum-Kulka (1986) found evidence that explicitations occurred more frequently in trainee translations than in those by professional translators. In studying translations into English from different source languages, Laviosa-Braithwaite (1996) similarly found that trainee translators opted for explicitations and other presumed translation universals more often than professionals did. The assumption that explicitation is indicative of non-expertise finds support in Pym's hypothesis that "the harder the source text, the harder the translator works, and the more likely they are to make their renditions explicit" (Pym 2005, p. 39). However, other studies have suggested that explicitation is a feature of expertise. Examining explicitation in French to Danish translations by advanced trainees, Denver (2002) found that the more knowledgeable the trainees were, the more likely they were to opt for explicitation techniques. Englund Dimitrova (2005) examined explicitations of implicit textual links in Russian to Swedish translations by language students, translation trainees, and professional translators. Her findings revealed that the professional translators performed explicitations in a more automatic (i.e. non-problematic) manner than both of the student groups did, thus suggesting that explicitation was linked to expertise. Using Think-Aloud-Protocols, Hjort-Pedersen and Faber (2010) examined explicitation techniques in eight trainee translations (Danish to English) and found that explicitations of system-bound terms occurred automatically without prior mental explicitation (i.e. verbal explicitations of the complexities of the source text in the cognitive processing phase). In contrast, explicitations of nominalisations, passives and elliptical phrases were all preceded by mental explicitations. Based on this finding, the authors concluded that there was a link between explicitation and expertise in the sense that trainees gradually acquired explicitation techniques through practice. As mentioned in the introduction, Krogsgaard Vesterager (2017) examined explicitations in Spanish to Danish translations of a judgment produced by ten professional translators, five of whom were experts and five non-experts (according to parameters proposed in previous literature, see previously). The findings revealed that explicitation techniques were used more frequently in expert translations, and, as such, explicitation was indicative of translation expertise. As already stated, the present study builds on Krogsgaard Vesterager (2017) to examine the explicitations performed by the participants in more detail. The study is presented in the following section.

4 The study

The following sections outline the data on which the study is based (section 4.1), the participants (section 4.2), and the set-up and methodology (section 4.3).

4.1 Data

The study draws on an experimental study from a PhD thesis by Krogsgaard Vesterager (2011). The purpose of that thesis was to examine whether the participants opted for a literal or free translation. Thus, the purpose was different from the one pursued in this chapter. The data consisted of a Spanish source text and ten translations into Danish by professional Danish translators. The source text was an excerpt from the grounds (i.e. the legal justifications for the result of the judgment) of a Spanish judgment and consisted of 885 words. The source text was an appellate judgment concerning disciplinary dismissal, that is, dismissal due to misconduct or non-compliance on the part of the employee. Examples of legal grounds for a disciplinary dismissal include repeated insubordination, physical or verbal abuse, breach of contractual good faith, and habitual drunkenness or drug addiction negatively affecting job performance (Estatuto de los Trabajadores, articles 54 and 55). In the source text, several references were made to the judgment of the first instance court.

4.2 Participants

As has already been stated, the participants were ten professional Danish translators, that is, translators who earn their living translating. The details of the participants' translation experience and area of specialisation are summarised in Table 5.1.

According to the criteria adopted in previous literature (see section 3), translators 1, 3, 4, 5, and 8 can be defined as *experts*, having a minimum of ten years'

Table 5.1 Background information on participants (Krogsgaard Vesterager 2017)

Experts/non-experts	*Translator no. (corresponds to translation number)*	*Experience*	*Area of specialisation*
Experts	1	24 years	Legal texts
	3	15 years	Legal texts
	4	21 years	Legal and technical texts
	5	12 years	Legal texts
	8	31 years	Legal and medical texts.
Non-experts	2	2 years	None
	6	20 years	Medicine and EU texts
	7	15 years	EU texts
	9	3 years	None
	10	5 years	None

experience and specialising in legal translation. Conversely, translators 2, 6, 7, 9, and 10 can be defined as *non-experts* since they had less than ten years' experience and/or did not specialise in legal translation.

4.3 Set-up and methodology

The study was experimental in nature and involved participants recruited by the major translation agencies in Denmark, all of whom worked as full-time employees at the agencies, or as freelance translators. To help ensure the ecological validity of the study, the experiment was conducted in a naturalistic setting, although with the reservation that the translation task was not authentic but had been constructed for research purposes. Thus, the translators did not know that they were participating in a study, except for translators 8 and 10, to whom I was referred directly by the translation agencies. Although the two translators knew that they were participating in an experimental study, they were not informed of the purpose of the study.

The translation agencies assigned the task to their respective translators, except for translators 8 and 10, to whom I assigned the task myself. The participants were given the source text in its full length but were not provided with further translation instructions in the form of a brief. It was possible for the participants to request a brief; however, none of them did so. A deadline of two weeks was set for the translation task.

The data for the present study were analysed using complimentary approaches. More specifically, the translations were first analysed qualitatively using contrastive text analysis (see section 5.1), and, subsequently, a quantitative synthesis of the results was performed (see section 5.2). By combining qualitative methods with quantitative approaches, the study aims at developing a comprehensive understanding of the explicitation techniques used by the participants defined as experts and non-experts of the study. While the qualitative approach allows for an in-depth analysis of the explicitations performed by the participants, the quantification provides summary results in numerical terms, which can help identify clear explicitation patterns in the participants' translation products.

5 Analyses and results

In this section, the results of the qualitative analyses of explicitations (section 5.1) and the quantitative synthesis (section 5.2) are presented.

5.1 Qualitative analyses

Since the present study uses a longer source text than Krogsgaard Vesterager (2017) and examines all explicitation techniques (whereas the previous study only examined selected focal points), a new qualitative analysis was carried out. First, the ten target texts were compared to the source text to identify all explicitations made by the translators. Second, obligatory explicitations were identified and excluded from the results. For instance, in translating the gerunds of the source text, some translators had opted for structural changes, often adding conjunctions to their target text. The remaining explicitations (i.e. optional explicitations) were related to nominalisations, legal terms, elliptical phrases, anaphoric adjectives and demonstrative pronouns, and prepositional phrases expressing manner. In the following, the results of the analyses of each of these categories will be presented.

5.1.1 Explicitations of nominalisations

In linguistics, the term nominalisation (nom.) refers to the use of a word, which is not a noun (typically a verb, but also an adjective, or an adverb), as a noun, or as the head of a noun phrase. While nominalisation is a general characteristic of legal language, this linguistic phenomenon is more frequent in Spanish than in Danish, as is typical of Romance languages (e.g. Spanish) in comparison with Germanic languages (e.g. Danish) (Korzen 2005).

The results of the analyses reveal that explicitations of nominalisations are relatively rare. The explicitations performed are mainly identified in translations by experts, and all are in the form of additions, as illustrated in Example 1:

Example 1[1]

ST: (. . .) la tolerancia del empresario no genera un derecho al incumplimiento del trabajador (. . .)

[(. . .) the employer's tolerance does not justify non-compliance on the part of the employee (. . .)]

TT 8: (. . .) tolerance fra arbejdsgiverens side ikke berettiger den ansatte til **at misligholde aftalen** (. . .)

[(. . .) the employer's tolerance does not give the employee the right **to not comply with the contract** (. . .)]

In Example 1, the nominalisation of the source text *incumplimiento* (i.e. non-compliance) has been translated with the finite verb *misligholde* (to not comply with), followed by the noun *aftalen* (the contract), the latter of which has been added to the target text. By opting for this solution, the translation is in accordance with the stylistic preferences of Danish, which is less prone to linguistic nominalisation than Spanish is, as has already been mentioned.

5.1.2 Explicitations of legal terms

High density of legal terminology is one of the most characteristic features of legal language as a language for special purposes (LSP) (e.g. Šarčević 2000). According to the analyses, all of the target texts include explicitations of legal terminology, although they are especially prevalent in expert translations.

Most of the explicitations relate to translations of legal institutions, laws and general legal principles such as *good faith*, and they are all in the form of addition, as illustrated in Example 2:

Example 2

ST: (. . .) el Estatuto de los Trabajadores (. . .)
[(. . .) the Statute of Workers' Rights (. . .)]
TT 7: (. . .) den **spanske** arbejdslov (**Estatuto de los Trabajadores**) (. . .)
[(. . .) the **Spanish** Labour Act (**Estatuto de los Trabajadores**) (. . .)]
TT 9: (. . .) **Estatuto de los Trabajadores** (Loven om arbejdstageres forhold) (. . .)
[(. . .) **Estatuto de los Trabajadores** (Act on Workers' Conditions) (. . .)]

In Example 2, translator 7 has added the localising generic adjective *spansk* (Spanish) to the target text and included the Spanish term in brackets to explicitate to the Danish recipient that we are dealing with the Spanish Labour Act, not the Danish one. Other translators (both experts and non-experts) have included the Spanish term in brackets, and yet others (both experts and non-experts) have borrowed the term from the source text and added the descriptive Danish equivalent in brackets, as exemplified in target text number 9.

5.1.3 Explicitations of elliptical phrases

In linguistics, ellipsis refers to the omission of one or more words whose meaning may be recovered from the context. According to the analysis, explicitations of elliptical phrases are present in all the target texts, with a slight predominance of experts over non-experts. All explicitations are in the form of addition, and they relate to explicitations of reduced relative clauses of the source text, as exemplified in Example 3:

Example 3

ST: (. . .) todas las circunstancias constitutivas de grave antijuricidad (. . .)
[(. . .) all the circumstances constituting serious unlawfulness (. . .)]
TT 4: (. . .) alle de omstændigheder, **som udgør** alvorlig retsstridighed (. . .)
[(. . .) all the circumstances, **which constitute** serious unlawfulness (. . .)]

In Example 3, the elliptical phrase *constitutivas de grave antijuricidad* (constituting serious unlawfulness), which modifies the noun phrase *todas las circunstancias* (all the circumstances), constitutes a reduced relative clause headed by the adjective *constitutivas.* In the target text, the relative clause has been marked by the explicit relative pronoun *som* (which), which has been added to the text, followed by the finite verb *udgør* (constitute).

In addition, the analysis revealed two explicitations of agency[2] (both in the form of addition), as exemplified in Example 4:

Example 4

ST: (. . .) actos realizados en el clima de tolerancia (. . .)
[(. . .) actions carried out in a climate of tolerance (. . .)]
TT5: (. . .) handlinger, der foretages **af den ansatte** i et tolerant klima (. . .)
[(. . .) actions, which are carried out **by the employee** in a tolerant climate (. . .)]

In Example 4, the reduced relative clause *realizados en el clima de tolerancia* (carried out in a climate of tolerance) has been marked by the explicit relative pronoun *der* (which) followed by the finite verb *foretages* (are carried out), both of which have been added to the target text. In addition, the translator has added the prepositional phrase *af den ansatte* (by the employee) indicating that the employee is the agent in connection with the action described by the verbal passive (cf. Marco and Marín 2015, p. 242) of the source text *realizados* (carried out).

5.1.4 Explicitations of anaphoric adjectives and demonstrative pronouns

Anaphors are words and phrases (e.g. pronouns, nouns, adjectives, etc.) that refer back to words or phrases used previously in a text. The analyses of the target texts reveal that almost all the translations include explicitations of anaphoric adjectives and demonstrative pronouns, with experts explicitating more than non-experts do. All explicitations performed are in the form of specification.

According to the analyses, the vast majority of the explicitations relate to translations of anaphoric adjectives used as nouns, that is, when an adjective stands alone, acting as a noun, or, more specifically, having the function of a noun, as exemplified in Example 5:

Example 5

ST: (. . .) tales como la antigüedad del trabajador en la empresa, el perjuicio económico en su caso sufrido por **la misma** (. . .)
[(. . .) such as the seniority of the employee in the company, the potential financial loss suffered by **the same** (. . .)]
TT 6: (. . .) f.eks. arbejdstagerens anciennitet i virksomheden, den økonomiske skade, som **virksomheden** eventuelt har lidt (. . .)
[(. . .) such as the seniority of the employee in the company, the financial loss that has potentially been suffered by **the company** (. . .)]

In Example 5, the anaphoric adjective of the source text *la misma* (the same) functioning as a noun has been translated with the noun *virksomheden* (the company) in the target text, explicitating that the agent of the action expressed by the passive construction of the source text is the company. A more literal translation would include the Danish demonstrative pronoun *denne* (this).

In addition, one specification involves explicitation of an anaphoric demonstrative pronoun, as illustrated in Example 6:

Example 6

ST: (. . .) para que resulte lícita **aquella sanción** (. . .)
[(. . .) for **such a sanction** to be legitimate (. . .)]
TT 5: (. . .) for at en **afskedigelse** er lovlig (. . .)
[(. . .) for a **dismissal** to be legitimate (. . .)]

In Example 6, the Spanish demonstrative pronoun *aquella* (such), which functions as a determiner to specify the noun *sanción* (sanction), constitutes an anaphoric reference to the sanction of dismissal (*la sanción de despido*) mentioned previously in the source text. In the target text, the translator has opted for a solution involving the noun *afskedigelse* (dismissal), thus specifying that the sanction we are dealing with in this context is dismissal.

5.1.5 Explicitations of prepositional phrases expressing manner

Prepositional phrases consist of a preposition, which is the head of the phrase, and a postmodifier. Prepositional phrases modify nouns and verbs, expressing various relations (usually time, manner, or place) between the subject and the verb. According to the analyses, explicitations of prepositional phrases expressing manner are found in two translations (one by an expert, and the other one by a non-expert), and both are in the form of specification, as exemplified in Example 7:

Example 7

ST: (. . .) el enjuiciamiento del despido disciplinario debe abordarse de forma gradualista (. . .)
[(. . .) the adjudication of disciplinary dismissals should be addressed in a gradualist manner (. . .)]
TT 7: (. . .) skal behandlingen af en disciplinær afskedigelsessag således ske i henhold til **proportionalitetsprincippet** (. . .)
[(. . .) the treatment of disciplinary dismissal cases must therefore be in accordance with **the principle of proportionality** (. . .)]

In Example 7, the translator has translated the prepositional phrase *de forma gradualista* (in a gradualist manner) with the prepositional phrase *i henhold til proportionalitetsprincippet* (in accordance with the principle of proportionality). In the translation, reference is made to the principle that the sanction must be proportional to the violation, more specifically *el criterio de proporcionalidad* mentioned later on in the same paragraph of the source text, thus constituting a specification.

5.2 *Quantitative synthesis*

After the qualitative analyses had been carried out, a quantitative synthesis was made. According to the quantification results, the ten target texts included 217 explicitations, making the average number of explicitations per text 21.7.

Figure 5.1 is a pie chart representing the distribution across categories of the explicitations performed in the ten target texts.

As we can see from the chart, the explicitations were distributed somewhat unevenly across the five categories of analysis. Explicitations of elliptical phrases, legal terms, and nominalisations by far outnumbered those of the remaining two categories, constituting 41 percent, 29 percent, and 20 percent, respectively, of all explicitations performed in the ten target texts. In contrast, explicitations of anaphoric adjectives and demonstrative pronouns constituted eight percent of all explicitations performed, and prepositional phrases expressing manner accounted for one percent of the explicitations.

As for types of explicitations performed, the analyses showed that addition constituted 91 percent (198 of 217) of all explicitations, whereas specification

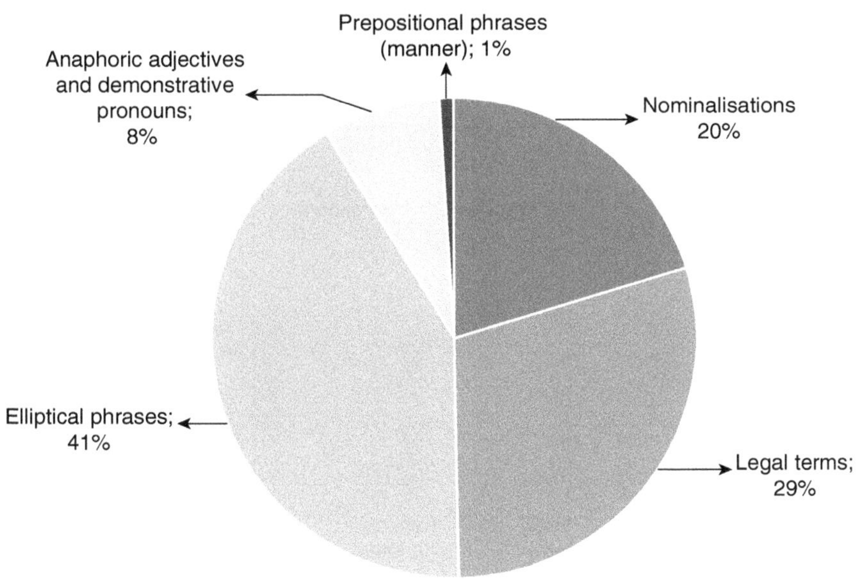

Figure 5.1 Representation of explicitations performed in the target texts, as distributed across categories

only accounted for nine percent (19 of 217). Table 5.2 illustrates the distribution of additions and specifications across categories.

According to Table 5.2, only addition is used in explicitations of nominalisations, legal terms, and elliptical phrases. Conversely, only specification is used in explicitations of anaphoric adjectives and demonstrative pronouns and prepositional phrases expressing manner.

When comparing the explicitations performed in the target texts to the participants' expertise in translation, the results revealed that experts generally explicitated more than non-experts did. According to the analyses, experts accounted for 63 percent (136 of 217) of all explicitations, whereas 37 percent (81 of 217) of the explicitations were found in performances of non-experts. In other words, experts explicitated almost twice as much as non-experts did. In addition, the results revealed significant differences in explicitation patterns between the two groups, as summarised in Figure 5.2.

As we can see from Figure 5.2, experts explicitated more than non-experts did in all categories but one, that is, prepositional phrases expressing manner.

Table 5.2 Additions and specifications as distributed across categories

Category	*Number of additions*	*Number of specifications*	*Total number of explicitations*
Nominalisations	44	0	44
Legal terms	64	0	64
Elliptical phrases	90	0	90
Anaphoric adjectives and dem. pronouns	0	17	17
Prepositional phrases (manner)	0	2	2
Total	**198**	**19**	**217**

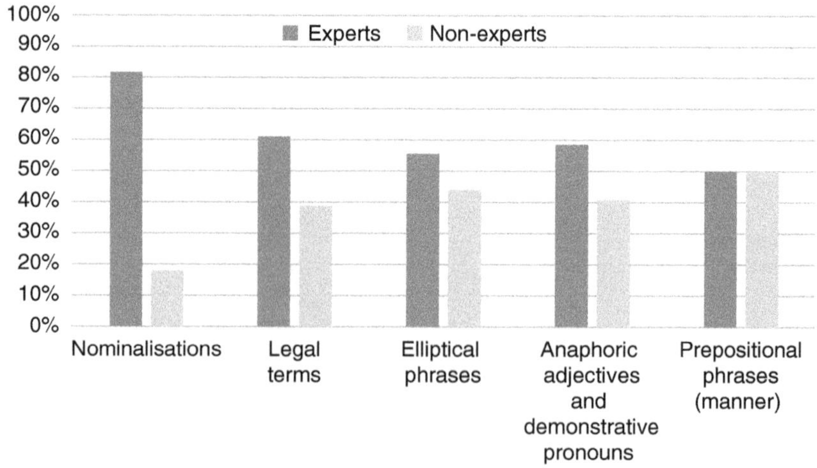

Figure 5.2 Representation of explicitations by experts and non-experts

The most significant differences were observed in nominalisations and legal terms, with experts performing 82 percent of explicitations of nominalisations and 61 percent of explicitations of legal terms. When it comes to the remaining categories, experts performed 59 percent of explicitations of anaphoric adjectives and demonstrative pronouns, 56 percent of explicitations of elliptical phrases, and 50 percent of explicitations of prepositional phrases expressing manner. Non-experts, on the other hand, performed 18 percent of explicitations of nominalisations, 39 percent of explicitations of legal terms, 41 percent of explicitations of anaphoric adjectives and demonstrative pronouns, 44 percent of explicitations of elliptical phrases, and 50 percent of explicitations of prepositional phrases expressing manner.

When looking at the individual translation products, the results showed that the participants in the expert group performed approximately the same number of explicitations, whereas there were significant individual differences in the non-expert group, as displayed in Figure 5.3.

As we can see from Figure 5.3, the experts performed between 24 and 31 explicitations in their target texts, with an average of 27.2 explicitations in this group. In the non-expert group, on the other hand, translators 6 and 7 performed 26 and 27 explicitations, respectively (average 26.5), whereas the three other non-experts performed between six and 11 explicitations (average 9.3). Thus, two of the non-experts performed approximately the same amount of

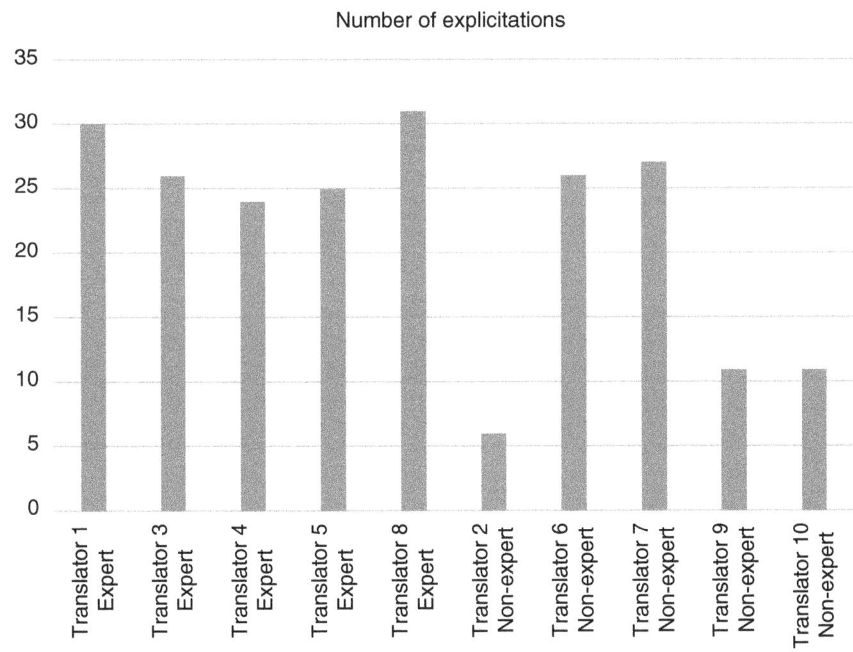

Figure 5.3 Representation of explicitations by individual participants

explicitations as the experts did, whereas the remaining non-experts performed significantly fewer explicitations.

6 Discussion and conclusion

Building on a previous study by the same author, the present study examined explicitation techniques used by Danish translation experts and non-experts in their translations of an excerpt from a Spanish judgment. According to previous literature, two criteria for expertise were used in this study: 1) number of years' expertise (a minimum of ten years' experience) and 2) domain-specific experience (i.e. legal translation).

Overall, the results of the qualitative analyses and the quantitative synthesis revealed that explicitations were relatively rare in the ten target texts. Drawing on the results from previous studies, one plausible explanation for this finding may be that translators generally resort to literal translation as a first solution at all expertise levels (e.g. Tirkkonen-Condit 2005).

As regards explicitation types, the analyses revealed that addition constituted 91 percent of all explicitations, whereas specification only accounted for nine percent, which is in line with the previous study (Krogsgaard Vesterager 2017).

According to the analyses, the explicitations actually performed in the target texts were significantly more frequent in the translation products of experts than in those of non-experts, with experts accounting for 63 percent of all explicitations performed. According to the results, experts explicitated more than non-experts did in all the categories except for prepositional phrases expressing manner. Thus, explicitation seems to be indicative of translation expertise in this study, supporting the results of Krogsgaard Vesterager (2017) and other studies that have found a positive link between explicitation and expertise in translation (e.g. Englund Dimitrova 2005; Denver 2002). According to the results, the differences between the two groups were especially significant with respect to nominalisations and legal terms. This supports the notion of explicitation as a feature of expertise developed gradually through extensive practice, as has been suggested by translation scholars (see section 3).

Although the results showed that there were considerable differences between the two groups, a look at the individual performances of the participants revealed important differences among the non-experts. While the non-expert group as a whole explicitated significantly less than the expert group did, the results revealed that two non-experts (translators 6 and 7) performed approximately the same number of explicitations as the experts did, thus displaying expert behaviour. The two translators in question have extensive translation experience (20 and 15 years' experience, respectively), but do not meet the domain-specific criterion, having worked with translations of medical and EU texts. If, on the other hand, expertise is defined only in terms of the number of years' experience (i.e. minimum ten years), thus excluding the domain-specific criterion, translators 6 and 7 are to be defined as experts, which would help explain the results of the study. In further support of this definition of expertise, if the participants are ordered according to the number of years' experience, an almost perfect upward trend can be observed in terms of explicitations performed. Thus, the results of the study suggest that legal translators' explicitation techniques develop gradually through practice in translation in any domain, not only legal translation. In conclusion, the study reminds us that translation expertise is a complex concept in need of further research and clarification.

In interpreting the results of the study, it is important to keep in mind that explicitations may not go hand in hand with expertise in all countries, but rather may depend on the translation culture in each country, which could help explain the conflicting findings in literature. This may be especially true in a legal context, where literal translation has generally been the norm (e.g. Šarčević 2000).

The limitations of the study point to directions for future research. First, since it involved a relatively small sample and only included Spanish–Danish translation, further studies (using the same and other language pairs) are needed to examine the possible link between the use of explicitation techniques and translation expertise in different countries. Second, the present study only examined the translation product, not how the recipient, that is, Danish judges or lawyers perceived the translations. Thus, research examining whether translations including explicitations are still regarded as legal text types by Danish legal experts are needed. Such research may include a survey in which translations with and without explicitations are submitted to legal experts.

Although the study has its limitations, it contributes to filling a research gap by providing empirical evidence of Danish professional translators' use of explicitation techniques. Apart from its academic contribution, the study may foster a more conscious praxis and decision-making process among professional translators (especially non-experts) and translation trainees who may want to emulate expert behaviour from the start.

Notes

1 In the examples, the excerpts of the source text are included to provide a context. The source-text excerpts are preceded by the abbreviation ST (for *source text*). The excerpts from the target text are preceded by the abbreviation TT (for *target text*) followed by the number of the translator in question (1–10). Following each excerpt, a literal translation into English is provided in square brackets. Some examples include excerpts from more than one target text. The explicitations of the examples are indicated in boldface.

2 In Krogsgaard Vesterager (2017), these two instances were described separately as explicitations of passives because they concern the agent of the action expressed by the sentence. However, since they also constitute elliptical phrases, the two explicitations are analysed as explicitations of ellipsis in this article.

References

Alcaraz Varó, E. and Hughes, B. (2002). *El español jurídico*. Barcelona: Ariel.

Angelone, E. (2010). Uncertainty, uncertainty management and metacognitive problem solving in the translation task. *In*: G. Shreve and E. Angelone, eds. *Translation and cognition*. Amsterdam: John Benjamins, pp. 17–40.

Baker, M. (1996). Corpus-based translation studies: The challenges that lie ahead. *In*: H. Somers, ed. *Terminology, LSP and translation: Studies in language engineering, in honour of Juan C. Sager*. Amsterdam: John Benjamins, pp. 175–186.

Becher, V. (2010). Abandoning the notion of 'translation-inherent' explicitation: Against a dogma of translation studies. *Across Languages and Cultures*, 11 (1), pp. 1–28.

Bernardini, S. (2001). Think-aloud protocols in translation research: Achievements, limits, future prospects. *Target*, 13 (2), pp. 241–263.

Blum-Kulka, S. (1986). Shifts of cohesion and coherence in translation. *In*: J. House and S. Blum-Kulka, eds. *Interlingual and intercultural communication. Discourse and cognition in translation and second language acquisition studies*. Tübingen: Gunter Narr Verlag, pp. 17–35.

Chesterman, A. (2000). Teaching strategies for emancipatory translation. *In*: C. Schäffner and B. Adab, eds. *Developing translation competence*. Amsterdam: John Benjamins, pp. 77–89.

Denver, L. (2002). On the translation of semantic relations: An empirical study. *Revista Brasileira de Lingüística Aplicada*, 2 (2), pp. 25–46.

Englund Dimitrova, B. (2005). *Expertise and explicitation in the translation process*. Amsterdam: John Benjamins.

Enríquez Raído, V. (2014). *Translation and web searching*. New York: Routledge.

Estatuto de los Trabajadores, Real Decreto Legislativo 2/2015. Available at: www.boe.es/buscar/act.php?id=BOE-A-2015-11430.

Faber, D., *et al.* (1997). *Introduktion til dansk juridisk sprogbrug – metode og analyse*. Frederiksberg: Handelhøjskolens Forlag.

Göpferich, S. (2009). Towards a model of translation competence and its acquisition: The longitudinal study transcomp. *In*: S. Göpferich, *et al.*, eds. *Behind the mind. Methods, models, and results in translation process research*. Copenhagen: Samfundslitteratur, pp. 11–37.

Göpferich, S. and Jääskeläinen, R. (2009). Process research into the development of translation competence: Where are we, and where do we need to go? *Across Languages and Cultures*, 10 (2), pp. 169–191.

Hansen, G. (2003). Controlling the process: Theoretical and methodological reflections on research into translation processes. *In*: F. Alves, ed. *Triangulating translation*. Amsterdam: John Benjamins, pp. 25–42.

Hjort-Pedersen, M. and Faber, D. (2010). Explicitation and implicitation in legal translation. A process study of trainee translators. *Meta: Translators' Journal*, 55 (2), pp. 237–250.

Jääskeläinen, R. (1989). Translation assignment in professional vs. non-professional translation: A think-aloud protocol study. *In*: C. Séguinot, ed. *The translation process*. Toronto: H.G. Publications, pp. 87–98.

Jääskeläinen, R. (1990). *Features of successful translation processes: A think-aloud protocol study*. Unpublished licentiate thesis. University of Joensuu, Savonlinna School of Translation Studies.

Klaudy, K. (2009). Explicitation. *In*: M. Baker and G. Saldanha, eds. *Routledge encyclopaedia of translation studies*. London: Routledge, pp. 104–108.

Krogsgaard Vesterager, A. (2011). *The translation of judgments: An examination of potential translation challenges in translating judgments from Spanish into Danish*. Unpublished thesis (PhD). Aarhus University.

Krogsgaard Vesterager, A. (2017). Explicitation in legal translation – a study of Spanish-into-Danish translation of judgments. *The Journal of Specialised Translation*, 27 (1), pp. 104–123.

Korzen, I. (2005). Endocentric and exocentric languages in translation. *Perspectives: Studies in Translatology*, 13 (1), pp. 21–37.

Laviosa-Braithwaite, S. (1996). Comparable corpora: Towards a corpus linguistic methodology for the empirical study of translation. *In*: M. Thelen and B. Lewandowska-Tomaszczyk, eds. *Translation and meaning: Part 3*. Maastricht: Euroterm, pp. 153–163.

Marco, C. and Marín, R. (2015). Origins and development of adjectival passives in Spanish: A corpus study. *In*: I. Pérez-Jiménez, *et al.*, eds. *New perspectives on the study of ser and estar*. Amsterdam: John Benjamins, pp. 239–266.

Muñoz, R.M. (2014). Situating translation expertise: A review with a sketch of a construct. *In*: J. Schwieter and A. Ferreira, eds. *The development of translation competence: Theories and methodologies from psycholinguistics and cognitive sciences*. Newcastle: Cambridge Scholars Publishing, pp. 2–57.

Øverås, L. (1998). In search of the third code: An investigation of norms in literary translation. *Meta: Translators' Journal*, 43 (4), pp. 571–590.

Pápai, V. (2004). Explicitation: A universal of translated texts? *In*: A. Mauranen and P. Kujamaki, eds. *Translation universals. Do they exist?* Amsterdam: John Benjamins, pp. 143–164.

Pym, A. (2005). Explaining explicitation. *In*: K. Károly and A. Fóris, eds. *New trends in translation studies*. Budapest: Akadémiai Kiadó, pp. 29–43.

Šarčević, S. (2000). *New approach to legal translation*. The Hague: Kluwer Law International.

Shreve, G. (2006). The deliberate practice: Translation and expertise. *Journal of Translation Studies*, 9 (1), pp. 27–42.

Tirkkonen-Condit, S. (1996). What is in the black box? Professionality in translational decisions in the light of TAP research. *In*: A. Lauer, *et al.*, eds. *Übersetzungswissenschaft im Umbruch: Festschrift für Wolfram Wilss zum 70. Geburtstag*. Tübingen: Narr, pp. 251–257.

Tirkkonen-Condit, S. (2002). Translationese – a myth or an empirical fact? A study into the linguistic identifiability of translated language. *Target*, 14 (2), pp. 207–220.

Tirkkonen-Condit, S. (2005). The monitor model revisited: Evidence from process research. *Meta: Translators' Journal*, 50 (2), pp. 405–414.

Tirkkonen-Condit, S., *et al.* (2008). The translation process: Interplay between literal rendering and a search for sense. *Across Languages and Cultures*, 9 (1), pp. 1–15.

6 Critical Discourse Analysis and the investigation of the interpreter's own positioning in a court hearing

A case study from an Austrian criminal court

Karolina Nartowska

1 Introduction

The fundamental interest of Critical Discourse Analysis according to Fairclough (1995, 2001) consists of the (critical) exploration of transparent and non-transparent structural relations of supremacy, discrimination, power and control between different social groups, which manifest themselves in language use and are legitimised by language use (cf. Wodak and Meyer 2009, p. 10).[1] CDA is, therefore, a particularly suitable instrument for the analysis of an interpreter-mediated criminal court interaction, which is based on (institution-)specific power and control relations. However, there is no research on court interpreting based on CDA, and only a few studies focus on interpreters' actions in court interactions.

Most of the discourse analysis-oriented or authentic data-oriented research concentrates primarily on the interpreter's performance and its linguistic aspects, i.e. rendition of the language register and style, forms of address, pragmatic meaning, or interpreting of questions (e.g. Berk-Seligson 1990; Jacobsen 2003; Hale 2004; Lee 2011). The analysis of an Austrian civil case (Kadrić 2009) is presented as an exceptional example which shows that the interpreter caused communication problems owing to her misinterpretation of the judge's strategies due to lack of institutional knowledge. Communication difficulties also arose when there were substantial divergences between lawyers' perceptions of the interpreters' role and those of the interpreter herself.

The first critical-discourse-analytical investigation in interpreting studies, which explores interpreters' actions in asylum interrogations (Pöllabauer 2003), shows that interpreters are active and equal participants in the interaction, that they intervene in the interrogation and take over the conversation. In a conflict situation, interpreters have been observed to be less oriented to follow official codes of conduct, especially the principle of impartiality, and to fit in with the expectations of the officials.

Nor has the self-positioning of interpreters in a court interaction been the subject of empirical research thus far, although the interpreters' own role perception is of great significance for their actions in the courtroom (e.g. Jansen 1995; Anderson 2002; Angelelli 2004; Kadrić 2009). The few studies on the self-image of court interpreters show that practicing interpreters perceive their role very differently and they do not seem to have a definite role identity. For example, court interpreters in an Australian study (Lee 2009) saw themselves as communication facilitators, language experts, or translation machines and they unanimously rejected the role of advocacy for one of the parties. Although most of the interpreters stated that they tried to achieve a complete and adequate interpretation, they simplified lawyers' questions and explained legal terms in the courtroom (Lee 2009, see also Christensen 2011). Conversely, the surveyed interpreters in Norway saw themselves on the side of the foreign language speaking person or identified with the role of institutional representatives (Falck 1987 cited in Niska 1995).

Interpreters' own role understanding can be shaped by several factors, including ethical standards, legal provisions, their internalised theoretical role conception, or expectations of the lawyers in the courtroom. At the same time, interpreters always bring their own role identity and their self to an interaction so that their role behaviour has an individual character. The aim of this study is to investigate the subjective positions that are adopted by an interpreter and to analyse to what extent the interaction is influenced by the interpreter's own positioning.[2] Simultaneously, it will show how CDA can contribute towards the understanding of interpreter-mediated interactions.

2 CDA as research method

Critical Discourse Analysis (CDA)[3] according to Norman Fairclough (1995, 1998, 2001) is "[a] problem-oriented, interdisciplinary approach" (Wodak and Meyer 2009, p. 2), the roots of which are in rhetoric, text linguistics, anthropology, philosophy, sociopsychology, cognitive and literary studies, sociolinguistics, applied linguistics, and pragmatics. Together with semiotics, pragmatics, psycho- and sociolinguistics, the ethnography of speech, conversation analysis, and discourse studies, it is one of the new, closely related disciplines which evolved in social sciences and the humanities in the 1960s and 1970s; disciplines which all pay attention to discourses in spite of their differences in theoretical backgrounds, research methods, and research objects (cf. Wodak 2008, p. 3). A common feature of these approaches is no longer the exploration of abstract language systems but characteristics of natural language use in real interactions. CDA, therefore, deals with the (partly) linguistic-discursive character of social and cultural processes and structures (cf. Fairclough and Wodak 1997, p. 271).

The term *critical* refers to the Frankfurt School, especially Jürgen Habermas, and to the common tradition of Critical Linguistics. *Critique* in the Frankfurt School "is the mechanism for both explaining social phenomena and changing them" (Fairclough *et al.* 2013, p. 80). Therefore, a "critical" social theory is considered to be oriented not only towards understanding and explaining, like the traditional theory, but also towards criticism and societal change. A critical science, though, must be self-reflexive, i.e., it must take into consideration the underlying interests and the historical context in which linguistic and social interactions take place (Fairclough and Wodak 1997, p. 261). Critical Linguistics assumes that language use can lead to the (ideological) distortion of social events and this can be shown by a systematic analysis (Wodak and Meyer 2009, p. 7).

2.1 Discourse definition, order of discourses

In his definition of discourse, Fairclough (cf. 2001, p. 19f.) distinguishes between text and discourse: the term *text* is used for language use in both speaking and writing, and is understood as a product of the text production process. The term *discourse*, however, is broader and refers to the entire process of a social interaction. This process also includes the production process of which the text is a product, and the interpretation process for which the text is a resource.[4]

Language use as *discourse* is regarded as "a form of social practice" (Fairclough 1995, p. 131). This implies, on the one hand, that language use is a kind of action and, on the other hand, that this action is always socially and historically embedded. The embedding in the social context has a dialectical character:

> Describing discourse as social practice implies a dialectical relationship between a particular discursive event and the situation(s), institution(s) and social structure(s) which frame it. A dialectical relationship is a two-way relationship: the discursive event is shaped by situations, institutions and social structures, but it also shapes them.
>
> (Fairclough and Wodak 1997, p. 258)

This three-dimensional discourse concept is shown in Figure 6.1.

Following Halliday's view of language as multifunctional within Functional-Systemic Linguistics, Fairclough (cf. 1998, p. 64f.) assumes socially constituent characteristics of linguistic use (of texts and discourses), which create social identities and social relationships, as well as knowledge and belief systems. Discourses influence social structures and can contribute to social continuity or social change.

Discourses are socially determined by underlying conventions and language norms. Fairclough (1995, p. 132) summarises these conventions in his concept *order of discourses*, based on Foucault: "The order of discourse of some social domain is the totality of its discursive practices, and the relationships (of complementarity, inclusion/exclusion, opposition) between them (. . .) ". Just as the order of discourses of the whole society structures the orders of discourses of different social institutions in a certain way, the order of discourses of a social institution structures individual discourses of this institution in a certain way (cf. Fairclough 2001, p. 25). Every social institution is "an apparatus of verbal interaction, or an 'order of discourse' " with its own repertoire of communicative events, different settings in which discourse takes place, social roles in which people can participate in the discourse (identities of participants and relationships

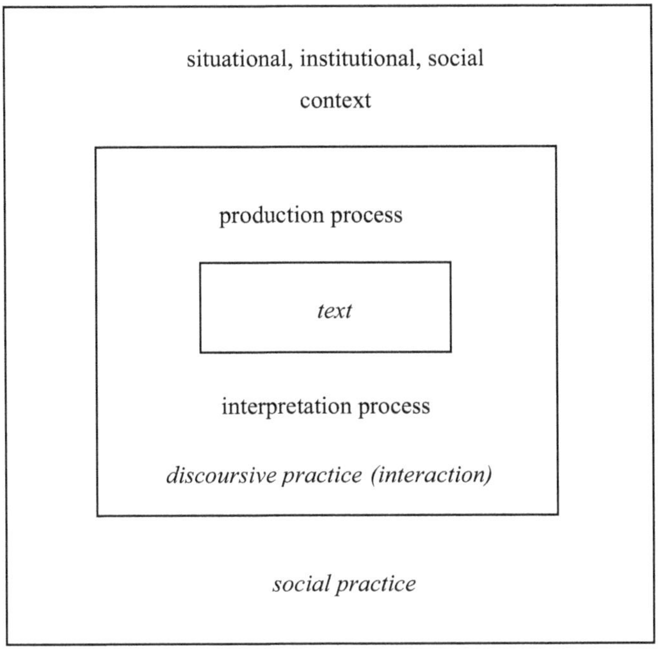

Figure 6.1 Discourse as text, interaction and context according to Fairclough (1995, p. 98)

between them), specific objectives (topics), and discourse types (norms) (cf. Fairclough 1995, p. 38).

Discourse types of a social institution determine "positions of subjects" (Fairclough 1995, p. 38). The filling of these positions implies the carrying out of certain discursive rights and obligations intended for the position taken, including what someone may and may not say within the discourse type, what is expected of him/her, etc. Social institutions, thus, facilitate social practice, in particular verbal interaction, and at the same time restrict it (cf. Fairclough 2001, p. 23).

Critical Discourse Analysis tries to explore the tension between these two dimensions of language use, i.e. that language is socially constitutive and, at the same time, socially determined (Fairclough 1995, p. 131).

2.2 Power and ideology

The way in which orders of discourses are structured is determined by changes in power relations in social institutions. Fairclough (2001, p. 36ff.) distinguishes between *power in discourse* and *power behind discourse*: in the first case, the discourse is seen as a place of actual power exertion, in which powerful discourse participants control and restrict contributions of powerless participants; in contrast, power behind discourse refers to how orders of discourses are constituted and determined by power relations.

A particular kind of power struggle in discourse is the struggle between ideologically different discourse types in social institutions. Institutional (including discursive) practices may contain assumptions which contribute to maintaining unequal power relationships and which legitimise them directly or indirectly. Such conventions, which appear to be universal and commonsensical, can often become ***naturalized*** but, originating in the dominant class, they function ***ideologically*** (cf. Fairclough 2001, p. 27).

Since different ideologies coexist simultaneously, they compete in order to establish themselves as the universally valid one so that they are shared by most members of a society or an institution. Consequently, it comes to an ideological struggle for dominance, which takes on a linguistic form. Enforcing or maintaining a discourse type (meaning systems, interactions, subjects and situations of a discourse type) in a social institution as predominant means implementing or maintaining certain ideological assumptions as universally valid (cf. Fairclough 2001, p. 75f.). Thus, ideologies, understood as "particular ways of representing and constructing society" (Fairclough and Wodak 1997, p. 275), can contribute to the reproduction of unequal power and dominance relationships.

2.3 Analytical framework

For his three-dimensional discourse concept, Fairclough (1995, 1998) develops an analytic, also three-dimensional, apparatus in which he links Bakhtin's theory of genres and the hegemony concept of Gramsci: "Any discursive 'event' (i.e. any instance of discourse) is seen as simultaneously being a piece of text, an instance of discursive practice, and an instance of social practice" (Fairclough 1998, p. 4).

The textual level (*textual analysis*) involves the analysis of the content, form and organisation of a text (Fairclough 1995, p. 4) as form and content are inseparable. Thus, the descriptive analysis includes the general structure of the text (e.g., phonology, grammar, lexis, semantics and cohesion) as well as higher levels of textual organisation in terms of interaction systems (including turn-taking, interaction control, politeness and face-threatening strategies, argumentation and generic structures).

The analysis of discoursive practice (*discourse praxis analysis*) is the link between the text and the socio-cultural practice, and it concerns sociocognitive aspects of the two processes: text production and text interpretation (cf. Fairclough 1995, p. 97f.). The analysis is interpretative and includes both the explanation of how the interaction partners interpret and produce texts (microanalysis) as well as the analysis of relations of the discursive event to the orders of discourses, that is interdiscursivity (macroanalysis) (cf. Fairclough 1998, p. 85). The interdiscoursive analysis, which bridges the gap between text and context, refers to the heterogeneity of texts which are based on a combination of different genres and discourses (cf. Fairclough 1999, p. 184).

The analysis of the discursive event as a social practice (*social discourse analysis*) refers to all levels of social organisation: the given situation, the institutional, and the social context related to the society as a whole, focusing on power and hegemonic relations at all contextual levels (Fairclough 1995, p. 134).

Although Fairclough's perspectives have been developed and/or critiqued by other authors, it is beyond the scope of this chapter to consider the various strands within CDA.

3 Outline of the study

The aim of this chapter is to describe the self-positioning of a professional court interpreter and its influence on the court interaction. Since discourses are not produced without context and can not be understood without consideration of the context (Titscher *et al.* 1998, p. 181), the study has been triangulated through ethnographic methods: an observation of the trial, a post-interview with the interpreter, and a survey among the participants in the proceedings. By doing so, not only is the linguistic dimension of the interpreter's actions taken into account but also the dialectical relationship between the interpreter's role behaviour and the institutional and interactional framework.

The core of the study is the analysis of a trial at the Regional Court for Criminal Matters in Vienna, in which a Polish interpreter was involved. The subject of the hearing was a dangerous threat and resistance to state authority. The trial was audio-recorded. The agreement of all participants was obtained at the beginning of the hearing, and the interpreter was contacted by telephone before the appointment.

The trial was transcribed using EXMARaLDA according to the HIAT-method (Ehlich and Rehbein 1976). The peculiarity of the "semi-interpretive work transcription" (in German HIAT) lies in its notation convention, namely the score notation (cf. Rehbein et al. 2004, p. 6). Each interaction partner is assigned his/her own action line – a score. In addition to a verbal and a translation track, the transcripts contain several annotation tracks, in which non-verbal communication, way and speed of speaking, volume and actions of the communication partners are recorded. The transcription should be a detailed, "natural" reproduction of the recorded interaction, in which such aspects of oral communication as hesitation, thinking aloud, self-corrections, and dialectal formulations are depicted as accurately as possible (see "literary transcription", Rehbein *et al.* 2004, p. 11).[5] All utterances in Polish were translated into German. All names and personal data were replaced by cover names, numbers or a description. Each speaker was assigned an abbreviation derived from their function: Judge = J, Defence Counsel = DC, Prosecutor = Pr, Defendant = D, and Interpreter = I.

The role perception of the court interpreter involved was investigated by a semi-standardised guideline interview following the hearing. The guideline consisted of open questions and included several thematic areas, i.e., career, conception of one's own role, and norms of professional ethics.

In order to examine the participants' expectations of the court interpreter, a qualitative questionnaire was carried out after the hearing. Through a series of open and semi-open questions, the first part of the questionnaire examined the participants' expectations and their perception of the interpreters' role. In the second part, a selection of tasks and functions of court interpreters was presented to them for evaluation of their importance on a four-point scale.

The study results are only valid for the case under investigation and they cannot be generalised to the entire court action context. There is no claim to representativeness of the data.

4 Analysis

4.1 Self-perception of the interpreter

The enlisted interpreter is a certified court interpreter for the Polish language. He has a master's degree in translation and interpreting studies and has nearly 35 years of professional experience. Court interpreting forms the bulk of his professional activity and he regards the Regional Court as his "second home". He enjoys a special status there and is well known to most of the lawyers.

When asked what the role of court interpreters is, the interpreter answers: "The interpreter is the person, the helper both of the judge and of the defendant". This could mean that he perceives himself simultaneously on both sides, as advocate of the judge (or rather the court) and the accused person. However, it is also possible that he sees his role as a link between two parties, as "the man in the middle" (Anderson 2002, p. 208) who only supports them in as much as this is necessary for the establishment of communication. The interpreter's firmly intonated statement "I'm on nobody's side!", although appearing contradictory at first glance, speaks in favour of this.

Concerning the most important rules of conduct, the interpreter says: "Objectivity, absolute objectivity. (. . .) Absolute impartiality. We must not show partiality", and he means both in the rendition and in the interpreter's behaviour. In his opinion, the preservation of impartiality is always possible, provided that interpreters focus exclusively on the interpreting task. He affirmed this with the words: "There are no emotions in my case".

For the interpreter, the norm-compliant, literal interpretation is the interpreter's ideal: "In my case, every word has to be conveyed". However, he provides a summary of testimonies for the defendant only if the judge requests it.

4.2 Lawyers' expectations of the interpreter

The lawyers involved in the trial believe that interpreters are visible, active participants in the proceedings. They are seen primarily as language and communication mediators whose main task is to accurately render what is being said in the courtroom. The judge explains that a "complete and correct" interpretation of all statements is particularly important so that "the (mental) 'path' from me to the accused is reduced to a minimum". In the opinion of the judge and the prosecutor, the exact rendition means that interpreters convey the meaning of a statement and not just its verbal level. However, they should not "gloss over" grammatical mistakes or confused utterances of the person speaking a foreign language and they should also render offensive statements and emotions of the communication partners. In addition, all three expect interpreters to take their own initiative to facilitate communication, if necessary, including independent explanations and inquiries.

The judge also supports "a bit" the role of interpreters as advocates for the foreign-language speaking person, while the defence counsel and the prosecutor speak out against it. However, the prosecutor and the judge believe that interpreters should build trust in the person speaking a foreign language.

The judge also sees in interpreters the function of court assistants. In his opinion, they should support the court in its work by performing certain actions, such as verification of the foreigner's personal data. The defender expects interpreters to "independently carry out the explanation of the instruction on rights of redress". Only the prosecutor takes the opposite view and emphasises that interpreters should act as "intermediaries" between the court and the defendant and not to be on the court's side.

The common expectation of all three lawyers of interpreters are impartiality and neutrality. The defender states in this context: "Under no circumstances must they bring in their own opinion!"

4.3 *Actual actions and the self-positioning of the interpreter in the courtroom*

The following part discusses the findings which emerged from the three-dimensional analysis presented previously.

Since the defendant has admitted that he had recently been sentenced, which is not mentioned in the file, the judge is trying to figure this out. He conducts an electronic search, then familiarises himself with the content found and finally confirms that the information provided by the defendant is "really" correct (Example 1, 40–42). His colloquial formulation "What do we have?"/"Was hamma?" with the inclusive we-structure shows that the finding of a judgment copy represents a common problem of all participants. The judge deals with the result with great concentration, so that the defence counsel's question is not heard (Example 1, 42).

As the interpreter does not interpret, the defendant cannot participate in the events. In one moment, the interpreter interrupts the silence, not to provide an interpretation, however, but to express his own opinion (Example 1, 42–43). He allows himself a judgmental comment on the defendant, of whom he speaks distantly in the third person singular. The use of the personal pronoun ("he") and not the name of the role in the trial (defendant) emphasises the character of his statement declaring the defendant incapable. At the same time, the interpreter signals his affiliation to the powerful institution representatives, and the fact that he also speaks in dialect reinforces this impression. He seems to assume that his opinion will be believed, in contrast to the defendant's statements which are constantly subjected to the examination of credibility. By usurping the right to

[40]

J [v]	Na ja, schau ma mal nach! Äääh Krawczyk. ((2,4s))
J [en]	Well, let's have a look! Ermm Krawczyk.
J [k]	((typing))
[k]	*((pages flicking, mouse clicking))*

[41]

J [v]	(Mit) folgender Begründung... ((2,2s)) Was hamma? Hundert C elf
J [en]	(On) the following grounds... What do we have? Hundred C eleven
J [k]	((reading out)) ((to himself))
[k]	*((keyboard noise))*

[42]

J [v]	((2,4s)) Ääh jo, • • • tatsächlich. ((6,6s))
J [en]	Oh yes, • • • really.
DC [v]	Wo woa des?
DC [en]	Where was it?
I [v]	Er
I [en]	He

[43]

J [v]	Vierzehn null fünfundzwanzig. Jǎ. Er ist offensichtlich
J [en]	Fourteen zero twenty-five. Yes. He is obviously
I [v]	sogt (()) wahrheits(gemäße) Angaben.
I [en]	says (()) truth(ful) statements.

[44]

J [v]	ein sehr wahrheitsliebender Mensch. ((1,6s))
J [en]	a very truth-loving person.

Example 1

have a say, stepping out of his role, and becoming a judgmental authority, the interpreter exercises power and takes the side of the lawyers.

The judge perceives the interpreter's interjection, which is different to the defence counsel's question, and answers: "Yes. He is obviously a very truth-loving person". The judge not only accepts this powerful intervention, but, by expressing his agreement with this judgment (in the third person singular), he takes the same stand. Whether the judge would have felt tempted to assess the defendant without the interpreter's impulse remains open. In any case, this creates an alliance between the interpreter and the judge, and the already well-founded position of the interpreter as an equal player in the trial is underpinned. The powerless defendant is excluded from this dialogue. The other lawyers react to the interpreter's behaviour with passivity.

The judge asks the defendant what he would do after a possible release (Example 2, 267–270). With his alternative question, he signals to the defendant what kind of response is desired and, at the same time, gives him the opportunity to answer without suggestions. The interpreter interrupts the judge forcing him to break off another open question (Example 2, 270). He interprets the first judge's question as an open question; however, instead of the passive without subject, he introduces a precise subject into the conditional clause ("if they") emphasising the role of the decision-making authorities. The interpreter clarifies the judge's alternative question by adding whether the defendant is going to Germany (instead of "going somewhere else"), which limits the defendant's answer. This addition seems to be the interpreter's own conclusion. Finally, he asks independently about the defendant's intentions (Example 2, 272), as if he were trying to guess the judge's purpose in his interrupted question.

The defendant starts his reply by saying that he would take his belongings and his girlfriend who is waiting for him (Example 2, 273), but does not complete

[267]
J [v] Na eh, aber die
J [en] Well, anyway, but the

[268]
J [v] Frage ist die: Sollt/ wenn Sie wieder enthaftet werden, Herr/ Herr Kro/
J [en] question is this: Should/ if you are released again, Mister/ Mister Kro/

[269]
J [v] Krawczyk, was werdenS dann machen? • • BleibenS dann in Österreich oder
J [en] Krawczyk, what will you do then? • • Do you stay then in Austria or

[270]
J [v] möchtenS woanders hingehn? Oder was/ wie/ wie...
J [en] would you like to go somewhere else? Or what/ how/ how...
I [v] Co Pan będzie robił,
I [de] Was werden Sie machen,
I [en] What will you do,

[271]
I [v] gdyby/ w przypadku, gdyby Pana dzisiaj zwolnili? • • Przy/ będzie/ pozostanie
I [de] wenn/ im Falle, wenn sie Sie heute entlassen würden? • • Kom/ werden/ bleiben noch in
I [en] if/ in the case if they released you today? • • Will you co/ be/ stay

[272]
I [v] jeszcze w Austrii czy Pan wyjedzie do Niemiec? Jakie zamiary Pan ma?
I [de] Österreich oder werden Sie nach Deutschland fahren? Welche Absichten haben Sie?
I [en] still in Austria or will you go to Germany? What intentions do you have?

[273]
I [v] Ich nehme/ packe
I [en] I take/ pack
D [v] Biorę swoje rzeczy, dziewczynę, która na mnie czeka tutaj...
D [de] Ich nehme meine Sachen, meine Freundin, die hier auf mich wartet...
D [en] I take my things, my girlfriend who is waiting for me here...

[274]
I [v] meine sieben Sachen, nehme mein Mädchen mit.
I [en] my stuff, take my girl with me.
D [v] • • • Mein Mädchen wartet
D [en] • • • My girl is waiting

[275]
J [v] • • Und?
J [en] • • And?
I [v] ((1,1s)) Ich hoffe!
I [en] I hope so!
D [v] hier • • • yy • • • aaaa ((1,1s)) chyba. Ja.
D [de] • • • äh • • • aahh wohl.
D [en] here • • • er • • • eerm probably. Yes.

[276]
J [v] Gehen wieder zrück nach Polen oder was?
J [en] Are you going back to Poland or what?
I [v] I dalej? Pan wraca do Polski?
I [de] Und weiter? Sie gehen nach Polen zurück?
I [en] And further? You are going back to Poland?

[277]
D [v] Naaach Deutschland. Nach Keln ich fahre... M/ muszę odzyskać pracę.
D [de] Ich m/ muss meine Arbeit
D [en] Tooo Germany! To Cologne I'm going... I/ I have to get back my work!

[278]
D [v] • • • Do Polski nie wracam! ((1,1s)) Jadę do Niemiec.
D [de] zurückbekommen. • • • Nach Polen gehe ich nicht zurück! Ich fahre nach
D [en] • • • I'm not going back to Poland! I'm going to Germany.

[279]
I [v] (Ich...) Ich reise dann nach Deutschland.
I [en] (I...) I travel then to Germany.
D [v] Jadę do Niemiec odzyskać pracę!
D [de] Deutschland. Ich fahre nach Deutschland die Arbeit zurückbekommen!
D [en] I'm going to Germany to get my work back!
D [k] ((louder))

Example 2

the sentence because of the interpreter's intervention. He tries to present himself positively by addressing the topic of family and his serious plans. Although his answer is incomplete, the interpreter makes a complete sentence in the rendition (Example 2, 273–274). The colloquial phrases ("pack his stuff", "my girl") make the defendant's statement seem less serious while the information serving his positive image (that is, the comment that his girlfriend is waiting for him in Vienna) is left out by the interpreter. The defendant, however, seems to have understood that the interpreter did not convey everything. Thus, he delivers the omitted information directly in German: "• • • My girl is waiting here • • • er • • • aahh ((1,1 s))" but reaches the limits of his knowledge of German and, finally, after a long search for a correct word, he articulates his doubts in Polish (Example 2, 275). Since he has been in custody for a long time, he is uncertain whether his girlfriend is still in Vienna. However, his interjection shows the meaning of this statement for him, so that he even renounces the support of the interpreter and acts independently. After that, a longer break arises as if the interpreter was not sure of his action strategy, but finally he does not repeat the defendant's statement in German and only renders his last interjection (Example 2, 275).

It is not clear whether the defendant's statement is comprehensible to the judge, but it is not the desired answer. Therefore, the judge asks again if the defendant will go back to Poland or what he wants to do (Example 2, 275–276). The interpreter only partially interprets the question: "And further? You are going back to Poland?" By this statement with increasing intonation, he leaves no alternative open to the defendant but suggests that an affirmative answer is expected.

The defendant replies insisting (first in German, then he switches to Polish), that he is going back to Germany, that he must get his job back there and, after a pause, he adds loudly and determined that he will not go back to Poland (Example 2, 277–278). The defendant wants to prompt the interpreter into acting with his tone as the interpreter remains silent. But even when the defendant has clearly finished his statement, the interpreter does not provide any interpretation. After another longer break (1.1 s), the defendant repeats his statement again to force the rendition ("I'm going to Germany. I'm going to Germany to get my work back!"). The certain, loud tone indicates that he becomes impatient due to the interpreter's neglect and, simultaneously, that it is of importance for him to convey this information to the court. This time the interpreter reacts but of all the defendant's utterances he merely renders the last sentence: "(I. . .) I travel then to Germany". With this general wording and the omission of "travel" reasons, the interpreter intervenes significantly in the defendant's statement. It also contains an implicit negative assessment of the defendant by the interpreter.

The defendant draws a positive image of himself as a citizen who has a solid standing in family and professional life, bears responsibility, and lives an orderly life implying that the committed offense was a singular event. He, thus, credibly answers the judge's question about his plans. The interpreter does not convey the information most relevant to the defendant, his goals, and future plans. Nor does the interpretation sound credible, and it makes the defendant appear as if he were unwilling or unable to give a desired answer. This means that the interpreter not only does not convey the positive image of the defendant but conveys the opposite, a distorted, negative image. He changes the character of the interaction and creates two parallel worlds in the courtroom, in which the German-speaking lawyers and the Polish defendant are each situated.

In her closing speech, the defence counsel emphasises all mitigating circumstances that serve the defence of the defendant and his presentation in a positive light. She begins with the reference to the defendant's remorseful confession, as it is fundamental to the assessment of punishment: she emphasises the adjective "remorseful" and the fact that "it worked anyway". By using the inclusive we-structure ("we've seen"), she makes his confession an indisputable fact that all participants have already experienced. The strong, repeated emphasis of the confession ("he has fully confessed in terms of content") can also be seen as an attempt of the defence counsel to offset the not quite clearly conveyed confession. By the subsequent reference to the fact that the defendant was heavily intoxicated, she appeals to the common presupposition that one does irresponsible things while

[355]	DC [v]	Hohes Gericht! Sehr geehrte Frau Stootsanwältin! • •
	DC [en]	Your Honour! Dear Mrs. Prosecutor! • •
[356]	DC [v]	Na jo, wir habn gesehn, es is ja eh gegangen mit dem reumütigen
	DC [en]	Well, we've seen, it worked anyway with the remorseful
[357]	DC [v]	Geständnis. Er hot holt, obwohl er so stoak alkoholisiert woa - zwei Komma
	DC [en]	confession. He had just, although he was so heavily intoxicated – two hundred
[358]	DC [v]	acht Promille ist, glaub i, auch in Polen einigermoßen tüchtig - • • • äh • • er
	DC [en]	eighty millilitres alcohol level is, I think, also in Poland reasonably sizeable - • • • er • • he
	DC [k]	((laughing))
[359]	DC [v]	hot sies... - wo/ wobei die Alkoholisierung, • • die woascheinlich/ die is
	DC [en]	has... – bu/ but the intoxication, • • that probably/ that is
[360]	DC [v]	sicherlich in ana gewissen Weise mildernd zu werten - er hat sich, wie gsogt,
	DC [en]	surely in a certain way to rate as mitigating – he has, as mentioned,
[361]	DC [v]	voll inhaltlich geständig • • verantwortet. Mildernd ist weiters, dass es nur zum
	DC [en]	fully confessed in terms of • • content. Mitigating is further, that it only partially
[362]	DC [v]	Teil beim/ zum äh Versuch äh geblieben is. • • Äh es woa des Gaunze hoit a
	DC [en]	remained at the/ to the er attempt. • • Er it all was just a
[363]	D [v]	bleede Gschicht. • • Er hot jetzt a erkannt, • • dass • • er • • net wieder nach
	DC [en]	stupid story. • • He has now also realized, • • that • • he • • will not
[364]	D [v]	Österreich kommen wird und sich ähnlich benimmt. Er hot jetzt hoch und heil/
	DC [en]	come to Austria again and behave similarly. He has now faithf/
[365]	D [v]	heilig versprochen, sich in die nächste Eisenbahn zu setzen • • • und noch
	DC [en]	faithfully promised to get on the next train • • • and
[366]	D [v]	Deutschland zu faon. • • Ich hätte gemeint, • • • man sollte die Strafe so
	DC [en]	go to Germany. • • I would have thought, • • • the punishment should be so
[367]	D [v]	bemessen, • • • dass er möglichst boid enthoftet wird • • • und die Republik
	DC [en]	assessed • • • that he will be released as soon as possible • • • and
[368]	DC [v]	verlossn kaun. Ein mildes Urteil bitte schön!
	DC [en]	can leave the Republic. A lenient punishment, please!

Example 3

being under the influence of alcohol, and suggests that this strong intoxication is considered a mitigating circumstance. Due to the jovial nature of her statement as well as the colloquial language, the defence counsel tries to mitigate the gravity of the offense. Subsequently, she points out that it was "merely" an attempt, describes the incident as "a silly story", and emphasises its singular character. By repeatedly using the impersonal subject "it" and not making the defendant an agent, she shifts the guilt away from the defendant. Then, the defence counsel refers to the defendant's promise that he will immediately go to Germany and not come back to Austria. She emphasises this circumstance as being particularly relevant, as when the defendant leaves the country the problematic case will be resolved. Therefore, she is making a case for a judgment which would enable the defendant to leave Austria as quickly as possible.

The routine interaction, which is strongly oriented towards institution-specific conventions, takes place at a fast pace only among the lawyers. The defendant remains only a passive observer of the events until the interpreter intervenes after the speech with the rendition:

Although in the beginning the interpreter mentions (though the sentence is not entirely comprehensible) mitigating circumstances named by the defence counsel (the remorseful confession, the intoxication, and the attempt), he does not deal with them (Example 3, 369–370). Instead, he focuses on the final part of the speech, the defendant's promise (Example 3, 370–372). The interpreter, however, does not report on an event that has already happened in perfect tense but makes a deictic shift by addressing the defendant directly ("You promise that

[368]

I [v]		Pani prokurator utrzymuje
I [de]		Frau Staatsanwältin hält den Strafantrag
I [en]		Mrs. Prosecutor upholds

[369]

I [v]	wniosek o ukaranie, tak jak na piśmie, natomiast pani obrońca (())
I [de]	aufrecht, so wie schriftlich, hingegen Frau Verteidigerin (())
I [en]	the penalty petition as written; however, Mrs. Defender (())

[370]

I [v]	wszelkiej sprawy okoliczności łagodzące:	Pan obiecujee, że Pan wsiądzie w
I [de]	jeglicher (Sache) Milderungsgründe.	Sie versprecheen, dass Sie in den nächsten
I [en]	any (case) mitigating circumstances.	You promise that you will get on the

[371]

I [v]	następny pociąg, wyjedzie do Niemiec • • • i że na przyszłość Pan uwzględni
I [de]	Zug einsteigen, nach Deutschland fahren • • • und dass Sie in Zukunft das berücksichtigen und nicht w/
I [en]	next train, go to Germany• • • and in the future you will take

[372]

I [v]	to i nie b/ powróci do przestępstwa • • • i wn/ • • • i wnosi o możliwie najniższy
I [de]	zu einem Verbrechen zurückkommen werden • • • und be/ • • • und beantragt das möglichst geringe
I [en]	it into consideration and will not b/ return to a crime • • • and re/ • • • and requests the smallest

[373]

I [v]	wymiar kary.	Przyłącza się Pan do wypowiedzi swojego obrońcy?		
I [de]	Strafausmaß.	Schließen Sie sich der Äußerung Ihres Verteidigers an?		
I [en]	possible	punishment. Do you go along with the statement of your defender?		
D [v]			Ja.	Ja.
D [en]			Yes.	Yes.
D [k]				((louder))

[374]

I [v]	• • Ja, ich schließe mich an.
I [en]	Yes, I go along with it.

Example 4

you . . . ") and renders, using the present, what are supposedly the defendant's own words. By using only verbs with the perfect aspect (literally "wsiąść"/"will get in", "wyjechać"/"will leave", "uwzględnić"/"will take into consideration", "powrócić"/"will return"), the statement has a purely futuristic meaning with which the interpreter clearly indicates that the illocution, the given promise, applies unabated and without restrictions. Due to the change in tense, the indirect speech, and the use of perfect verbs in his interpretation, the interpreter places a demand on the defendant to fulfil the promise. Thus, the interpreter creates a different effect than that produced by the defence counsel, who presented the defendant in a positive light by reporting on the promise given by him.

Moreover, the interpreter omits the second part of the promise that the defendant will not come back to Austria and will not behave in a similar way; however, he seems to be aware of this because, after a pause, he adds on his own: "and in the future, you will take it into consideration and will not return to a crime". This means, in addition to the previous demand, that the rendition also includes a lesson or reprimand of the defendant independently brought in by the interpreter. His fast speech tempo and strong tone reinforce the expressiveness of the warning, just like the negatively connoted noun "crime" (compared to "behave similarly"). It is, at the same time, a judgmental, negative attitude of the interpreter towards the defendant.

After the rendition, the interpreter, on his own initiative, asks the defendant whether he goes along with the defender's statement (Example 3, 373). By this question, the interpreter assumes a lawyers' task and acts in the powerful, trial-leading role of the judge. He anticipates the impending course of the proceedings showing himself to be an expert, a co-lawyer, who is well acquainted with court processes and supports the work of the court contributing to the efficiency of the proceedings. By forcing the defendant to react (Example 3, 373), the interpreter influences the course of the interaction. The defendant's positive answer can be seen not only as an automatic affirmation to this question and, thus, to the closing speech of his defender but rather as to the interpreter's entire admonishing remarks. The interpreter conveys his monosyllabic answer with a necessary explication: "Yes, I go along with it" as the lawyers know nothing of his independent actions. It remains unsolved whether the judge would have actually asked the same question to the defendant or whether he would have given him the last word before the verdict. In any case, the passive response of the lawyers to the interpreter's own initiative indicates that they do not disapprove of his active actions. The interpreter retains full control over the situation.

5 Conclusions

The study shows that applying CDA as a research method enables to investigate the subjective positions adopted by the interpreter and to analyse how the interaction is influenced by his own positioning. The given examples of the interpreter's actions show that the interpreter is aware of his active role in the courtroom; however, he does not identify himself with the interpreter's role but with the role of the institutional representatives. This is a result not yet achieved in the previous research.

The analysis demonstrates both his power in discourse and power behind discourse. Power in discourse manifests itself, among others, in the reservation of the interpreter's right to decide what and how to interpret. He intervenes and introduces modifications both in the judge's questions, so that the communication is not straightforward, which gives rise to two communication levels, as well as in the defendant's statements, conveying a distorted image of him. Power behind discourse manifests itself in different forms of the interpreter's actions. The interpreter changes the interaction and the usual power relations in the courtroom acting as a co-lawyer who claims for himself the right to have a say. He usurps the judge's power and, by independently asking the defendant questions and prompting him to act, he fulfils the role of the proceedings' leading judge. He also supports the court, e.g. by independently carrying out instructions or supplying protocol-suitable answers. The active, intervening role of interpreters in court or asylum-related interactions (Jansen 1995; Kadrić 2009; Pöllabauer 2003) is, thus, confirmed.

The three-dimensional analysis reveals the interpreter's ideological assumptions which contribute to the maintaining of unequal power relations. On the one hand, he emphasises in his interpretations the powerful role of the court towards the defendant, e.g. by inserting a subject related to the deciding authority even if the judge does the opposite and eliminates the power imbalance using passive formulations and we-structures. On the other hand, the changed renditions turn the interpreter into an instructive, admonishing authority, which also shows his negative, judgmental attitude. He behaves powerfully towards the defendant, acting as a judge without a robe, who co-accuses, co-instructs and co-punishes him. This behaviour manifests itself in selected interpretations and omissions, blaming reproaches, in his strong, harsh tone, as well as in his valuating comment about the defendant.

By embedding the interpreter's actions into the social context, the analysis shows that the interpreter's power and independent actions remain mostly invisible and uncontrollable for the lawyers. However, even if his actions are visible and he clearly acts against the lawyers' expectations (accurate and complete interpretation, impartiality, see section 4.2), they do not react. They do not seem to question the interpreter's special status at the Regional Court and tacitly accept his powerful position in the courtroom. His behaviour even seems to fulfil their expectations to show the interpreter's own initiative and to take on the role of a court-assistant, though it conflicts with the professional ethics of court interpreters. It turns out that interpreters' actions can, but do not always have to, be influenced by expectations of other participants (cf. Jansen 1995).

The analysed examples also show that the interpreter's own role perception (see section 4.1) differs from his actual role behaviour in the courtroom, which confirms Christensen's findings (2011). Although he considers neutrality and "interpretation of every single word" as the highest professional standards, his actions reveal substantial deviations and contradictions. Although the interpreter has completed relevant studies, where one might think that he had internalised the correct behaviour patterns and norms for court interpreters, his decades of professional experience seem to have an effect on his role conception. He has, in the meantime, internalised practices and behaviour patterns of the institution and he adopts a role of an institutional representative.

The study shows that interpreters are power figures in the courtroom. An analysis based on CDA of the implications of their actions enables to highlight the need to meet professional standards, even when relations of trust allow interpreters to overstep their limits. Simultaneously, it becomes clear that CDA as a research method opens new horizons and provides new insights into authentic interpreter-mediated court interactions.

Notes

1 Its research interests include feminism, anti-Semitism, fascism, xenophobia, but also language in politics, and language use in organisations and institutions.
2 In this paper, only selected results of the comprehensive study on the role behaviour of professional court interpreters in criminal proceedings are presented (see Nartowska 2014, 2015, 2017).
3 Since CDA is based on a series of approaches with different theories and methods, more recent works differentiate conceptually between various CDA approaches, including Fairclough's *Dialectical-Relational Approach* (see Wodak and Meyer 2009; Wodak 2013).
4 In his later work, Fairclough prefers the alternative term "semiosis" to "discourse" (Fairclough 2009, p. 163; Fairclough *et al.* 2013, p. 79).
5 The following transcription conventions were applied:

• a micropause
•• a break up to 0.5 second
••• a break up to 1 second
((2,5 s)) a break over 1 second
. . . breaking off
/ repair
<u>instit</u>ution emphasis
() hardly audible
(()) inaudible
((whispers)) non-verbal features or explanatory comments
CAPITALS anonymous information

References

Anderson, R.B.W. (2002). Perspectives on the role of interpreter. *In*: F. Pöchhacker and M. Shlesinger, eds. *The interpreting studies reader*. London: Routledge, pp. 206–214.

Angelelli, C.V. (2004). *Revisiting the interpreter's role. A study of conference, court, and medical interpreters in Canada, Mexico, and the United States*. Amsterdam: John Benjamins.

Berk-Seligson, S. (1990). *The bilingual courtroom. Court interpreters in the judicial process*. Chicago: University of Chicago Press.

Christensen, T.P. (2011). User expectations and evaluation: A case study of a court interpreting event. *Perspectives: Studies in Translatology*, 19 (1), pp. 1–24.

Ehlich, K. and Rehbein, J. (1976). Halbinterpretative Arbeitstranskriptionen (HIAT). *Linguistische Berichte*, 45, pp. 21–41.

Fairclough, N. (1995). *Critical discourse analysis: The critical study of language*. London: Longman.

Fairclough, N. (1998). *Discourse and social change*. Cambridge: Polity Press.

Fairclough, N. (1999). Linguistic and intertextual analysis within discourse analysis. *In*: A. Jaworski and N. Coupland, eds. *The discourse reader*. London: Routledge, pp. 183–211.

Fairclough, N. (2001). *Language and power*. Harlow: Longman.

Fairclough, N. (2009). A dialectical-relational approach to critical discourse analysis in social research. *In*: R. Wodak and M. Meyer, eds. *Methods of critical discourse analysis*. Los Angeles: Sage, pp. 162–200.

Fairclough, N., *et al.* (2013). Critical discourse analysis. *In*: R. Wodak, ed. *Critical discourse analysis. Concepts, history, theory*. Los Angeles: Sage, pp. 79–101.

Fairclough, N. and Wodak, R. (1997). Critical discourse analysis. *In*: T.A. van Dijk, ed. *Discourse as social interaction. Discourse studies: A multidisciplinary introduction*, Vol. 2. London: Sage, pp. 258–284.

Hale, S. (2004). *The discourse of court interpreting. Discourse practices of the law, the witness, and the interpreter*. Amsterdam: John Benjamins.

Jacobsen, B. (2003). Pragmatics in court interpreting: Additions. *In*: L. Brunette, *et al.*, eds. *The critical link 3. Interpreters in the community. Selected papers from the third international conference on interpreting in legal, health and social service settings, Montréal, Québec, Canada 22–26 May 2001*. Amsterdam: John Benjamins, pp. 223–238.

Jansen, P. (1995). The role of the interpreter in Dutch courtroom interaction: The impact of the situation on translational norms. *In*: J. Tommola, ed. *Topics in interpreting research*. Turku: University of Turku, pp. 11–36.

Kadrić, M. (2009). *Dolmetschen bei Gericht. Erwartungen – Anforderungen – Kompetenzen*. Wien: Facultas.

Lee, J. (2009). Conflicting views on court interpreting examined through surveys of legal professionals and court interpreters. *Interpreting*, 11 (1), pp. 35–56.

Lee, J. (2011). Translatability of speech style in court interpreting. *The International Journal of Speech, Language, and the Law*, 18 (1), pp. 1–33.

Nartowska, K. (2014). *Rollenhandeln von DolmetscherInnen in strafgerichtlichen Verfahren. Eine diskursanalytische Studie im Ländervergleich Österreich und Polen*. Thesis (PhD). Universität Wien.

Nartowska, K. (2015). The role of the court interpreter: A powerless or powerful participant in criminal proceedings? *The Interpreters' Newsletter*, 20, pp. 9–32.

Nartowska, K. (2017). The role of court interpreters in criminal proceedings in the context of the right to a fair trial. *In*: A. Liimatainen, *et. al.*, eds. *Legal translation and court interpreting: Ethical values, quality, competence training*. Berlin: Frank & Timme, pp. 95–123.

Niska, H. (1995). Just interpreting: Role conflicts and discourse types in court interpreting. *In*: M. Morris, ed. *Translation and the law*. Amsterdam: John Benjamins, pp. 293–316.

Pöllabauer, S. (2003). *Translatorisches Handeln bei Asylanhörungen. Eine diskursanalytische Untersuchung*. Thesis (PhD). Karl-Franzes-Universität Graz, Graz.

Rehbein, J., *et al.* (2004). *Handbuch für das computergestützte Transkribieren nach HIAT*. Hamburg: Universität Hamburg.

Titscher, S., *et al.* (1998). *Methoden der Textanalyse. Leitfaden und Überblick*. Opladen: Westdt. Verl.

Wodak, R. (2008). Introduction: Discourse studies – important concepts and terms. *In*: R. Wodak and M. Krzyżanowski, eds. *Qualitative discourse analysis in the social sciences*. Basingstoke: Palgrave Macmillan, pp. 1–29.

Wodak, R., ed. (2013). *Critical discourse analysis. Concepts, history, theory*. Los Angeles: Sage.

Wodak, R. and Meyer, M. (2009). Critical discourse analysis: History, agenda, theory, and methodology. *In*: R. Wodak and M. Meyer, eds. *Methods of critical discourse analysis*. Los Angeles: Sage, pp. 1–33.

7 How to apply comparative law to legal translation[1]

A new juritraductological approach to the translation of legal texts

Sylvie Monjean-Decaudin and Joëlle Popineau-Lauvray

1 Introduction

Since the 1950's, translation has gained momentum in a newly rebuilt and increasingly globalised world, either because of international reasons linked to WWII or national ones. Countries exchange political views, have trading relationships and share economic, financial and legal ideas, leading to a higher demand for translation. Legal texts are thus translated in different legal contexts and meet the requests of international or national institutions, companies or individuals for specific purposes.

The legal translator is therefore entrusted with the task of transferring a wide range of legal texts from one language to another, with each of them having specific legal effects based on a specific context. How should the translator deal with a legal text? Should s/he evaluate its level of legal complexity to be able to estimate the issues and stakes in his/her translation? How can s/he assess that s/he has gained enough experience to face the challenges posed by transferring the meaning between the source law and the target law systems? How should s/he deal with it?

Juritraductology (or the science of legal translation) offers a new conceptual framework to translation studies applied to law: this chapter presents it as the basis of a new theoretical and methodological tool for analysing translation and its process. Prior to this, the translator must analyse the legal text to translate, its legal context and assess its level of legal complexity. Juritraductology offers a three-step process in which comparative law plays an important role.

2 Juritraductology: a new conceptual framework in law and translation sciences

Juritraductology is a cross-interdisciplinary field of study that emerged in France in the early 21st century (Monjean-Decaudin 2012). This novel approach differs from Legal Translation Studies, or *traductologie juridique* in French, which mainly focus on the complexity of a legal translation and/or the translation of legal concepts. Legal Translation Studies are a subdivision combining (juri)linguistics and translation studies and offer various interesting and worthy approaches and solutions. Besides Legal Translation Studies, comparative law specialists have developed their own approach to find solutions when translating concepts of law in a specific legal system.

However, both theories have developed in a distinct way and to a certain extent remain independent: translation theories are disconnected from theories of law.

Juritraductology, a field of study developed by the CERIJE[2] in 2012, offers a new crossdisciplinarity, building bridges between translation studies and law, but rooted in both fields. Combining theories makes it thus possible to establish the required connection between the legal right to translation and legal translation, which form the bedrocks of juritraductology. In other words, the juritraductological thinking is conceived as a science enabling ideas to interact with each other without any disciplinary frontiers. The approach can encompass all laws and all languages, because only a broader approach can help nurture the epistemological debate in this field of study and thus enrich the targeted applications.

Juritraductology has several epistemological founding principles, as shown in Figure 7.1.

Law and linguistics, which are the two "nourishing" sciences, merge to form legal linguistics. Linguistics is one fundamental pillar in translation studies, which became an independent field of study in the 1970s.

The legal right to translation has its roots in Law. And legal translation has it roots in legal linguistics and translation studies. Both combine and create the two main fields of study in juritraductology.

The field is undoubtedly a cross-disciplinary area. Two remarks can be made: firstly, juritraductology does not place disciplines side by side but instead combines them; secondly, law has a determining influence on translation, thus

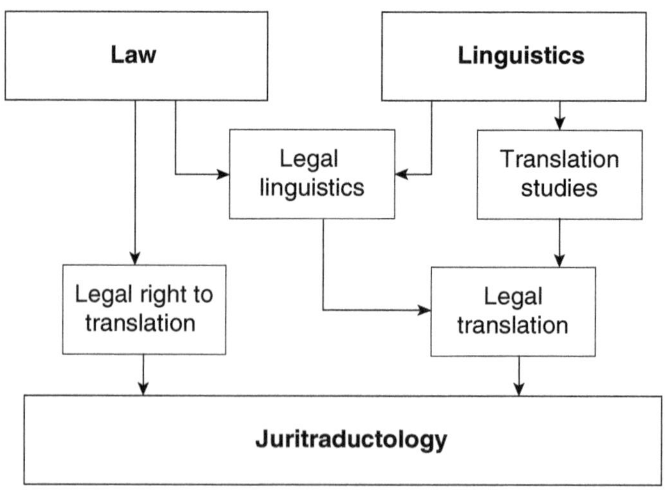

Figure 7.1 Juritraductology and its epistemological founding principles

explaining the consequences on legal translation, which have remained unexplored up to now.

Juritraductology as a cross-disciplinary field of study shares common knowledge with the three other areas already mentioned at different levels. Firstly, juritraductology shares focus and knowledge with linguistics and translation studies. Both build the general framework for the conceptualisation and application phases leading to juritraductology. A juritraductological approach does not need to fully put into practice all approaches and concepts used in linguistics and translation studies. Juritraductology selects particular aspects dealt with in TS which are especially useful for a juritraductological approach to legal translation.

For example, the founding principles and the methods used in translation studies seem particularly well-adapted to legal translation. The theories describing general translation problems and the approaches developed in translation studies help define the field of study of juritraductology.

Secondly, juritraductology projects itself as an approach strongly connected to law in general and comparative law in particular. Juritraductology must meet the demanding requirements set by law (law is both a "consumer" and "a producer" of legal translations). Juritraductology embraces all the linguistic and translational demands contained in law. It aims at describing all legally relevant translation issues and thus expands the scope of legal translation. It covers in principle all branches of international, European and national law. Moreover, the fields of law juritraductology are closely associated with legal language.

Thirdly, the combined interactions of fields that define the scope of study of juritraductology is legal linguistics. Legal linguistics assists juritraductology in the role it may play as an auxiliary branch of law. As it is the case for translation studies, it forms the discursive environment in which juritraductology is designed. Gérard Cornu uses a metaphor to say that a legal translator picks a word studied by general linguistics as a farmer would pick a tool at a large department store (Cornu 2005, p. 26). Likewise, juritraductology can choose the most fertile and appropriate fields among the branches of general linguistics and translation studies. Therefore, juritraductology deals with theoretical and practical questions in legal translations whenever they are of legal interest, among which are questions which have arisen before translating.

3 Steps to be taken before translating in juritraductology

It is commonly accepted that we translate legal texts for a purpose, which is mainly pragmatic and sometimes mandatory due to a legal context, and for legal specific needs. In most cases, law is translated because a legal situation arises, an act or a deed requires it (Monjean-Decaudin 2010). Juritraductology aims at exploring the translation carried out in various legal contexts. In addition, it shows the varying levels of legal effect. This approach is a novel approach as it has never been explored before. It highlights the impact of law and its consequences on translation. In practical terms, this approach presents itself as a targeted or functionalist activity (Monjean-Decaudin 2016) and offers an introductory framework for any translation process.

Before translating, the translator must understand the legal context in which the source text has been written to fully understand the issues involved in the text and its translation. In other words, s/he must (1) understand why, for whom and for what purpose law is being translated in a context, then (2) be able to measure its level of legal complexity, depending on the context.

3.1 *What are the different contexts for translating law?*

There are mainly four legal contexts for which a translation is required.

a. In international public law

Translation is carried out within the framework of institutions and organisations, both at international and regional level. Translating helps create a supranational regime in several languages, for example when drafting an international treaty.

Each international or regional organisation adopts its own language system to determine the official languages it has. The number of official languages determines both the language pairs and the volume of translation.

The language system used in the International Monetary Fund is different from that of the European Union. By declaring English the only official language, the world of finance has deliberately become unilingual at institutional level. Translations carried out by the IMF's language services mainly have an informative role for interstate communication. As a result, these translations do not involve any legal consequences, as evidenced by the introductory IMF disclaimer stating: "While every effort is made to ensure the accuracy of translations, the version of any document used by the IMF is the English version, as American English is the working language of the IMF".

On the contrary, the European Union is a paradigmatic example of institutional multilingualism, soundly described by Umberto Eco in his famous motto: "Translation is the language of Europe". Today, with 24 official languages and 552 language combinations, the European Commission's Directorate-General for Translation is one of the world's largest translation services. The texts written in all the official languages of the Member States are published in the Official Journal of the European Union to produce legal effects in the legal orders of the Member States. The decisions made by the Court of Justice of the European Union are published in all the official languages in order to ensure a uniform law enforcement across the EU (Monjean-Decaudin 2015, p. 95).

b. In international private law

Cross-national exchanges between physical and/or legal persons with different nationalities are governed by private international law. Increased exchanges have led to a dramatic increase in legal translation. Key economic players expand their trade across borders, people travel and work in a foreign country, they marry foreigners or even commit crimes and offenses abroad: daily life brings about many acts and deeds that need a translation. When you adopt a child abroad you need a translation; when you transfer your patent to a foreign company, you need a translation; when you hire a foreign worker, you need a translation. There are many cases in which translations are needed, be it administrative documents, private deeds or authentic instruments. Under private international law, people need a translation to assert their rights or to acknowledge their status at a local government office in a foreign country (for example, when foreign nationals get married or divorced, when a property located in a foreign country is left to a person, etc.). All these translations have legal effects. However, they are limited to the legal situation of each person involved.

c. In a judicial context

In a globalised world, people subject to trial can travel abroad, where again international justice and legal cooperation is based on translation. In this context, legal translation is most frequently carried out by sworn translators for justice services.

Judicial translation can be used in all types of proceedings, in civil, criminal or administrative matters. Both written and oral translations fulfil two distinctive functions (Monjean-Decaudin 2012).

Firstly, judicial translation is a communication tool for the judicial system. In this case, the translation may circulate or not. When there is a cross-border dispute, the translation travels to the foreign country. It is carried out to help judicial cooperation when exchanging acts and information between judicial authorities. The translation of a European arrest warrant or an international letter rogatory is, by its nature, a "circulating" translation. Where the translation allows the national court to understand the content of a document written in a foreign language, the translation is, in this case, a "non-circulating" one. It is not carried out to be sent to another State but to inform the national judge about the content of a document provided to the court. Documents may be testimonies, contracts, code articles, etc.

On the other hand, translation is a procedural safeguard for suspects/defendants speaking a foreign language. It is more obvious in criminal than in civil matters, and in oral than written translations. However, in all cases, translating a document aims at safeguarding the right to a fair trial to individuals who do not understand the language of the proceedings. The Directive 2010/64/EU of the European Parliament and of the Council of 20 October 2010 on the right to interpretation and translation in criminal proceedings reasserts the importance of the right to interpretation and translation in criminal proceedings (Monjean-Decaudin 2011).

d. In a scientific context

We all live in a multilingual and translated world but we also work in a context of multilingual and translated law. Translation is used to expand legal knowledge on legal doctrine or normative texts (constitution, code, laws, etc.) and court decisions. Legal translation is carried out when law is imported and exported. We can either know a foreign law or make our own law known to the rest of the world through translation. Translation is also an integral part of comparative law. Examples which prove this include, for example, the translation of the description of major contemporary legal systems into different languages, the drafting of bilingual dictionaries or the publication of the Henri Capitant Law Review (Goré 2011, p. 114).

In this context, the translator is generally both a lawyer and a comparative law specialist (Sacco 2011, p. 23) and the effects of translation are important for law.

Once the context has been clearly defined, let us consider the *degré de juridicité*.

3.2 Le degré de juridicité – *the level of legal complexity in a text*

All translations do not systematically lead to legal consequences, but all legal translations, *per se*, have some legal complexity. Depending on the context, these consequences are more or less significant. From a methodological point of view, before translating a legal text, the translator must assess the level of legal complexity of a text (Decaudin 2007, pp. 94–95).

To assess this level, s/he must study two distinct indicators. The first indicator takes into account the scope of legal knowledge which is required to understand and translate the text and/or legal concepts. The second indicator identifies the resulting legal consequences when the translation is done. Thus, the more the text contains law and legal concepts – i.e. the more it requires in-depth legal knowledge to be understood – the higher its level of legal complexity. Moreover, the more legal consequences the translation involves – i.e. if the rule or concept contained in the text is binding and has legal consequences – the higher its complexity.

When translating, two cases may arise: the legal text to translate contains only one of the two previously mentioned criteria or it contains both of them. Let us consider examples containing only one criterion.

In a first example, the number of highly specialised terms in the source text requires a sharp law knowledge to understand and translate them. For instance, a book on procedural law written by a law professor contains many legal concepts requiring an accurate knowledge when translating. On the other hand, a university textbook for lawyers (students, teachers, etc.) has no binding force or legal effect and, therefore, the resulting translation has no legal effect. Another example is about translating a holographic will and testament written in French and containing only some words: "Je donne toute ma fortune après ma mort à . . . " ["I leave all my property to . . . when I am gone" (my translation)]. This is an example of a will and testament in France. The French text does not contain legal concepts and is therefore quite easy to translate *at first sight*. While a rather simple vocabulary does not require a sharp legal knowledge or a highly specialised terminology, nonetheless, legal consequences will be effective after translating this will and testament.

Let us now consider texts containing both criteria. In that case, legal effects add up to a highly specialised terminology, resulting in a sharper complexity and the utmost legal value a text may have. Translating laws, court decisions, some agreements and contracts are examples of this. The translator must make sure to transfer the correct meaning of texts while taking into account the challenges and stakes of his/her translation. The legal complexity of a translation will therefore depend on its clients and function. Translating a final judgment of a court has a lower legal complexity than translating a European regulation: the effects of a final judgment concern the parties involved in the trial whereas European regulations will apply to all EU Member states.

From the very beginning of the legal translation process, the series of steps depends on the legal complexity of the text. A methodology specifically designed for legal translation makes it possible to overcome the difficulties shown in legal terms and concepts.

4 How to translate a legal text?

Prior to any other task, the translator must carefully read the text where terms and legal concepts are spotted. S/he will put the text in a specific legal culture (for example, common law culture, Romano-Germanic culture) and in the subdivision of law covered by the source text (e.g. public law, private law, criminal law, civil law). When reading is completed, the comparative-law step takes place, in which the translator simultaneously takes into account the source language and law system, with the aim of translating a text from a source law system to a target law system. As a result, a text may be more or less difficult to translate, depending on the extent of differences to be bridged in the transfer between language and legal systems. Common law and the French law system share common roots. Translating from English into French needs less negotiation of differences than translating from English into Chinese, for example. The lack of common references between two distant law systems may be a further difficulty for the translator (Monjean-Decaudin 2013, p. 6).

Whatever the legal systems concerned, comparative law consists in comparing two systems with a view of performing the translation process of a legal text. Among the different approaches described by authors, comparative law is part of the translation process (Gémar 1979; Šarčević 1997).

More precisely, the methodological approach chosen and developed in legal translation studies (Bocquet 2008, p. 80) is a 3-step approach comprising a semasiological step, a comparative-law step and an onomasiological step. Such an approach has been implemented in translation classes (Popineau *forthcoming*).

We will exemplify each step by giving pairs of English and French terms:

- *Crime* (in English) and *crime* (in French);
- *Copyright* and *droit d'auteur*;
- *Act of God* and *catastrophe naturelle*.

The 3-step approach will answer the following questions: is the English term *crime* an equivalent of the French term *crime*? Can the French term *droit d'auteur* be translated by the English term *copyright*? Are *Act of God* and *catastrophe naturelle* comparable, and therefore translatable?

The 3-step approach requires language in both source and target languages, each step being explained in the corresponding language. Quotations in French and English are part of the demonstration and may not always be translated.

Step 1: the semasiological step

In the semasiological step, the goal is to understand the source text and its building blocks both on semantic and conceptual levels. As these blocks contain legal knowledge, the semasiological step requires in-depth documentary research into the legal system of the source language. Understanding is a dual concomitant process: it implies understanding both source and target languages and systems, conveying a meaning in words. "*Les mots sont un passage obligé pour les concepts juridiques*" [words are a necessary step for conveying legal concepts] (Legeais 2008, p. 267). The abstract approach that is part of legal translation consists in legally defining a concept. To this end, this step consists in carrying out a documentary research to define and put a legal concept into a context.

Let us give a first example: *crime* (in French).

In French law, *crime* is part of a trilogy: *contravention, délit et crime*. In the first semasiological step, a documentary research leads to finding definitions. In French criminal law, *contravention* is "une espèce d'infraction appartenant à une catégorie située en bas de l'échelle de la gravité" (Cornu 2016, p. 263) [a kind of wrongdoing with a less severe punishment]; a *délit* is a "espèce d'infraction moins grave que le crime et plus grave que la contravention" (Cornu 2016, p. 320) [a wrongdoing less severe than *crime* but more severe than *contravention*]; and finally, *crime* is a "espèce d'infraction pénale appartenant à la catégorie des plus graves d'entre elles" (Cornu 2016, p. 288) [the most severe wrongdoing of the group]. The definitions show that the French term *infraction* is a general hypernym into which *contravention*, *délit* and *crime* fall, with severity being the classifying criterion.

Crime in French is often translated by and compared to *crime* in English. Are they true synonyms? Comparing French *crime* in source law to English *crime* in target language will be carried out in Step 2.

We can also show how significant this step is by giving a second example: *droit d'auteur.*

The same documentary approach is followed. In French law, *droit d'auteur* is defined as

> droit de propriété incorporelle exclusif et opposable à tous, qui comprend l'ensemble de prérogatives morales (droit de divulgation, droit à la paternité, droit à l'intégrité de l'œuvre, droit de repentir ou de retrait) et patrimoniales (droit de reproduction, droit de représentation, droit de suite) dont jouit

> l'auteur sur son œuvre du seul fait de sa creation. [Summary: *Droit d'auteur* comprises two types of rights: a moral right and a patrimonial right].
>
> (Cornu 2003, p. 66)

Droit d'auteur is usually translated by *copyright* into French. Are they true cognates or false friends?

Finally, yet importantly, a documentary research on *Act of God* shows that:

- *Act of God* is "a natural and unavoidable catastrophe that interrupts the expected course of events".[3]

When a distributor contract between an English and a French firm needs to be translated, what is the best equivalent of *Act of God* in a French distributor contract?

Once the semasiological phase is completed, once the meaning of a concept in the source language and law is found, the second step is to find a *possible* equivalent concept in the target law and language: the comparative-law step begins.

Step 2: the comparative-law step

> "Comparer consiste à établir des rapports de ressemblances et de différences entre les termes d'un savoir, puis à en mesurer l'ampleur, à en chercher les raisons et à en apprécier la valeur" [Comparing is finding how similar and different terms may be in a field of study, evaluating how significant their differences are, explaining the underlying reasons for such differences and finally evaluating them].
>
> (Laithier 2009, introduction)

In this respect, and prior to a correct translation, legal concepts usually require an in-depth comparative study. The legal translator becomes "*le savant exégète qui s'abîme dans les profondeurs du texte écrit*" [a scholarly expert who delves into the depths of the written text] (Ost 2009, p. 111) and who ventures into the legal system and meaning conveyed by the source language. Before any translation, the translator should look for a *possible* equivalent in the target language. This *possible* equivalent should fulfil the first and foremost role of translation: conveying the source text meaning to the audience reading the target translated text.

Let us turn back to our first example: *crime* (in French)

The documentary research carried out in Step 1 shows that *crime* in French belongs to a triplet, with *infraction* being the hypernym in French (Figure 7.2); a severity criterion ranks them from less to more severe punishment.

Let us now turn to the English term *crime*. Is *crime* in English a possible equivalent to *crime* in French or a false friend? Step 2 aims at comparing legal concepts in both source and target language.

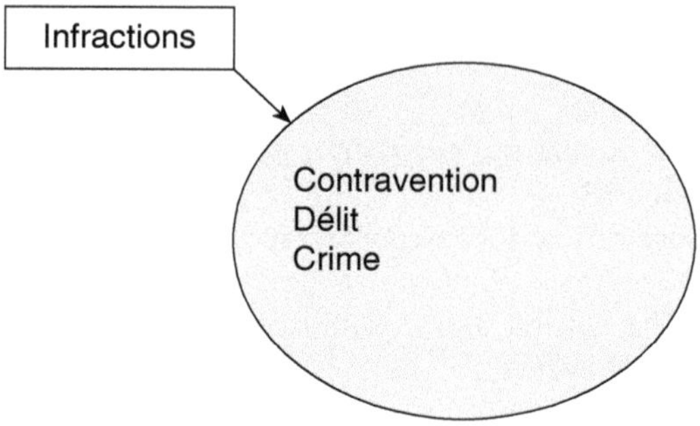

Figure 7.2 What are infractions in French law

Crime in English is "an offense against public law usually excluding a petty violation". Furthermore, *felony* and *misdemeanour*[A] are words accompanying the definition: a *crime* can be a *felony* or a *misdemeanour* according to the dictionary. Our documentary research continues with definitions of the previously mentioned words: a *felony* is "a crime that has a greater punishment imposed by statute than that imposed on a misdemeanour" and *misdemeanour* is "a crime that carries a less severe punishment than a felony"; again, severity is a ranking criterion for each word. *Crime* seems to be a hypernym for both words.

Both are hypernyms, into which two terms can be found in English (*misdemeanour* and *felony*) and three terms in French (*contravention, délit* and *crime*). If we compare definitions, similarities do appear: severity is a significant criterion for both words; moreover syntax shows comparatives in both English and French (more . . . than . . ., less . . . than . . .; *moins . . . que, plus . . . que*):

> *Espèce d'infraction moins grave que le crime et plus grave que la contravention*
>
> *Espèce d'infraction pénale appartenant à la catégorie des plus graves d'entre elles*

> a crime that has a greater punishment imposed by statute than that imposed on a misdemeanor
>
> a crime that carries a less severe punishment than a felony

Step 2 shows that *crime* in French and *crime* in English share similarities.

Let us take the second example.

Droit d'auteur in French is commonly translated by *copyright* into English. Are they true equivalent concepts?

Firstly, they have deeply different founding principles:

> Tandis que le droit d'auteur se consolide en Europe, les Etats-Unis adoptent un corpus législatif d'une autre nature autour de la notion de copyright.

Leurs fondements respectifs sont profondément distincts. [Our translation: While the French droit d'auteur is being strengthened in Europe, the United States is adopting different laws and legal texts dealing with copyright. They have deeply different founding principles.].

(Benhamou et Farchy 2009, p. 22)

Although both are proprietary rights, *copyright* is "utilitariste et économique" [a use-oriented and economic right] whereas "le juridique prime sur l'économique dans le droit d'auteur" [the legal side is heavier than the economic side in French droit d'auteur] (Benhamou et Farchy 2009, p. 23).

Secondly, *copyright* is more restrictive and is "the legal right to have control over the work of a writer, artist, musician, etc",[5] or in other words, "droits exclusifs du titulaire du *copyright* sur son œuvre" (Cornu 2003, p. 66) [the exclusive rights of the copyright owner on his/her work]. "If you own the copyright on something, it is your intellectual property, and other people must pay you to broadcas, publish, or perform it"[6] the Merriam-Webster dictionary says, without mentioning any moral rights.

The French *droit d'auteur* is indeed a dualistic right as it comprises two types of rights:

le droit d'auteur français est qualifié de droit dualiste en raison de la coexistence de droits de différentes nature: d'une part le droit moral appartenant à la famille des droits de la personnalité qui conserve à l'auteur un pouvoir de contrôle sur sa création même s'il en a cédé les droits, et d'autre part les droits patrimoniaux qui lui permettent de tirer profit de l'exploitation de son œuvre [The French droit d'auteur comprises two types of rights; on the one side, a moral right belonging to the rights of the personality by which the creator keeps a right of controlling his/her work even if s/he transferred proprietary rights; on the other end, proprietary rights by which s/he can financially profit from his/her work].

(Cornu 2003, p. 67)

Thirdly, The French definition lists many neighbouring rights: "*le droit de divulgation, le droit à la paternité, le droit à l'intégrité de l'œuvre, le droit de repentir ou de retrait sont les droits moraux entrant dans la sphère du droit d'auteur; s'y ajoutent le droit de reproduction, droit de représentation, droit de suite*". Translating these neighbouring rights into English is difficult because the French neighbouring rights do not exist in common law and no equivalents are given in comparative-law dictionaries (Cornu 2003, pp. 66, 81).

In this law comparative step, *copyright* appears to be a shortened, truncated French *droit d'auteur* with missing moral rights.

Finally, *Act of God* is commonly translated by *catastrophe naturelle* into French.

In French law[7] *catastrophe naturelle* is "un agent naturel ayant une intensité anormale"; [sont considérés comme catastrophe naturelle] "les dommages matériels directs ayant eu pour cause déterminante l'intensité anormale d'un agent naturel, lorsque les mesures habituelles à prendre pour prévenir ces dommages n'ont pu empêcher leur survenance ou n'ont pu être prises" [My translation: a *catastrophe naturelle* is a natural phenomenon whose intensity is beyond normality; [catastrophe naturelle comprises] direct damage whose determining cause is the abnormal intensity of a natural phenomenon, when usual precautions to avoid damage could not prevent it to occur or could not have been taken].

Both definitions mention a natural and unavoidable factor and the terms seem to be exact equivalents.

Step 3: the onomasiological step

A translation is given in this last – but not least – step. It is about deciding which criteria carry the equivalence. The choice consists in deciding on an acceptable term both on the linguistic and legal levels; a large variety of translations can be given.

Let us look at the French trilogy formed by *contravention, crime, délit.* We are facing a conceptual imbalance. As shown in Steps 1 and 2, three French terms refer to two English terms. The hypernym *crime* can be translated by its French counterpart *infraction;* but the number of hyponyms is different (two against three). The translator is facing a choice: s/he must decide which term s/he would choose or discard to keep a balance when translating.

Two translation strategies are possible:

- *Crime* is translated by the legally correct French term *infraction*;
- The translator decides to introduce an adjective to best describe the severity (*mineure* and *majeure*, minor and major) of the wrongdoing.

The latter seems a satisfactory solution: *infraction mineure* does legally correspond to misdemeanor, which is "defined as an offense punishable only by fines or by short terms of imprisonment in local jails[8]"; and *infraction majeure* does legally correspond to *felony*, which is "typically defined as a crime punishable by a term of imprisonment of not less than one year or by the death penalty", according to the Merriam-Webster dictionary.

Comparing the French *droit d'auteur* to common law *copyright* shows fundamental conceptual differences between the two words: when comparing both terms, *droit d'auteur* does not sound like a legally acceptable translation for *copyright* into English and vice-versa:

> Les mêmes termes de chacun des droits peuvent recouvrir des sens différents. L'exemple classique est le terme "droit d'auteur" qui, pour les Canadiens est la traduction de "Copyright" et qui n'est pas un équivalent du droit d'auteur belge et français. [Similar terms may have different meanings in different law systems. A standard example is the word "Droit d'auteur" which is translated

> by copyright in Canada and which is not an equivalent of the droit d'auteur in Belgium and in France].
>
> (Cornu 2003, p. 20)

However, the translator must translate, as it is his/her duty and what s/he is being paid for. Borrowing a foreign word is a possible strategy when terms have no equivalent counterparts in target legal languages. Borrowing the French term *droit d'auteur* into English and the English *copyright* into French contracts is a way of both transferring an odd meaning into a text and keeping the legal differences when no equivalent legal concept exists in the target language.

We can finally complete our onomasiological step with our third example: *Act of God* and *catastrophe naturelle*. Is *Act of God* the best possible and legally correct translation for the French *catastrophe naturelle*? It seems both are comparable, and thus translatable. Moreover, they both appear in contracts with long lists of "unexpected, disruptive event[s] that may excuse a party from performing duties under a contract", for instance in:

> [. . .] Company shall not be in default by reason of any failure in its performance under this Agreement if such failure results from, whether directly or indirectly, fire, explosion, strike, freight embargo, *Act of God* or of the public enemy, war, civil disturbance, act of any government, de jure or de facto, or agency or official thereof, material or labor shortage, transportation contingencies, unusually severe weather, default of any other manufacturer or a supplier or subcontractor, quarantine, restriction, epidemic, or catastrophe, lack of timely instructions or essential information from Distributor, or otherwise arisen out of causes beyond the control of the Company,

with the French translation being:

> [. . .] La Société ne saurait être tenue pour responsable de l'inexécution du présent contrat, dans le cas où ladite inexécution résulte de façon directe ou indirecte de: incendie, explosion, grève, embargo de marchandises, *catastrophe naturelle*, attentat terroriste, guerre, troubles, fait du prince *de jure ou de facto*, pénurie de matériaux ou de main d'œuvre, aléas liés au transport, conditions météorologiques extrêmes, inexécution émanant d'un fabricant, fournisseur et sous-traitant, mise en quarantaine, contingentement, épidémie ou désastre, défaut d'information en temps et en heure de la part du Distributeur, ou de toute cause indépendante de la volonté de la Société.

"Unforeseeable circumstances that prevent someone from fulfilling a contract", such as fire, explosion, labour shortage, etc, are the exact definition of the French legal concept *force majeure*, which is

> un événement imprévisible et irrésistible qui, provenant d'une cause extérieure au débiteur d'une obligation ou à l'auteur d'un dommage (force de la

nature, fait d'un tiers, fait du prince) le libère de son obligation ou l'exonère de sa responsabilité" [Our translation: in French, force majeure is an unforeseen and compelling event that frees the lienee from his/her obligation or exonerates the person who caused the damage from his/her liability (natural event, act of a third party, or government fiat].

(Cornu 2016, p. 471)

Force majeure is a hypernym into which both *catastrophe naturelle* in French and *Act of God* in English fit.

Therefore, the preceding contract can be translated in a shorter way into both French and English:

> [. . .] La Société ne saurait être tenue pour responsable de l'inexécution du présent contrat, dans le cas où ladite inexécution résulte d'un cas de force majeure.
>
> [. . .] Company shall not be in default by reason of any failure in its performance under this Agreement if such failure results from *force majeure.*

Force majeure is a frequent legal borrowing in English contracts, as *force majeure* clauses are acceptable in common law systems such as in the US and in the UK.

5 Conclusion

Proof has been given that translators may avoid usual translation pitfalls when applying the 3-step legal approach. Although the translation strategies suggested in the different cases may differ, the resulting translations are legally correct and consider both source and target legal contexts and systems after comparing them. Translators avoid false friends (*crime* and *crime*) as well, thanks to a complete and well-organised documentary research. Comparative law highlights major conceptual differences and eliminates common mistakes or mistranslations (*copyright* and *droit d'auteur*). Comparable and translatable concepts do exist (*Act of God* and *catastrophe naturelle*) and may sometimes fall into hypernyms to give shorter but still legally correct translations (*force majeure*). The three examples given in this chapter have shown that juritraductology is a legitimate academic discipline in a broader translation approach, which is both well-thought-of and well-suited for legal texts.

Notes

1 Thanks to Carol Jagot-Lachaume and Solweig Franzinetti for proofreading this article.
2 CERIJE (CEntre de Recherche Interdisciplinaire en JuritraductologiE) is the first interdisciplinary research centre dedicated to "juritraductology" (www.cerije.eu/).
3 www.memidex.com/.
4 www.merriam-webster.com/dictionary/crime#legalDictionary.
5 www.memidex.com/copyrighting.
6 www.merriam webster.com.
7 www.legifrance.gouv.fr/ – Loi n° 82–600 du 13 juillet 1982.
8 www.merriam-webster.com/dictionary/felony

Bibliography

Benhamou, F. and Farchy, J. (2007/2009). *Droit d'auteur et copyright*. Paris: Editions la Découverte.

Bocquet, C. (2008). *La traduction juridique. Fondement et méthode*. Bruxelles: De Boeck (coll. Traducto).

Cornu, G. (2005). *Linguistique juridique*. 3th ed. Paris: Montchrestien.

Cornu, G. (2016). *Dictionnaire juridique*. 11th ed. Paris: PUF.

Cornu, M. (2003). *Dictionnaire comparé du droit d'auteur et du copyright*. Paris: CNRS Editions.

Decaudin, S. (2007). Les parémies juridiques: Une version en espagnol et en français de leur traduction. *In:* G. Ruiz Yepes and C. Valderrey Reñones, eds. *Traducción y cultura: La paremia*. Málaga: Libros Encasa, pp. 93–114.

Gémar, J-C. (1979). La traduction juridique. *Meta: Translators' Journal*, 24 (1), pp. 35–53.

Goré, M. (2011). La traduction, instrument de droit comparé. *In:* M. Cornu and M. Moreau, eds. *Traduction du droit et droit de la traduction*. Paris: Dalloz, pp. 109–115.

Laithier, Y-M. (2009). *Droit comparé*. Paris: Editions Dalloz.

Legeais, R. (2008). *Grands systèmes de droits contemporains: Une approche comparative*. Paris: Litec.

Monjean-Decaudin, S. (2010). *Approche juridique de la traduction du droit*. Cerije [online]. Available at: www.cejec.eu/2010/01/13/approchejuridique-de-la-traduction-du-droit/ [Accessed 4 Oct. 2018].

Monjean-Decaudin, S. (2011). L'Union européenne consacre le droit à l'assistance linguistique dans les procédures pénales. *Revue Trimestrielle de Droit Européen*, 47 (4), pp. 763–781.

Monjean-Decaudin, S. (2012). *La traduction du droit dans la procédure judiciaire. Contribution à l'étude de la linguistique juridique*. Paris: Dalloz (Bibliothèque de la Justice).

Monjean-Decaudin, S. (2013). Réflexion sur l'inflexion du signifié dans la traduction juridique de Claude Bocquet. *Parallèles*, 25, pp. 19–29.

Monjean-Decaudin, S. (2015). Multilinguisme et traduction du droit. *In*: I. Pingel, ed. *Le multilinguisme dans l'Union européenne*. Paris: Pedone, pp. 89–99.

Monjean-Decaudin, S. (2016). Pourquoi traduire un code, hier et aujourd'hui? *Journal of Civil Law Studies*, 9 (1), pp. 191–204. Available at: http://digitalcommons.law.lsu.edu/jcls/vol9/iss1/9/ [Accessed 4 Oct. 2018].

Ost, F. (2009). *Traduire – Défense et illustration du multilinguisme*. Paris: Fayard (coll. Ouvertures).

Popineau, J. (*forthcoming*). La juritraductologie comme outil didactique pour la traduction des concepts en français et en anglais. *In:* B. Franck and S. Monjean-Decaudin, eds. *Aspects théoriques et pratiques de la traduction juridique et économique*. Paris: Garnier (coll. Translatio).

Sacco, R. (2011). Aperçus historique et philosophique des relations entre droit et traduction. *In:* M. Cornu and M. Moreau, eds. *Traduction du droit et droit de la traduction*. Paris: Dalloz, pp. 13–27.

Šarčević, S. (1997). *New approach to legal translation*. The Hague: Kluwer Law International.

8 A matter of justice

Integrating comparative law methods into the decision-making process in legal translation

Carmen Bestué[1]

1 Introduction

"I've got a pen and I've got a phone" was the well-known phrase pronounced by President Obama when exercising his authority and discretionary powers as President of the United States to expedite new "executive orders" with force of law. This power is more frequently used when Congress is not on the President's side, as was the case at the time. During his two-term mandate, President Obama approved a total of 276 "executive orders".[2] However, the frequency with which "executive orders" are discussed in Spanish news is notably higher with the present administration (although Donald Trump has only approved eight since he has been in office). Leaving political considerations aside, the normalisation of the calque *órdenes ejecutivas* in the majority of Spanish mass media is striking from a translation perspective. As a result of this normalisation, Spanish receivers are confronted with a new term that, far from providing a clue as to the nature of this legal institution, may generate suspicions of possible excessive use of legislative power by the executive branch. On coming across it for the first time, my own immediate question was "Is the President overstepping his authority?" This is the principal problem with calques: they draw attention to a strange term that sometimes, at least in this particular case, is not relevant to the media outlet's informative purpose. Surely the focus should be on the subject matter itself, rather than what an *orden ejecutiva* means in Spanish. Probably, the functional equivalent in Spain, *decreto* (decree or order), would be more appropriate for use in the context of mass-media communication.

In an attempt to tackle this type of issue, the objective of this chapter is to demonstrate how comparative law methods can be applied to terminology work for translation purposes, revealing not only the semantics of a legal term but also its connotations and possible reception in the target culture. Today it is frequently acknowledged that legal translation, as a discipline, is closely linked to comparative law (de Groot 1991; Šarčević 1997; Engberg 2013, among many other authors) but we must not forget that comparative law and legal translation do not share the same goal. Indeed, as the main goal of legal translation is to fulfil a specific communicative purpose we need to take into consideration the "intervening" role of the translator (Martín Ruano 2014, p. 15) and his/her prediction about the reception of the target text (TT) in the target legal culture. The focus is on the different factors that need to be addressed by the translator: diatopic variety of legal terms, the aspects that can mean the difference between a defective and an accurate translation depending on the function of the target text and applicable law, and the importance of the legal context. For the purpose of this chapter, legal translation is contemplated in the context of intersystemic translation "that operates not only between two languages but also between at least two legal systems" (Biel 2017b, p. 78). In this context the need to improve translators' decision-making process is greater, since most resources are developed for intrasystemic legal translation, as is the case in the European Union (EU) and some bilingual countries, like Canada.

The practical objective is therefore to propose a "ready-made" comparative research tool to be used by freelance legal interpreters and translators working in the private market, who are usually constrained by less advantageous work conditions than those of their counterparts in institutional or governmental settings.

The chapter concludes with a reflection on the need for academia and government agencies to conduct comparative analysis and create ready-made tools whose accuracy can be trusted not only to meet the linguistic needs of the TT receivers but also to ensure the full exercise of their rights as a matter of justice.

2 Comparative law: its methods and its application to legal translation

As stated by de Groot (1991, p. 409), "comparative law forms the basis for translating legal texts". It may be useful at this point, accordingly, to review the aspects of comparative law methodology that are relevant for legal translation purposes.

In an area where there are multiple intersections between law and language it is important to remember that since language itself is indeterminate, legal rules are, to some extent, also indeterminate. H.L.A Hart (cited in Carston 2013, p. 20) describes the concept of the "open texture" of law due to the "inherent limitations of language". His example was the rule "no vehicles in the park", with the question of whether things like bicycles or roller skates would constitute "vehicles" for the purposes of the rule. As Bix has pointed out, "linguistic meaning can be determinate or indeterminate, but the operation of other processes of legal reasoning can modify the initial linguistic meaning, making it more or less unsettled, and sometimes overriding the linguistic meaning entirely" (2013, p. 43). Indeed, within a legal system the meaning of legal texts is not a fixed feature since it is subject to revision, or interpretation, by legislators and judges. For instance, the term *cosa* (thing), which traditionally included animals in its meaning, is changing in line with modern thinking, and this has had an impact on the current revision of the Spanish Civil Code. Now, under Spanish law, a new category distinct from things and human beings – "living beings" (*seres vivos*) – has been created, thus allowing recognition of animals' right to special treatment.

Therefore, if potentially misleading translations arising from indeterminacy in the source and the target legal culture are to be detected, legal comparison is essential.

In addition, comparative law has been considered "the most influential strategy informing the study of foreign law" (Glanert and Legrand 2013, p. 515). Since any translation work starts out from an understanding of the foreign culture, recourse to comparative law methodology is widely accepted as the first step to legal translation. However, from a comparative perspective, the views on how to address the language issue can either allow or deny the possibility of legal translation. Some comparative law scholars are sceptical about the feasibility of translating from one legal system to another (David 1974; Sacco 1999; Legrand 2005), often perceiving it as an "act of violence" (Legrand 2005, p. 39), while others are more optimistic – accepting legal translation as a unidirectional activity (Kjaer 2004, p. 384). Quite often comparatist scholars come from a multilingual background and are confronted with the need for legal translation before comparing, which is the main reason why they describe language as the "camouflage" of law that has to be stripped by the comparatist (Husa 2011, p. 217) in order to get under the skin of the law. As has been pointed out by Husa, the differences between functional comparative law and legal translation hinge on different "knowledge-interests":

> The comparatist compares functions adopted in different systems to solve the same legal problem and seeks for similarities and differences. Ultimately they aim at solving what causes similarities and differences by looking for explanations in history, economy, politics, culture, even geography. The translator tries to translate unfamiliar law in a "legally correct manner". In both, it is a question of the same thing, ie [sic] a serious attempt to understand *foreign law*.
>
> (Husa 2011, p. 224)

In terms of methodology in comparative law, the functional method is an advance on the simple comparison of legal notions. As noted by Samuel (2004), comparing legal notions is a dangerous operation since notions like "trespass" or "natural obligation" are difficult to understand by strict definition. Functionality allows the comparatist to "investigate the facts behind the law", which is a better basis for comparison. However, in certain situations the same act may be performed by a particular rule of law in one legal system and by an extra-legal measure in a foreign system. Zweigert and Kötz (cited in Samuel 2004) illustrated this functional situation by explaining how the same goal, protection of future purchasers of land, is achieved by a particular rule of law in Germany – consulting the records of the German land registry – and by an extra-legal practice in the United States, where no land registry exists – through title insurance companies that have very comprehensive and reliable conveyancing files. Both systems are reliable and functional but the fact that one system is regarded by functionalist scholars as outside the law "seems to assume that the frontier between the legal and the extra-legal is the same with respect to both systems" (Samuel 2004, p. 39) and distorts the notion of law to make it conform to a specific legal culture.

According to Van Hoecke, "comparative law research may only be carried out meaningfully if it also includes the deeper level of underlying theories and conceptions" (2004, p. 191). Following these recommendations, comparative work is useful if it relies not only on pure descriptive or positivist points of view but also on historical analyses, sociological writings, critical writings, legal doctrine and court decisions. Therefore, comparing notions and concepts in two different legal systems, and occasionally checking in monolingual dictionaries, is not a sufficient basis for an informed translation decision. In line with this point of view, scholars of legal translation in the past decade have been more oriented towards a deeper comparative analysis. In this chapter, based on Terral (2004), Bestué (2009) and Monjean-Decaudin (2012), I will suggest that conducting in-depth comparative research for specific points of law after creating a large comparable corpus is an extraordinarily useful way to expand the map of knowledge in the legal translation field. At the same time, as Martín Ruano has observed, legal translators need to perceive themselves as "fully fledged social actors, forging pacts between legal systems, cultures and languages" (2015, p. 148), not shackled by the constraints of the ST but endowed with a capacity of choice that necessarily has an impact on the acceptability of the TT.

3 Bridging the gap between comparative law and legal translation

Both translators and comparatists have to deal with problems of indeterminacy and lack of equivalence, but their approaches differ. As Engberg observes, "the interests and goals of comparative law and of translation studies are not identical" (2013, p. 20). Comparatists will be interested in the intricacies of a certain legal concept, looking for similarities or differences between it and other legal institutions in a different legal order, and their goals may range from genuine curiosity about other cultures to the search for valid models for their domestic regulations. For their part, translators will analyse the core elements of a legal term in order to identify the best possible translation to fulfil the communicative purpose of the TT. It is this communicative purpose that imposes certain strategies: sometimes more oriented to the TT, other times to the source text (ST). After a thorough comparative analysis, choosing a borrowing may appear to be the best solution. In certain cases, the translator needs to modify the usual syntactic patterns of the "host language" so the reader of the TT is aware of the existence of a "non-present text", the ST (Glanert and Legrand 2013, p. 517). However, this should not be regarded as a renunciation of translation but as a recognition of the complexities of the task defined by Glanert as "an assemblage in motion" (2014, p. 268). Here, I will focus on a few examples put forward by some legal scholars and then suggest some translations techniques that can be adopted in different contexts.

The first example is provided by the work of Geeroms (2002), centred on the study of the differences between the terms *cassation*, *revision* and "appeal" in the French, German and English legal systems and their "high courts". As a comparatist focusing on the differences in final judicial review matters, it makes sense for her strategy to be a "renunciation of translations" (2002, p. 202). Her justification is that the differences outweigh the similarities between the terms used in the legal orders being compared. As Geeroms has been able to demonstrate, terms like *cassation*, *revision* and "appeal", beyond certain similarities, are not identical. In view of the disparity between the terms shown by Geeroms, and drawing on her findings about the French term *cassation*, translators may adopt different translation strategies, always depending on the brief. Table 8.1 shows some proposals for translation.

Considering the multiplicity of potential situations, the use of the functional equivalent should possibly be reserved to situations where readers do not expect scrupulous accuracy in those terms. This is the case when several TTs are to be seen as "renderings of an original in different languages", in which case "if disagreement appears between source text and translation, this can be resolved by looking at the source text" (Engberg 2014, p. 148). The functional equivalent serves to provide only superficial information about the term – the fact that *cassation* is the last resort in both jurisdictions apart from other possible constitutional reviews. Functional equivalents transfer more semantic information to the TT reader than calques or borrowings but, on the other hand, the risk of possible misunderstandings is higher whenever the target reader is unable to learn about the source legal culture.

Table 8.1 Proposals of translation techniques for the French term *cassation*

Context	*Translation technique*	*Proposed translations*
Research paper on comparative law	Borrowing	*Cassation*
Judicial resolution translated for informative purposes	• Combination of borrowing and gloss • Paraphrasing with a descriptive equivalent • Gloss	• Cassation appeal • Highest French civil and criminal appeal • Quashing of judgment
Newspaper or other documents addressed to non-experts	Functional equivalent adding a descriptor	• Appeal to the French Supreme Court • Appeal
Rogatory Letter or other documents addressed to experts	Borrowing or calque combined with explanatory note, if needed	• Cassation appeal • *Cassation* • Translator's note: the function of the *pourvoi en cassation* is to verify that the decisions of the lower courts do not conflict with some point of law. It does not make any fresh assessment of the facts.

As for the translation of the terms "Supreme Court" and *Cour de cassation*, in the examples provided by Geeroms (2002, p. 203), or *Tribunal Supremo* in the Spanish judicial system, the translation decision also depends on the translation brief. Contrary to Geeroms, who suggests the use of the generic term "high courts" to translate both the German and the French terms in any situation, I propose that the strategy should vary depending on the communicative purpose. When the goal is to stress the fact that the supreme courts in common law systems perform more than the review function typical of most civil law countries, the use of the borrowings *Cour de cassation* or "Supreme Court" would be more accurate. Alternatively, as Geeroms suggests, when the goal is not to stress the differences, "the closest term available" (i.e. the functional equivalent) will be a correct strategy. In this case, translating *Cour de cassation* by the functional equivalent in English, Supreme Court, or "marking it" (Hickey 1998, p. 220–221), French Supreme Court, outlines the similarities between both institutions as they are the highest ordinary judicial bodies in each country. In the case of Spain, where a double jurisdiction exists (the *Tribunal Constitucional* and the *Tribunal Supremo*), both institutions could work as functional equivalents, but preference should probably be accorded to the less culture-specific translation modified by a descriptor, "Spanish Supreme Court".

The second example is extracted from the work of Sage-Fuller *et al.* (2013) in teaching the peculiarities of the French criminal law system to Irish law students. When the goal of the comparatist is to show foreign legal experts the peculiarities of their criminal law system, attention is usually drawn to certain words that express "tradition's understanding of virtues, and in particular justice" (2013, p. 55). In this case, for those scholars to stress the importance of the 1993 amendment to French criminal procedure, it was crucial to communicate the incorporation of a more respectful system of presumption of innocence in the examination of suspects, which meant using the term *mise en examen* in the French law relating to charging someone accused of an offense, instead of the less neutral previous word: *inculpation*. According to Sage-Fuller *et al.* (2013, p. 55), the selection of the functional equivalent "charged" to translate the term *mise en examen* would truncate the meaning of the expression in the French culture and the development experienced in the presumption of innocence. A calque in English, "put under examination", would be probably the best communicative solution, drawing the attention of the target reader to the foreign notion.

These problems presented as matters of untranslatability are in fact due to the lack of identicalness. As noted by Alcaraz Varó (2004, p. 202), legal translation reveals a high degree of anisomorphism in which "we do not seek identicalness but, rather equivalence". This concept of equivalence aims at communication through translation in which the limiting factor for the translator in making a choice between different strategies is the need to avoid misleading solutions in the TT. It is in this respect that comparative law, as Engberg (2013, p. 22) observes, becomes the key to successful mediation between legal systems once its methods and approaches are adjusted to the specific interests of legal translators. However, as shown by the preceding examples, this method is extremely sophisticated and it requires in-depth specialisation in the comparative techniques and the subject matter to avoid the possible pitfalls. In translating law, we are not just confronting linguistic problems. Legal translations are produced and scattered throughout the Internet more than ever (see Megale 2015; Bestué 2016) and this has led not only to an increase in volume of the translation market but also in the coining and spreading of equivalent legal terms in other languages. Furthermore, most of the time these translations are not TT-oriented, do not take into consideration the target legal system and "trivialize" borrowings as the most acceptable translation for legal terms (Megale 2015, p. 46). In our opinion, among other factors to be considered, translation strategies and techniques should vary to ensure that translated terms satisfy the legal requirements prevailing in the target context. A foreign language in contact with a foreign court of justice is unfortunately also a context where the rights of less favoured citizens may be compromised. Accordingly, high quality standards need to be attained in intersystemic legal translation, similar to those achieved in institutional settings.

4 Legal translation: a methodological proposal

It is important to note that translation, as an object of study, can be considered an *art d'exécution* (Gémar 2015, p. 478) or a *praxeologie* (Dullion 2007, p. 18). In that sense Translation Studies is not a pure search for universals but also a reflection on translation practices.

In taking indeterminacy as a starting point in legal translation, "linguistic compliance can only ever be partial" (Glanert and Legrand 2013, p. 517) and some translations are possible only by introducing modifications in the "host languages" or overusing foreign features in the TT. Indeed, in certain cases the translation exercise will be ST-oriented to be really communicative in the case of a target readership consisting of legal scholars, for instance. On the part of translators, however, there is a need for a comprehensive understanding of how legal translation is evolving with globalisation and how information mining in the Internet cannot be a substitute for rigorous documentation. I believe this exercise has to go beyond the purely linguistic one of checking coined translations in glossaries, dictionaries and on the internet. Seen in this light, legal translation is possible but needs to be modulated in order to communicate in the TT culture, in accordance with function, context, diatopic variation, legal field and applicable law.

Indeed, even though translators share the heavy burden of the comparatists in seeking the meaning in the ST, their load is lighter, since the TT receiver may often take on some of the responsibility for discovering the meaning of particular terms in the source culture, at least in the case of translation for informative purposes where applicable law is that of the ST. Here, translators can rely on more ST-oriented strategies to help readers in this endeavour without getting involved in legal hermeneutics, but to be aware of this possibility they must have the deep understanding of the ST. This understanding can be attained through a comparative law methodology.

As mentioned previously, translators' decisions are conditioned by different factors that need to be taken into consideration: function of the TT, context, diatopic variation, legal field, and applicable law. This is not an exhaustive list: as pointed out by Biel (2017a), other factors determine the "communicative dimension" of translation. Indeed, depending on the translation brief and their expertise in the specific field, translators do take other factors into account, like text type, syntax, phraseology and other patterns that need to be "convergent to target recipients' expectations" (Biel 2017a, p. 321). Additionally, de Torres Carballal (1991, p. 439) includes time and ideology: two factors that could be similar to those highlighted by Engberg (2013, p. 20) regarding the necessary profiling of certain legal concepts. I will not describe all the factors in detail here, but rather point to some examples of context-related problems and link them to the use of different translation strategies.

4.1 Context

Legal terms are created for a specific legal system but, once translated, they are not static. Insofar as translation takes an element from one particular cultural system and introduces it into another, it may serve as a cultural "pollenizer" (Rotman 1995, p. 190).

Only rarely, in the context of multilingual organisations, and legal systems with one legal order and co-drafted multilingual instruments, can we find examples of total equivalence in legal translation, as is the case between Catalan and Spanish procedural rules – for instance, the Spanish word *auto* is the total equivalent of the Catalan term *interlocutòria* ("order"). At the same time, legal terms created

Example 8.1 Translation of "assault and battery"

English	*Spanish*	*Italian*	*French*
that the criminal law of European Union Member States should treat the practice of sexual mutilation of women as an aggravating factor in the crime of **assault and battery**.	y que el Derecho penal de los Estados miembros de la Unión Europea trate la práctica de la mutilación sexual de las mujeres como un factor agravante en el **delito de la violencia y la agresión ilegítima.**	e che nella legislazione penale dei Paesi membri dell'Unione la pratica delle menomazioni sessuali verso le donne sia prevista come circostanza aggravante nel reato di **lesioni personali dolose**.	et de considérer la mutilation sexuelle des femmes dans le droit pénal des États membres de l'Union européenne comme une circonstance aggravante dans les **délits de voies de fait.**

Source: European Parliament (2005)

in a context of multilingual international organisations, because of their prestige and ready availability on the internet, are more easily recovered by translators and re-used in different contexts without taking into consideration their system-specificity (Groot and Van Laer 2006, p. 66). This is why it is essential, when translating legal terms, to analyse the specificities of each legal institution in the source culture and the target culture, which, in turn, requires research into the corresponding sources of law (i.e. common law, equity, statute law, etc.) and other doctrinal sources.

Merely searching for equivalents in "reliable" sources may end up in validation of solutions previously used but also lead to some serious misunderstandings, as shown in the following example, extracted from the debates conducted at the European Parliament and that are easily recovered from Linguee:

In the preceding example, the English version employs two terms from established criminal law ("assault and battery"), whereas the Spanish version uses a sort of paraphrase that is not a typified crime under Spanish law nor an established term in legal doctrine: *delito de violencia y la agresión ilegítima* [crime of violence and illegitimate aggression]. Both the Italian translation, *lesioni personali dolose* [wilful personal injury], and the French version, *delits de voies de fait* [crime of assault], could be considered to be functional equivalents. The concept of "assault and battery" is generally defined to cover both the threat of violence and actual physical violence, which is also the case in the Italian translation. However, the French and Spanish translations do not include the aspect of actual harm. In our view, in a case of sexual mutilation, physical harm is the core element of the crime.

Based on a comparative law methodology, our proposals for the Spanish translation of "assault and battery" in this context are the functional equivalents of Spanish law, as follows:

- Solution 1: *delito de lesiones* (which includes physical and psychological harm)
- Solution 2: *delito de amenazas y lesiones* (physical and psychological harm, and threats)

5 The translation-oriented terminological entry

As previously stated, our proposal is to provide a model of a ready-to-use translation-oriented entry where the translator can find different strategic choices which take into account the skopos of the TT, context, diatopic variations, legal field, applicable law and other explicit information which may help the translator to select a precise translation for a concrete situation. The model has been tested and is available on the internet. Although unfortunately the number of entries completed up to now is limited, in our view it opens up a pathway towards greater quality in legal translation that governmental entities and translators' organisations would do well to prioritise. The proposal has been developed in two research projects,[3] named Law10n and TIPp, respectively, which were conceived for greatly differing contexts but use the same methodological approach, which aims to highlight the choices of the translator in different scenarios. The methodological usefulness of this proposal lies in the fact that it presents a comparative analysis of a specific legal term oriented to help address the challenges that the translator faces in each particular situation, while also including contextual examples of use. In order to suggest appropriate translation techniques, the entry stresses the information load of the source legal term that best informs the TT receiver considering the specificities of the TT legal system. Two goals are achieved simultaneously through the implementation of this methodological proposal: first, the production of translations that are of high quality not only linguistically but also in legal terms; and second, increased recognition among legal professionals, since, by contacting legal experts to assess the validity of the solutions proposed, the intricacies of the translation process become more visible. As mentioned, the focus in the existing experiences was especially laid on cases in which the choice of a certain translation could not only compromise the information load of the target text but, moreover, the rights of the receiver.

5.1 Legal translations addressed to consumers

An approach based on a mixed method of qualitative and corpus research tools was applied in order to identify the field and the restrictions imposed by consumer protection laws on a specific legal genre: translation of end-user licence agreements. Consumer law in Europe establishes some legal requirements on how legal documents need to be drafted. With different wordings, almost all jurisdictions have enacted laws that include a duty to express in "plain and intelligible language", and "legibly", the content of all documents addressed to consumers.[4] The hypothesis of the project was that translations of terms and conditions addressed to consumers in Europe, with their abuse of calques and borrowings, do not comply with this requirement.

Another underlying assumption of the project was that a term included in a translated contract or a document addressed to consumers that cannot be traced back to a proper source of Spanish law is, at least, open to suspicion of unfairness. As a methodological proposal, the project advocated that "translating" certain foreign legal terms demands a substantial intervention in the TT, transforming a single term into a much longer formulation in the target language, or the opposite: simply removing it. Following traditional conceptions of translation, this task could be considered beyond the realm of translators but in reality it is not only performed by them but, most of the time, conducted within localisation processes involving computer-assisted translation (Torres-Hostench and Bestué 2015, p. 287; Orozco-Jutorán 2017, p. 141). Hence, our suggestion was to create a translation record in which different translation options were proposed. In our view, the function of the TT in this legal genre is conditioned by applicable law and the profile of the subjects to which the contract is addressed. When the contract is regulated by Spanish law and the receiver is a consumer, the translation brief should be instrumental in nature (Nord 1997, pp. 45–52, 127). In this case, the translator should verify that the TT achieves translational equivalence not only linguistically but also legally.

The research conducted by creating an extended ST and TT corpus of end-user licence agreements (Bestué 2009, 2013) enabled us to identify the features of the legal genre and the legal field, applying the methodology of comparative law to analyse the contract in depth (by searching in legal sources and legal scholars' treatises, and by consulting specialists in the field) and to detect the legal terms that, if translated, could potentially be affected by the instrumental or documentary function of the TT. From among the translation problems detected, eleven legal terms were selected, and a translation-oriented terminological entry was created. Different translation techniques were proposed for three of these terms (merchantability, non-infringement and strict liability) depending on the function of the TT. In the case of the term "tort", the functional equivalent was proposed as the most communicative strategy for an instrumental translation, but recognising that a borrowing or lexical expansion could be acceptable in a documentary translation. For the other six terms (consideration, fault, remedy, representation, severability, statute and subsidiary), after considering that the function of the TT did not interfere in the strategy of translation in the case of these particular contracts, the final proposal was to recommend the same translation techniques for both instrumental and documentary translations. The explanations and legal reasoning underlying each recommended translation may be consulted on the web page created for this project, where other resources, such as an aligned corpus, bibliography etc., may also be found for the translation of end-user software licence agreements. All the terms dealt with that deserved special attention were culturally bound terms (Šarčević 2009, p. 127).

The elaboration of this entry required a thorough analysis of the legal context of the source legal culture, and of the regulatory instruments for the matter in the target legal system, including consultation with legal scholars in both jurisdictions. Since the main aim is to facilitate the translator's decision-making process and its justification, the entry states the nature of the translation recommended in each case, i.e. a functional equivalent, borrowing, descriptive translation, neologism, etc. As shown in Figure 8.1, with an example of an entry proposed for an instrumental translation of the term *non-infringement*, the recommended TT-oriented translations, in this particular context, are different proposals of descriptive translations. The legal term *non-infringement* does not exist as such in Spanish but its legal content can be converted into a descriptive translation in accordance with Spanish law. Our recommended translation, in the absence of a neologism, when the applicable law is Spanish law, is *garantía de no infracción de los derechos de propiedad intelectual, industrial u otros derechos registrados de terceros* [warranty of non-infringement of intellectual and "industrial" property rights and other third-party registered rights]. Since these contracts are often the basis of computer-assisted translation assignments, the goal of these proposals is to help translators in their day-to-day efforts to confront the ready-made translations offered by the translation memory and to justify their decisions on legal grounds.

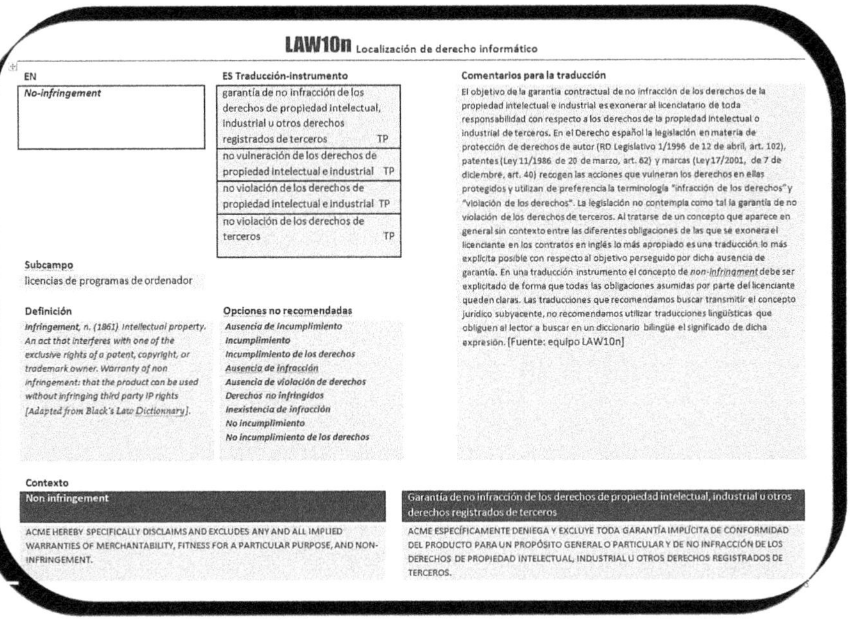

Figure 8.1 Example of translation-oriented entry for an instrumental translation of the term *non-infringement*

5.2 *Legal language in court interpreting*

Using a methodology of corpus analysis, one of the main goals of the TIPp project was to describe the real situation of court interpreting in criminal courts in Barcelona. The starting point was to create a sufficiently representative corpus of real criminal trial proceedings, analyse criminal court interpreting, detect areas of intervention that needed to be addressed and then propose specific solutions for raising the standards of quality in court interpreting. After detecting different factors that can influence interpreters' decision-making process we decided to formulate the following proposals:

- In relation to unidirectional interpreting, problems of conceptual inconsistency should be addressed, prioritising the actual legal sources of the Spanish legal system (mainly the criminal code and the criminal procedural act) over dictionaries or other terminological tools, which may not be up to date or which may take into consideration other jurisdictions.
- Taking into account the large number of participants not using their first language, especially in cases of English and French users, interpreters are recommended to double-check with the speaker and to favour lexical expansion in these situations.

- As for legal terms, and as the goal is to ensure that most speakers of the target language understand the legal term, when possible, the recommendation is to avoid legal terms that are highly specific to a single jurisdiction. Thus, preference should be given to "prosecutor" instead of "attorney general", and "theft" instead of "larceny".
- The context can affect the semantics of terms that seem to be non-specialised: real accuracy requires adapting to each particular legal context where the communication takes place. For example, specificities may be found in cases of violence against women, in juvenile courts, etc., making it necessary to pay special attention to terms that do not seem to have a specific legal meaning. As seen in the following example, in cases of crimes of violence against women in Spain, certain terms need to be translated in a very narrow way in order to be accurate, in accordance with the communicative situation:

Example 8.2 Triadic exchange extracted from the TIPp corpus

- Prosecutor: ¿Estaban Uds. en su **domicilio** cuando la discusión comenzó? [Were you at your domicile when the argument started?]
- Interpreter: Were you at the **flat** when the argument started?
- Witness: Yes, we were at the **flat**.
- Interpreter: Sí, estábamos en el **piso**. [Yes, we were at the flat].

Under Spanish law, crimes against women committed in the marital home are accorded an aggravating factor of criminal liability. In the preceding example, the prosecutor is using the very precise term *domicilio* (domicile, place of residence), which is translated merely as "flat". The example is rather significant since the defence counsel was trying to prove that there was no marital relationship or marital home in the case.

Court interpreting is a highly demanding field and interpreters work in a very rigid and demanding setting, where, paradoxically, they are regarded as a mere "peripheral presence" (Hale *et al.* 2017, p. 70). Under these circumstances, and without previous knowledge of the proceedings that they have to interpret for, the results of their work can often fall far short of the high quality standards that are current practice in other interpreting fields (see Arumí *et al.* 2017). Therefore, more comparative research needs to be conducted, especially on procedural law and the best translation solutions for certain legal terms. The entry created for criminal-case court interpreting includes the following fields: definition in Spanish,

Table 8.2 Summary of the main translation proposals, into English and French, for the Spanish term *sentencia firme* in the context of criminal trials

Spanish term	*English translation*	*French translation*
Sentencia firme	Final non-appealable judgment	*Jugement irrevocable* *Jugement inattaquable*

proposed translation with a definition, translation comments, original context with examples of use of the term and, finally, non-recommended translations.[5] An example of a term that needed this special attention was *sentencia firme*. When a plea bargain agreement has been reached, the Spanish judge pronounces *in voce* a final judgment that cannot be appealed by the parties. The closest equivalent (functional equivalent) to the Spanish term in English (see Table 8.2) is "final judgement" but the term does not convey the meaning that the judgment cannot be appealed. The development of this particular entry, which can be found on the web page developed for the project, was based on extensive comparative-law research and active consultation with legal scholars from different jurisdictions. As the Spanish term is a system-bound one, specific to Spanish procedural law, the recommended translations into English and French combine a functional equivalent and lexical expansion, emphasising the distinguishing element of the Spanish term: that this is a non-appealable decision. This lexical expansion, in our view, is a matter of accuracy and fits fully into the communicative dimension of legal translation and the right to information of the suspects, accused persons or victims of crimes.

Figure 8.2 shows an example of a translation-oriented entry for the Spanish term *sentencia firme* in English, highlighting the indeterminacy of the closest

Sentencia firme

Inglés | Francés | Rumano | Árabe | Chino

Definición

De acuerdo con lo establecido en los artículos 245.3 de la LOPJ y 141 de la LECr, tienen la consideración de sentencias firmes aquellas resoluciones contra las que no cabe ningún recurso (por no preverse ninguno o por haber transcurrido el plazo para recurrir, salvo supuestos de acciones de impugnación de la cosa juzgada).

La sentencia declarada firme en cuanto al fondo del asunto (es decir que se ha pronunciado sobre los hechos enjuiciados y no sólo sobre cuestiones de forma o procesales) pone fin al proceso penal y se termina con la condena o la absolución de la persona acusada.

La firmeza de la sentencia produce el efecto denominado de cosa juzgada, que puede ser formal o material. La cosa juzgada formal supone la imposibilidad de recurrir una sentencia firme. La cosa juzgada material supone la prohibición para otros jueces de volver a enjuiciar un asunto que ya ha sido resuelto, también denominado principio de *non bis in ídem* (Montero et al. 2013). En el corpus de TIPp este término suele aparecer en el contexto de la sentencia de conformidad, cuando las partes han llegado a un acuerdo sobre el reconocimiento del delito y la pena solicitada y el juez dicta la sentencia in *voce* advirtiendo de que se trata de una sentencia firme. Para una mayor información al acusado el juez debería advertir de que se trata de una sentencia que no se podrá recurrir, lo que no siempre sucede. No confundir con el término "sentencia definitiva" que en español sólo indica que es la sentencia que resuelve el asunto en la instancia y no implica la firmeza. En algunos ordenamientos esta distinción entre sentencia definitiva y sentencia firme no tiene un término específico y, por lo tanto, el calco o préstamo pueden llevar a ocultar el concepto y, por lo tanto, a no transmitir la información que lleva implícita sobre la imposibilidad de recurrir dicha resolución una vez aceptada. No existe el término "sentencia final" como concepto jurídico en español, aunque se utilice en ocasiones y, por lo tanto, no serviría para identificar el tipo de sentencia recaída.

Términos afines: cosa juzgada, principio de *non bis in ídem*

Traducción "Inglés"

Inglés: final non-appealable judgment
Definición: a definitive judgment is a judgment «which finally and completely ends and settles a controversy. A definitive sentence or judgment is put in opposition to an Interlocutory judgment.» (Black's Law Dictionary Online). Esta traducción perifrástica indica que la sentencia recaída además de resolver definitivamente un asunto (final), no podrá ser recurrido (non-appealable).
Términos afines: final non-appealable decision; final non-appealable decree

Campos

Derecho procesal

Comentarios

El término en inglés *final judgment* no recoge la precisión del español que distingue claramente entre "sentencia definitiva", es decir, la que pone fin a la instancia, y "sentencia firme", es decir no recurrible. Por ello proponemos realizar una traducción perifrástica, final *non-appealable judgment*, que recoja el sentido total del término español ya que se trata de un concepto sensible que puede dejar al receptor en una situación de indefensión si llega a aceptar una condena sin comprender que la resolución dictada no es recurrible. El término *definitive judgment* en la última versión del diccionario de referencia, Black's Law, indica que es tan sólo sinónimo de final *judgment*. La traducción correcta del término "sentencia" en inglés es *judgment*, o decree en procedimientos de divorcio, mientras que el término *sentence* significa "condena" o "pena" en español. En el procedimiento civil se utiliza el término en latín *res judicata*, que equivale a nuestro concepto de "cosa juzgada formal" y *double jeopardy* para designar el principio de non bis in ídem o "cosa juzgada material", es decir, la prohibición de enjuiciar un mismo asunto si ya ha sido resuelto.

Contexto

Ejemplo 1:
Juez : Pues a la vista de la conformidad manifestada por los acusados y sus respectivos letrados, se dicta sentencia condenatoria in *voce* en los términos del escrito de acusación modificado en el día de hoy por el ministerio fiscal, sentencia que se declara **firme** en este acto y que se documentará oportunamente.

Ejemplo 2:
Juez: En este acto se declara **firme** la sentencia contra la que no cabe ningún recurso.

Ejemplo 3:
Juez: Bien, pues ¿Están de acuerdo todas las partes con la sentencia? Se declara **firme.**

No recomendamos

Traducciones incorrectas: Firm jugdment; final judgment, definitive judgment

Figure 8.2 Example of translation-oriented entry for the term *sentencia firme*

equivalent *final judgment* and its implications in relation to the information load that has to be conveyed in this particular context, as well as the reasons to exclude the term *definitive judgment* as a valid solution.

6 Final remarks

In this contribution we have tried to clarify a methodology of legal translation that applies principles of comparative law and considers the different factors that need to be addressed by legal translators. While this discussion may not include all the potential parameters that should be taken into consideration on assessing the quality of a translation product (matters of syntactic formulation, register, genre, etc.), it tries to transcend sometimes unproductive discussions about translatability and untranslatability, and ST- or TT-oriented strategies. The translation-oriented terminology entry that we have presented here aims at reaching high standards of quality in translation and interpreting by linking comparative-law analysis to the translation techniques that best fit the skopos of the translation or interpreting. This tool has been implemented in two very different fields: technology contracts addressed to consumers and court interpreting. The particularities of both fields have a clear impact in the translation techniques that can be considered acceptable. Indeed, with a standard of higher legal protection of consumers' rights and the recognition of the rights of non-native speakers of the language of the court to be on an equal footing, legal factors need to be considered in order to evaluate the quality of the translation. When the target text is actually the binding agreement for a consumer, or when an individual must be tried in a language that he or she does not understand, comparative analysis of the legal terms becomes essential not only to the translation process but to the actual operation of the law, as a matter of justice (Certomà 1986). Since a thorough comparative analysis for translation purposes may become a heavy burden – too much for a single translator in any translation assignment – it is important to help raise the quality of legal translations by crafting tools that take account of translation activity in all its complexity. As has been described, comparative law is the basis of this methodological approach. Certainly, the task to carry out deep-level comparative research is often performed by legal scholars who need relevant material to be found in historical analyses, sociological writings, critical writings, legal doctrine and court decisions (Van Hoecke 2004, pp. 191–192). Our purpose is to combine efforts: to create translation-oriented terminology entries in which the comparative work conducted leads directly to the proposal of different translation techniques, depending on the translation assignment. Indeed, unlike comparatist scholars, who quite often view translation pessimistically, as something "undesirable" or "just impossible" for technical concepts (Van Hoecke 2004, p. 174), the judiciary and legal professions in general are quite unaware of the scale of the efforts required of translators – they tend to oversimplify the task and consider that legal hermeneutics only comes into play once the translation is completed. If we are to improve the visibility of the work involved in translation, cooperation with legal actors becomes a necessity, particularly in cases where users of the translations might suffer the consequences of an incorrect assessment of the suitability of the legal equivalent by the translator. Creating *ex ante* materials allows the solutions proposed to be discussed in focus groups made up of members of the judiciary and court interpreters, which would help to highlight the importance of the latters' role and their expertise in issues related to target contexts. As evidenced by the Law10n and TIPp projects, when legal terms are translated for consumer contracts or for a foreign citizen involved in a criminal trial in a different country, the need for accuracy in translation is imposed not only by professional standards but, above all, by the legal order of the target country.

Acknowledgments

The author is very grateful to the anonymous reviewers and the editors of this book for their careful and meticulous reading on an earlier version of this work.

Notes

1 This chapter has been supported by the Department of Translation and Interpreting and East Asian Studies.
2 Source: https://en.wikipedia.org/wiki/Executive_order_(United_States) [Accessed 15 Dec. 2017].
3 The law10N Project (lawcalisation.com) and the TIPp project (http://pagines.uab.cat/tipp/) from the Universitat Autònoma de Barcelona were both funded by the Spanish Ministry of Science and Innovation.
4 See Consumer Rights Act 2015 in the United Kingdom.
5 The explanation and development of this particular entry, and others, can be found on this web page: http://interpretacionenprocesospenales.es/web/terminos.php

References

Alcaraz Varó, E. (2004). Anisomorfismo y lexicografía técnica. *El español lengua de traducción 2*. Available at: https://cvc.cervantes.es/lengua/esletra/pdf/02/021_alcaraz.pdf [Accessed 8 Jan. 2018].

Arumí, M., *et al.* (2017). *La qualitat de la traducció com a factor de garantia del procés penal: Desenvolupament de recursos per a intèrprets judicials (el projecte TIPp)*. Universitat Autònoma de Barcelona: Dipòsit Digital de Documents de la UAB. Available at: https://ddd.uab.cat/record/176075 [Accessed 12 Jan. 2018].

Bestué, C. (2009). *Las traducciones con efectos jurídicos. Estudio de la traducción instrumental de las licencias de programas de ordenador*. Thesis (PhD). Barcelona: Universitat Autònoma de Barcelona.

Bestué, C. (2013). *Los contratos traducidos. La traducción de los contratos de licencia de uso de programas de ordenador*. Valencia: Tirant lo Blanch.

Bestué, C. (2016). Translating law in the digital age. Translation problems or matters of legal interpretation? *Perspectives: Studies in Translatology*, 24, pp. 576–590.

Biel, Ł. (2017a). Enhancing the communicative dimension of legal translation: Comparable corpora in the research-informed classroom. *The Interpreter and Translator Trainer*, 11 (4), pp. 316–336.

Biel, Ł. (2017b). Researching legal translation: A multi-perspective and mixed-method framework for legal translation. *Revista de Llengua i Dret, Journal of Language and Law*, 68, pp. 76–88.

Bix, B.H. (2013). Linguistic meaning and legal truth. *In*: M. Freeman and F. Smith, eds. *Law and language*. Oxford: Oxford University Press, pp. 34–44.

Carston, R. (2013). Legal texts and canons of construction: A view from current pragmatic theory. *In*: M. Freeman and F. Smith, eds. *Law and language*. Oxford: Oxford University Press, pp. 128–150.

Certomà, G.L. (1986). Problems of juridical translations in legal science. *In*: A.E-S. Tay, ed. *Law and Australian legal thinking in the 1980s*. Sydney: University of Sydney, pp. 67–74.

David, R. (1974). *Les grands systèmes de droit contemporains*. Paris: Dalloz.

Dullion, V. (2007). *Traduire les lois. Un éclairage culturel. La traduction en français des codes civils allemande et Suisse autour de 1900*. Cortil-Wodon: Éditions Modulaires Européennes.

Engberg, J. (2013). Comparative law for translation: The key to successful mediation between legal systems in legal translation in context. *In*: A. Borja Albí and F. Prieto-Ramos, eds. *Legal translation in context: Professional issues and prospects*. Oxford: Peter Lang, pp. 9–25.

Engberg, J. (2014). General and specific perspectives on vagueness in law: Impact upon the feasibility of legal translation. *In*: B. Pasa and L. Morra, eds. *Translating the DCFR and drafting the CESL. A pragmatic perspective*. Munich: Sellier European Law Publishers, pp. 147–159.

European Parliament (2005). *Debates 10 March 2005. Follow-up to the platform for action on women*. Available at: www.europarl.europa.eu/sides/getDoc.do?pubRef=-//EP//TEXT+CRE+20050310+ITEMS+DOC+XML+V0//EN&language=EN [Accessed 15 Feb. 2018].

Geeroms, S.M.F. (2002). Comparative law and legal translation: Why the terms cassation, revision and appeal should not be translated. *American Journal of Comparative Law*, 50 (1), pp. 201–228.

Gémar, J.M. (2015). De la traduction juridique à la jurilinguistique: La quête de l'équivalence. *Meta: Translators' Journal*, 60 (3), pp. 476–493.

Glanert, S. (2014). Law-in-translation: An assemblage in motion. *The Translator*, 20 (3), pp. 255–272.

Glanert, S. and Legrand, P. (2013). Foreign law in translation: If truth be told. *In*: M. Freeman and F. Smith, eds. *Law and language*. Oxford: Oxford University Press, pp. 513–532.

Groot, de G.R. (1991). Problems of legal translation from the point of view of a comparative lawyer. *In:* Paul Nekerman, ed. *Translation, our future/La traduction, notre avenir. XIth world congress of FIT*. Maastricht: Euroterm.

Groot, de G.R. and van Laer, C. (2006). The dubious quality of legal dictionaries. *International Journal of Legal Information*, 34 (1), pp. 65–86. Available at: http://scholarship.law.cornell.edu/ijli/vol34/iss1/6 [Accessed 15 Feb. 2018].

Hale, S., *et al.* (2017). The effect of interpreting modes on witness credibility assessments. *Interpreting*, 19 (1), pp. 69–96.

Hickey, L. (1998). Perlocutionary equivalence: Marking, exegesis and recontextualisation. *In*: L. Hickey, ed. *The pragmatics of translation*. Clevedon: Multilingual Matters, pp. 217–232.

Hoecke, M. Van (2004). Deep level comparative law. *In*: M. van Hoecke, ed. *Epistemology and methodology of comparative law*. Oxford and Portland, OR: Hart Publishing, pp. 165–195.

Husa, J. (2011). Comparative law, legal linguistics and methodology of legal doctrine. *In:* M. van Hoecke, ed. *Methodologies of legal research: Which kind of method for what kind of discipline?* Oxford and Portland, OR: Hart Publishing, pp. 209–228.

Kjaer, A.L. (2004). A common legal language in Europe? *In*: M. van Hoecke, ed. *Epistemology and methodology of comparative law*. Oxford and Portland, OR: Hart Publishing, pp. 377–398.

Legrand, P. (2005). Issues in the translatability of law. *In*: S. Bermann and M. Wood, eds. *Nation, language, and the ethics of translation*. Princeton: Princeton University Press, pp. 30–50.

Martín Ruano, M.R. (2014). From suspicion to collaboration: Defining new epistemologies of reflexive practice for legal translation and interpreting. *The Journal of Specialised Translation*, 22, pp. 194–213.

Martín Ruano, M.R. (2015). (Trans)formative theorizing in legal translation and/or interpreting: A critical approach to deontological principles. *The Interpreter and Translator Trainer*, 9 (2), pp. 141–155.

Megale, F. (2015). Mondialisation et traduction juridique: Nouveaux parcours de recherche. *International Journal for the Semiotics of Law*, 28, pp. 31–52.

Monjean-Decaudin, S. (2012). *La traduction du droit dans la procedure judiciaire. Contribution à l'étude de la linguistique juridique*. Paris: Dalloz.

Nord, C. (1997). *Translating as a purposeful activity*. Manchester: St. Jerome Publishing.

Orozco-Jutorán, M. (2017). Efficient search for equivalents at your fingertips – the specialized translator's dream. *Meta: Translators' Journal*, 62 (1), pp. 137–154.

Rotman, E. (1995). The inherent problems of legal translation: Theoretical aspects, *Indiana International and Comparative Law Review*, 6 (1), pp. 187–196.

Sacco, R. (1999). Langue et droit. *In:* R. Sacco and L. Castellani, eds. *Les multiples langues du droit européen uniforme*. Italia and Isaidat: Harmattan, pp. 163–185.

Sage-Fuller, B., *et al.* (2013). Law and language(s) at the heart of the European project: Educating different kinds of lawyers. *In*: M. Freeman and F. Smith, eds. *Law and language*. Oxford: Oxford University Press, pp. 495–512.

Samuel, G. (2004). Epistemology and comparative law: Contributions from the sciences and social sciences. *In*: M. van Hoecke, ed. *Epistemology and methodology of comparative law*. Oxford and Portland, OR: Hart Publishing, pp. 35–77.

Šarčević, S. (1997). *New approach to legal translation*. The Hague-London-Boston: Kluwer Law International.

Šarčević, S. (2009). Translation of culture-bound terms in laws. *Multilingua – Journal of Cross-Cultural and Interlanguage Communication*, 4 (3), pp. 127–134.

Terral, F. (2004). L'empreinte culturelle des termes juridiques. *Meta: Journal des traducteurs*, 49 (4), pp. 876–890.

Torres Carballal, P.D. (1991). Trends in legal translation: The focusing of legal translation through comparative law. *In*: P. Nekeman, ed. *XIth world congress of FIT: proceedings*. Maastricht: Euroterm, pp. 447–450.

Torres-Hostench, O. and Bestué, C. (2015). Technology and e-resources for legal translators: The LAW10n project. *In*: O. Torres, P. Sánchez and B. Mesa, eds. *The coming of age of translation technologies in translation studies*. London: Peter Lang, pp. 285–306.

9 A mixed-methods approach in corpus-based interpreting studies

Quality of interpreting in criminal proceedings in Spain

Mariana Orozco-Jutorán

1 Introduction

The social context for our study was the new law passed in Spain in 2015 (*Ley Orgánica 5/2015, de 27 de abril*) to amend Spain's Code of Criminal Procedure. This new law was a result of the transposition of both Directive 2010/64/EU of the European Parliament and of the Council of 20 October 2010 on the right to interpretation and translation in criminal proceedings and Directive 2012/13/EU of the European Parliament and of the Council of 22 May 2012 on the right to information in criminal proceedings. As worded in this new Spanish law, it

> significantly reinforces procedural guarantees in criminal proceedings, by regulating the right to translation and interpreting in these proceedings and the right of accused persons to be informed of the purpose of the proceedings so that they can exercise their right of defence efficiently.[1]

Translation and interpreting thus became an essential component to ensure the right to effective legal protection in the exercise of lawful rights and interests before the courts.

However, the reality and quality of court interpreting in Spain's criminal courts were never studied in a systematic and rigorous way using a representative oral corpus. This task was undertaken by the research group MIRAS based at Universitat Autònoma de Barcelona, which specialises in public service interpreting, backed by researchers from four Spanish universities.[2] The project was funded by the Spanish Ministry of Economy and Competitiveness.[3]

2 Research methodology

The study adopted a mixed-methods approach, not only in the sense that it gathered quantitative and qualitative data, but also in that it combined features of different ontological and epistemological positions, usually related to quantitative and qualitative methodologies. On the one hand, it could be classified ontologically as objectivism, which:

> assumes a positivist epistemology, which asserts that social phenomena [in this case, court interpreting quality] can be objectively researched, data about the social world can be collected and measured, and the resulting observations must remain independent of the researchers' subjective understanding; that is to say, the researcher remains independent and has no impact on the data.
>
> (Saldanha and O'Brien 2013, p. 11, our words between square brackets)

In this sense, the approach was empirical, since it sought new information from the observation of data: the interpreting analysed had already taken place and had been recorded – as is the case in all the criminal proceedings in Spain. Thus, the researchers were non-participating observers: they were not present at the trials and had no impact on the data.

On the other hand, the study was not experimental because it did not seek to establish cause-effect relations, but rather to assess the quality of the existing reality. This recalls the ontological and epistemological position of realism, very commonly held in research in social sciences (Ormstorm *et al.* 2014, p. 15).

In respect of the methodology, the study was qualitative. Several features explain this. Firstly, the setting was natural: the researchers did not control any variables or intervene while the interpreting in the trials was taking place, so maximum ecological validity could be claimed. Secondly, once the oral corpus had been compiled and transcribed, a first explorative study was carried out to look at the data and develop and refine techniques to analyse it. Thirdly, the operationalisation of court interpreting quality proceeded in a cyclical fashion: indicators used to measure quality were tested and tailored to the nature of the data being observed, which is typical of qualitative methodology.

However, other features were aligned with a quantitative approach. For instance, the data sample used was not a small or already existing oral corpus, but a large, representative sample of real criminal proceedings that included interpreting. Another component involved creating and validating a measuring instrument, something clearly quantitative since it is deductive, aimed at measuring phenomena and sequential; additionally, there was a validation design which included a pilot study.

Therefore, if we understand methods to be "the practical means by which data are collected" (O'Reilly and Kiyimba 2015, p. 3) or "the practical 'tools' to make sense of empirical reality" (Saukko 2003, quoted in Saldanha and O'Brien 2013, p. 13) this was a mixed-methods study, since qualitative methods were used to collect data and quantitative methods were used to analyse them.

There is a growing interest in the use of corpus methods for comparative studies in Translation and Interpreting Studies (TIS) (see, for instance, Calzada Pérez 2017) and this is also true for Legal TIS (see Biel 2017; Pontrandolfo 2016;

Vigier and Sánchez 2017). However, in the case of this project, the term "corpus method" was avoided for two reasons. Firstly, we considered our oral corpus to be "only" the data gathered. While the corpus had to be designed, compiled and transcribed, and it was a time-consuming and complex task,[4] this is also the case with other types of data, such as questionnaires or interviews, in any kind of research. Secondly, when corpus-based studies are carried out in TIS, corpus linguistics tools are usually applied to measure frequency, keywords and concordances, including collocates and clusters (Calzada Pérez 2017, p. 236). We did not use any of these, because they were not suitable for our purposes, which were quality-oriented and legal ones, i.e. to describe to what extent the interpreting was fulfilling the right of information of the accused person.

3 Research question and dependent variables

The main objective of the project was to study the quality of court interpreting in criminal proceedings in Spain to determine to what extent the interpreting was fulfilling the right of information of the accused person. Therefore, the main research question was "What is the quality of court interpreting in Spain?", and the first task was to define and operationalise the theoretical construct of quality so that it could be turned into "tangible" or empirical units that could be observed.

After discussions and a literature review on the quality of public service interpreting and court interpreting,[5] we decided to adopt an *ad hoc* definition which was drafted by one of the leading team members, Carmen Bestué, and based partly on a judgment by the Supreme Court of Canada[6] mentioned in Roberts-Smith (2009, see Bestué 2018). The definition was as follows:

> To guarantee access to justice to the person with limited knowledge of the language being used in the courtroom, court interpreting should be continuous, precise, impartial, competent and contemporaneous. Precision is understood as fidelity, i.e. fulfilling legal equivalence, which means transferring the meaning of the message, including the repetitions, interruptions, errors, etc. and also reflecting the style, tone and register used by the speaker.

Out of the many possible theoretical frameworks in Interpreting Studies (see Pöchhacker 2016 for an overview) we chose Wadensjö's approach to dialogue interpreting to operationalise the construct. Wadensjö's approach (1998) goes beyond the monologic view (what she calls "talk as text") and complements it with the dialogic view ("talk as activity"), understanding interpreting not only as a translation task, but also as mediation and coordination. In this way, she accounts for the double role of dialogue interpreters: relaying original utterances (renditions) and coordinating conversation (non-renditions). In the words of Pöchhacker (2016, p. 79), Wadensjö launched "a new paradigm for the study of interpreting as dialogic discourse-based interaction". This paradigm inspired us to create two dependent variables, namely interaction problems and textual problems, based on the distinction between "talk-as-activity" and "talk-as-text" (Wadensjö 1998, p. 21). Textual problems refer specifically to issues regarding the precision or accuracy of the message conveyed, whereas interaction problems encompass all matters related to dialogue-building and multi-party encounters where the interpreter is an active participant in the conversation. These two dependent variables were then operationalised with scales and indicators so that they could be observed and measured, which will be discussed in further sections of this chapter.

4 Data collection and sampling

Random sampling where every subject of the population being studied has an equal chance of being selected as a participant in the study is considered to be an ideal scenario since it is the most reliable sampling technique for ensuring generalisation. In our case, the population consisted of the oral interventions in criminal trials with an interpreter, and therefore the "subjects" were not people but the trials, which were seen as composed of oral interventions.

Since the purpose of the study was to describe and assess court interpreting in criminal proceedings, the decision was made to use a random sampling of criminal proceedings with interpreters taking place in Barcelona. Barcelona was chosen for two reasons. Firstly, it is the place where the research team was based and where contacts with the judiciary were possible to obtain permission for access to recordings of the trials. Secondly, it is the second biggest city in terms of population in Spain, with 1,620,343 inhabitants[7] and it attracts a large number of immigrants and tourists,[8] who are the main defendants or witnesses with limited competence in the official languages in trial courts.

Regarding the size of the sampling, there are currently 28 Criminal Courts in Barcelona (known as *Tribunales de lo Penal* in Spanish), but only 24 of them are specifically trial courts that ask for interpreters when needed, since the other four deal with the enforcement of judicial decisions, which involves written proceedings only. Therefore, the question was what sample size should be used out of the total of 24 courts.

According to Creswell (1998, p. 64), there are no specific rules when determining an appropriate sample size in qualitative research, although obviously the bigger and the more representative the better. For phenomenological studies, for instance, Creswell recommends five to 25 cases. In TIS, however, corpora have been used long enough to have many scholars pondering on the size of a representative corpus. For example, Baker stresses quality over quantity:

> One consideration when building a specialised corpus in order to investigate the discursive construction of a particular subject is perhaps not so much the size of the corpus, but how often we would expect to find the subject mentioned within it (. . .) Therefore, when building a specialised corpus for the purposes of investigating a particular subject or set of subjects, we may want to be more selective in choosing our texts, meaning

> that the quality or content of the data takes equal or more precedence over issues of quantity.
>
> (2006, pp. 28–29, qtd. in Corpas Pastor and Seghiri 2010, p. 120)

In this sense, our corpus is specialised and includes full texts rather than extracts. Based on an extensive literature review, Corpas Pastor and Seghiri (2010, p. 122) clarify the concept of representativeness and agree, quoting Wright and Budin (1997), that the conclusions drawn from a corpus can be claimed to be meaningful, even if the size is not very large, if the subject of corpus is specialised because the vocabulary used in it is restricted. They also quote Ahmad and Rogers (2001, p. 736) to agree that a specialised corpus requires only tens of thousands of words, compared with the millions of words required for general-language lexicography.

Considering all the preceding, together with the resources available for transcribing (it takes between 40 and 50 minutes of work to transcribe one minute of trial), a decision was made to request the recordings available from 50 percent of the criminal courts in Barcelona for a specific period of time (January–June 2015). Therefore, out of the total of 24 such courts where interpreting is used, we requested video recordings from 12 courts, which were chosen randomly.

Owing to some technical and practical difficulties, which are explained in detail in Orozco-Jutorán (2018), recordings were provided by ten criminal courts, but the sample was still random. It would have been better to have the recordings of all 12 courts, but we still believe that the sample can be claimed to be representative, since it amounts to 190,000 tokens from 55 hearings, interpreted by 45 different interpreters – or, rather, since it is an oral corpus, 1,116 minutes – and it includes 41.6 percent of the total "population". It is also important to add that all the courts are very similar as regards the number of interpreted proceedings, the language combinations concerned and interpreters' background and experience, with the latter all coming from the same agency, which has an official agreement in place as an interpreting provider.

Naturally, it would be very interesting and necessary in the case of extrapolation to the whole of Spain to replicate the study and see to what extent the results obtained are corroborated. The research team plans to do it in Seville, the fourth Spanish city in terms of population, and is currently taking all the requisite steps to be able to develop another full-scale study using the same procedure to compile, transcribe and analyse the corpus.

Therefore, the final corpus consists of the transcription of all the trials with interpreters that took place between January and June 2015 in three language combinations (English, French and Romanian into Spanish) and in ten criminal courts in Barcelona. It included 1,116 minutes of trial recordings which, once transcribed, amount to 190,000 tokens, including all the monologic and dialogic parts of the trial that are audible (since some parts were interpreted using the "chuchotage" technique, far from the microphones of the courtroom and were thus not audible enough to allow transcription).

5 Operationalisation of the dependent variable *textual problems*

The first dependent variable was **textual problems** and the phenomenon to be observed and measured was the accuracy of the information transfer, i.e. the message conveyed by the interpreter. By problems, the researchers meant "areas" where interpreters encountered linguistic, cultural, or domain-related (for instance legal) difficulties in the oral discourse. The term "linguistic" is understood here in the broader sense of this word, including not only textual, syntactic and lexical levels, but also the pragmatic level, i.e. problems posed by register, tone or changes in the discourse and so on.

To measure this variable, two scales were created. The first of these was an interval scale regarding accuracy. Interval scales rank concepts and set the difference between them, just like the grading system that is used to evaluate students. In this case, the interval scale had three categories, shown in Figure 9.1.

The definition of the three categories included in the scale is as follows. An "adequate" solution means that the content and the form of the message is conveyed "adequately", i.e. precisely and accurately, by the interpreter. An "improvable" solution means that the interpreter conveys the message and the basic communicative objective is reached, but not in a complete way, so the solution could be clearly improved either in content or in form. An "inadequate solution" means that there is a serious distortion of meaning in the message conveyed. This may be due to several possible error types, such as serious omissions or additions, shift in meaning and so on, and that is why a second, descriptive scale was created to complement the data obtained from the first scale.

The second scale is categorical. Also called nominal data, categorical scales classify concepts without ranking them, so one category is not better or worse than any other. This scale is related to the usual accuracy scale and was created to quantify the type of solutions adopted by the interpreters to solve a textual problem. The indicators are shown in Figure 9.2.

These categories are explained and illustrated in detail in Orozco-Jutorán (2017). What should be emphasised is that a distinction was made between "serious" inadequate solutions (i.e. serious addition of information, serious omission, serious major shift in meaning) and other, "less serious" inadequate solutions. By "serious" we mean errors that might affect or interfere with the result of the criminal proceeding, as shown in Example 1, where we have included our translation of the Spanish oral interventions between square brackets and where the serious addition of information is underlined.

The solution applied by the interpreter when facing a textual problem was:
- (A) Adequate
- (M) Improvable
- (I) Inadequate

Figure 9.1 The interval scale created to measure accuracy in relation to textual problems

Types of solution applied by interpreters when facing a textual problem **Possible categories for "adequate" solutions:** – (EH) Established equivalent – (IM) Making some information implicit – (EX) Making some information explicit
Possible categories for "improvable" solutions: – (CR) Change of register – (NMS) Minor shift in meaning (compared to the source text)
Possible categories for "inadequate" solutions: – (O) Omission – (OG) Serious omission – (NT) Not translated – (AD) Addition of information – (ADG) Serious addition of information – (ITER) Inadequate terminology – (FS) Major shift in meaning (substantial distortion of meaning from that of the original message) – (FSG) Serious major shift in meaning – (SS) Incomprehensible (message is not understandable, does not make sense)

Figure 9.2 The categorical scale created to quantify types of textual solutions

Example 9.1 An example of serious addition of information

Judge – . . . *que si reconoce los hechos y está conforme.*
[Does he acknowledge the facts and agree?]
Interpreter – Do you accept?
Defendant – *Sí.*
[Yes]
Interpreter – Yeah? And do you agree?
Defendant – Yeah.
Interpreter – *Sí, <u>es culpable.</u>* [Yes, <u>he is guilty.</u>]

6 Operationalisation of the dependent variable *interaction problems*

The second dependent variable was **interaction problems** and the phenomena to be observed were related to the oral interaction conducted by the participants in the criminal proceedings: judge, counsels, prosecutor, interpreter, defendant, witnesses, etc. This variable includes three aspects of the oral interaction: conversation management, non-renditions (as defined by Wadensjö 1998, p. 25) and direct or reported speech, corresponding to three different scales created. Figure 9.3 shows the categorical scale used to observe conversation management.

These three categories, based on the existing literature on court interpreting (see Angermeyer 2015), include: (1) overlaps: that is, when two or more members of the judicial staff speak at the same time, or when the interpreter's voice overlaps with that of the judge or any other judicial staff, causing the latter to stop talking; (2) interruptions: that is, when the interpreter is interrupted by any member of the judicial staff, leaving his or her rendition unfinished; and (3) long turns: that is, when a member of the judicial staff speaks for more than two minutes in a single turn.

The second instrument was designed to observe non-renditions, that is, renditions that do not correspond to the original utterance. These can be used to manage turn-taking or dialogue and are then justified, but may also be used for other reasons which are not justified. Therefore, as in the case of textual problems, an initial interval scale measures acceptable non-renditions (justified) and non-acceptable non-renditions (unjustified) and then a second, categorical scale classifies possible types of non-renditions, as shown in Figure 9.4.

Finally, the third instrument regarding interactional problems was designed to observe speech style, both by the judicial staff and the interpreter. The purpose

Types of conversation management problems: – (S) Overlap – (I) Interruption – (DL) Long turn

Figure 9.3 The categorical scale created to quantify types of conversation management problems

The types of non-renditions by the interpreter (I.)
Possible categories for justified non-renditions: – (P) Pause (I. asks for a pause to be able to interpret) – (Cl) Clarification (I. asks for clarification or explains something that was expressed ambiguously) – (Co) Confirmation (I. seeks to confirm that s/he understood or heard the information clearly) – (R) Retrieval (I. is aware that he or she is missing some information and asks to retrieve it)
Possible categories for unjustified non-renditions: – (A) Warning (I. gives advice or instructions on how to behave or warns the defendant) – (Res) Answer (I. answers on behalf of the defendant) – (Extra) Extra information (I. gives information to any of the participants or asks questions not posed in the original utterances)

Figure 9.4 The categorical scale created to quantify types of non-renditions

Possible nominal categories for speech style:
(DIR) Direct speech Example: **Defendant**: No, I wasn't there. **Interpreter**: *No, no estuve allí.* [No, I wasn't there.]
(INDIR) Indirect speech Example: **Defendant**: No, I wasn't there. **Interpreter**: *No, no estuvo allí.* [No, he wasn't there.]
(RS) Reported speech Example: **Defendant**: No, I wasn't there. **Interpreter**: *Dice que no estuvo allí.* [He says that he wasn't there.*]*

Figure 9.5 The categorical scale created to quantify the speech style

of including this information in the observations was to see if participants were consistent with their own style during a trial. The categorical scale shown in Figure 9.5 was thus applied twice in every trial observed, once for the judicial staff and a second time for interpreters.

The categories are explained in detail in Arumí and Vargas-Urpí (2018).

7 Validation of measurement instruments through a pilot study

Our intention was to create a measuring instrument for court interpreting quality, with a focus on assessing whether the rights of accused persons are respected. For this purpose, we ensured the measurement validity, which "refers to the techniques we use to acquire our research data and to the appropriateness of the scales we use to measure that data" (Saldanha and O'Brien 2013, p. 33), by creating and describing the indicators with care and ensuring that the scales were consistent and could be applied to real situations (i.e. the oral corpus with interpreters' intervention in criminal proceedings).

To ensure the validity, after the scales and indicators were created and described, a pilot study was carried out with a subcorpus of 18 trials – out of the 55 trials that made up the whole sample to be analysed – six in each of the three language combinations (English, French and Romanian into Spanish), in which different experts used the same instruments and annotated the same trials to check if the results obtained were the same. Where differences were found, some changes were made to the instruments to ensure consistency in the results. Other pilot study results are explained in Arumí and Vargas-Urpí (2018) and Vargas-Urpí (2017).

The measuring instruments take the form of an annotation system that could be used by filling in a grid or, as was done in the TIPp project, annotating the corpus in a software package that allows such annotation and then exporting this information into Excel files in which the indicators can be quantified.

To give an example of what an annotated file looks like, Figure 9.6 shows a screenshot of the EXMARaLDA software,[9] with the transcription and annotation of a small fragment of a trial.

As can be seen in Figure 9.6, one tier or row is devoted to each type of problems, both textual and interaction problems. In the example, at the top of the screen, there are all the tiers or rows devoted to the speakers and the transcription of what they said. Below these rows, starting in tier 17, the annotation tiers can be seen, the first of which is called *PROBLEMA*. This tier is where the researchers tag the fragment in which there is a textual or interaction problem. For instance,

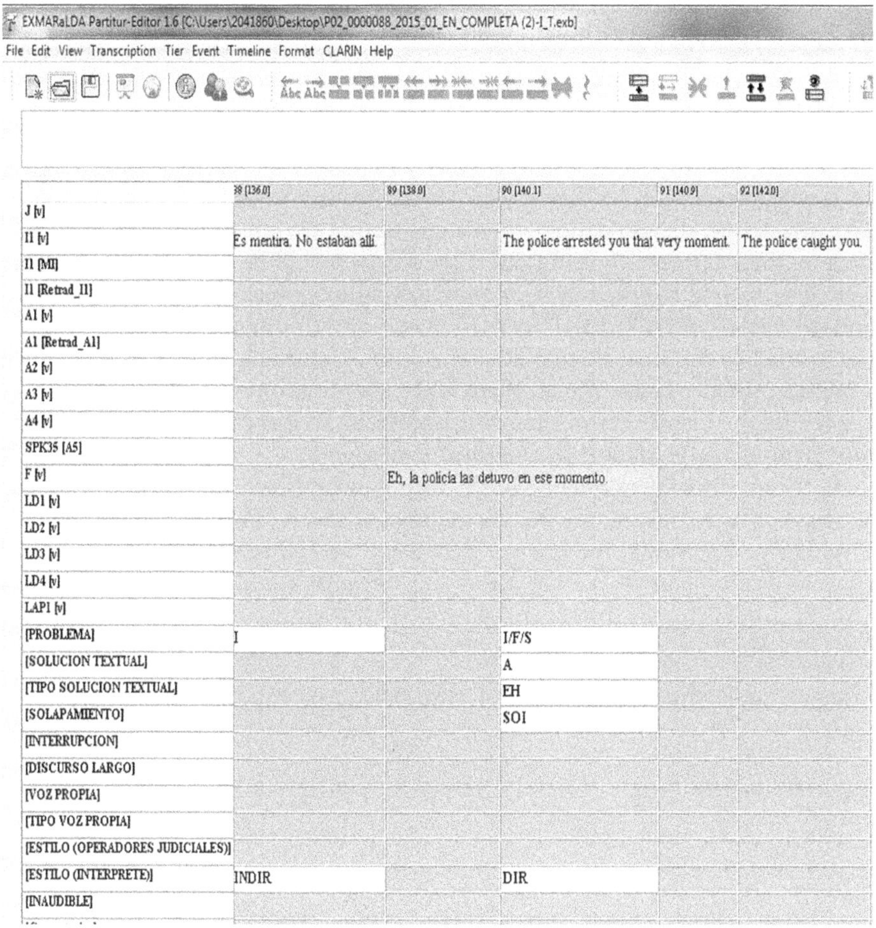

Figure 9.6 A fragment of a trial transcribed and annotated using the measuring instruments

in the first grey column, below where the interpreter says *Es mentira. No estaban allí* [That is a lie, they weren't there], there is an *I*, meaning that there is an "interaction problem" in this sentence. Then, some rows below, in the tier devoted to speech style, there is an annotation *INDIR*, meaning that the interpreter is using indirect speech (saying '*They* were not there' instead of using the same speech style used in the original sentence by the defendant, which would be '*We* were not there'). In the next column, to the right, the prosecutor speaks, saying *Eh, la policía las detuvo en ese momento* [Eh, the police arrested them at that moment] with no annotation or tag below because the interpreter does not face any problem in this case. In the next column, the interpreter renders the prosecutor's words but starts speaking before the prosecutor finishes his sentence. This overlap between the speakers is marked by the tag *I* in the tier *PROBLEMA*, since there is an interaction problem, and then there is the tag *SOI* in the tier belonging to *SOLAPAMIENTO*, which means "overlap" in Spanish. This *SOI* stands for "an overlap caused by the interpreter" and is differentiated from an overlap between the Judge and the prosecutor or the defence attorney, which would be annotated as *SOJ*. There are two more annotations in the same sentence. The first one is not an interaction problem but an observable phenomenon in the interaction (and that is why, in the tier for *PROBLEMA*, next to the *I*, there is an *F*, which stands for *Fenómeno*, which is the Spanish word for "phenomenon"). The observable phenomenon is then annotated in the style tier, tagged as *DIR*, because the interpreter is using direct speech, as would be recommended in this case. The second annotation is of a textual nature, which is why, next to the *I* and the *F* in the *PROBLEMA* tier there is also an *S* (meaning "Solution"). In the tier just below this one, there is an annotation *A*, meaning "adequate solution". Finally, in the tier below the *A*, there is the specification of the type of solution applied by the interpreter to the textual problem, in this case, *EH*, which stands for "Equivalente Habitual" [Established equivalent].

All the information annotated in the corpus as explained previously, for 55 trials, was converted into Excel files, an example of which can be seen in Figure 9.7.

As Figure 9.7 shows, the rows or tiers from the EXMARaLDA software were converted into columns so that filters and formulas could be applied to obtain

	A	B	C	D	E	F	G	H	
1	PROBLEMA	SOLUCION_	TIPO_SOLUCION	SOLAPAMIEN	INTER	DISCURS	VOZ_PROPIA	TIPO_VOZ_PROPIA	ESTILO_OPERAD
2	F								DIR
3	I								INDIR (FP)
4	I								
5	I								INDIR (FP)
6	F								
7	I								INDIR (FP)
8	I/T	I	NT				NJ	INFOEXTRA	
9	T	I	NT						
10	F						J	ACLAR	
11	I				IR				

Figure 9.7 Details of an Excel file with annotations

quantifiable data like that shown in the Results section. One Excel sheet was created for each trial and one Excel file containing all the trials in one language combination. Finally, a "bigger" Excel file was created, linked to the three sheets, containing the total data for each language and combining the results of the three language pairs that were analysed. This system proved to be very useful because it provided researchers with quantifiable data that enabled them to describe real practice systematically rather than anecdotally.

The pilot test and the analysis of the whole corpus with the measuring instruments showed that the differences between researchers when using the measuring instrument would be very small. Of course, there is always some room for interpretation on the part of the person assessing or using the measuring instruments. However, that never happened when dealing with indicators like "adequate" or "improvable", but rather with allocating items to the different inadequate solution types. Therefore, it would be very useful to have other researchers use the measuring instruments and replicate the study as the way to move forward, both in terms of research methodology and scientific gain for TIS.

8 Results

8.1. How much of the trial is interpreted?

One important finding of the corpus analysis is that a substantial part of the trial is not actually translated for the person with limited competence in the official languages of the court, who is usually the defendant. This is measured by one of the categories created under "inadequate textual solutions": "not translated" (NT). To be annotated as NT, there needs to be a whole intervention, not only a word or a sentence, by one of the participants which has not been interpreted at all. Thus, there is an important difference with respect to omissions, which affect only a word or a sentence that has not been translated. Table 9.1 shows the quantity of NT interventions found per hour and per minute in the corpus.

Other data regarding the parts of the trial which are not interpreted are also alarming, as shown in Table 9.2 (for more details see Vigier, *forthcoming*).

Table 9.1 The number of "not translated" interventions (NT) in the corpus per hour and per minute of trial

Language	*Total of NT per hour*	*Total of NT per minute*
English	371	1.8
French	190	1.6
Romanian	555	3.7
Mean	**372**	**2.7**

Table 9.2 The percentage of time interpreted to defendants in 55 hearings covered by the corpus

Language	*% of interpreted time (aloud)*	*% of interpreted time (chuchotage)*	*% of time not interpreted in any way*
English	33	16	51
French	48	13	39
Romanian	22	17	61
Mean	**30**	**16**	**54**

Table 9.3 The number of textual solutions in the corpus per bilingual minute of trial

Language	*Adequate solutions*	*Improvable solutions*	*Inadequate solutions*
English	0.49/min	0.45/min	2.14/min
French	0.07/min	0.36/min	2.07/min
Romanian	0.44/min	2.77/min	3.99/min
Mean	**0.3/min**	**1.2/min**	**2.7/min**

The mean of the percentage of the trial which is not interpreted to the defendant in any way is 54 percent, and only 33 percent of the interpretation is recorded, since the other 16 percent is whispered to the defendant's ear and is thus not heard or recorded by the microphones in the courtroom. These findings demonstrate that the defendant's right of information is being violated.

How accurate is the translation of the interpreted part of the trial?

The next variable is the accuracy of interpreting. Table 9.3 shows the quantity of adequate, improvable and inadequate solutions observed in the corpus per minute of trial.

As can be seen in Table 9.3, the mean of inadequate solutions is almost three per minute while the mean of adequate solutions is one every three minutes, which implies that the interpreting is not accurate. The differences between the three language combinations observed in Table 9.3 and also in other tables in this section are significant, with interpreting into and from Romanian containing almost double the inadequate solutions of interpreting from and into English or French, suggesting that this is an important factor to be accounted for in future research.

Table 9.4 describes the number of serious inadequate solutions in the corpus, which is alarmingly large, because the mean of 21.1 serious errors per hour implies that there is one serious error, which could affect the result of criminal proceedings, every three minutes. The issue is not merely a lack of precision, but serious errors in the translation of the messages, which again violates the defendant's right of information.

Table 9.4 The number of serious errors in the corpus per bilingual hour of trial

Language	*Serious omissions per bilingual hour*	*Serious addition of information per bilingual hour*	*Serious major shift of meanings per bilingual hour*	*Incomprehensible sentences (SS) per bilingual hour*	*Total of serious errors per bilingual hour*
English	6.3	2.6	7.3	4.4	20.6
French	5.9	1.3	6.5	1.3	15.0
Romanian	12.6	4.8	7.3	1.0	25.7
Mean	**8.5**	**3.2**	7.1	**2.3**	**21.1**

8.2 How do participants interact during trials?

Table 9.5 shows the number of conversation management problems during the trial, namely overlaps, interruptions and long turns per hour of trial, while Table 9.6 shows the number and type of non-renditions per hour of trial.

Table 9.5 The number of conversation management problems per hour of trial

Language	*Judicial staff overlaps per hour*	*Interpreter overlaps per hour*	*Long turns per hour*	*Interruptions per hour*
English	18.9	36.1	0.81	24.4
French	17.1	45.7	0.63	48.9
Romanian	11.7	18.4	1.5	6.7
Mean	**15.0**	**32.2**	**1.1**	**24.6**

Table 9.6 The number and type of non-renditions per hour of trial

Language	*Justified non-renditions*	*Unjustified non-renditions*
English	26.3	50.2
French	14.4	11.9
Romanian	25.6	65.7
Mean	**22.8**	**45.5**

The number of overlaps between judicial staff, interruptions and long turns confirms the complexity of interpreters' work. This is also supported by other data related to the speech speed of the judicial staff: the researchers counted the trials in which one of the judicial staff exceeded 180 words per minute and it happened in 72% of the trials. However, this complexity does not explain or justify the alarming number of unjustified non-renditions observed, again with considerable differences between the three language combinations, with the interpreter advising, instructing, warning or asking questions of his/her own three times every four minutes.

Table 9.7 The percentage of the lack of consistency observed in the speech style of judicial staff and interpreters in each trial

Language	*Lack of consistency (interpreters)*	*Lack of consistency (judicial staff)*
English	74%	74%
French	67%	67%
Romanian	63%	74%
Mean	67%	73%

In respect of the speech style, Table 9.7 shows the lack of consistency observed in the judicial staff and interpreters when using direct, indirect or reported speech in the same trial. The inconsistencies were widespread in both groups, which adversely affects the clarity of interaction between the participants of criminal proceedings.

9 Discussion

The findings indicate that there is an unacceptably low quality of court interpreting in the random sample of 55 criminal proceedings observed in Barcelona's criminal courts in 2015 in three language combinations. The alarming numbers of errors and unjustified non-renditions suggest that interpreters are not adequately trained and do not follow a code of ethics, and that the judicial staff need to receive awareness-raising information or training to interact better with interpreters. The findings also show that the defendants' right of information is being systematically violated, firstly because less than half of the trial is being translated for them and secondly because the part that is interpreted has an unacceptable number of errors that can affect the result of criminal proceedings.

We hope that these findings shed light on the problems currently facing the quality of court interpreting in criminal proceedings in Spain. We would also like to contribute to the improvement of the quality of court interpreting by creating some tools, which can be found online at http://interpretacionenprocesospenales.es/web/index.php, and include translation-oriented terminological records, thesaurus and recommendations to both court interpreters and judicial staff based on the observations made on the corpus.

10 Conclusions

This chapter has demonstrated a mixed-methods approach to examining the quality of court interpreting, involving a qualitative overall design with quantitative data analysis techniques and the creation of a measuring instrument. The objective was to operationalise the quality of court interpreting, which was achieved through a range of variables and the creation of measurable, quantifiable indicators for each variable. Departing from the theoretical distinction made by Wadensjö (1998) between "talk-as-text" and "talk-as-activity", two dependent variables were defined: textual problems and interaction problems. These variables were then operationalised through a range of interval and categorical scales created *ad hoc* and piloted using our corpus data. To be more specific, two scales were created to measure the textual problems variable: one interval scale to measure accuracy of the information transfer and one categorical scale to quantify types of solutions applied by the interpreter. Regarding the interaction problems variable, three categorical scales were created: one to quantify types of conversation management problems, another to quantify types of non-renditions and a third one to quantify the speech style.

The proposed method should be further tested by replication in other contexts (other countries, other language pairs, court types, civil proceedings, etc.) to help us better understand the nature of constraints in court interpreting and, in the long term, to be able to gather comparable data in different contexts.

Notes

1 Our translation of a sentence taken from the law: *Ley Orgánica 5/2015, de 27 de abril por la que se modifican la Ley de Enjuiciamiento Criminal y la Ley Orgánica 6/1985, de 1 de julio, del Poder Judicial, para transponer la Directiva 2010/64/UE, de 20 de octubre de 2010, relativa al derecho a interpretación y a traducción en los procesos penales y la Directiva 2012/13/UE, de 22 de mayo de 2012, relativa al derecho a la información en los procesos penales.* [www.boe.es/boe/dias/2015/04/28/pdfs/BOE-A-2015-4605.pdf]

2 The research team was composed of the following researchers: Marta Arumí, Anna Gil Bardají (Universitat Autònoma de Barcelona), Anabel Borja (Universitat Jaume I), Mireia Vargas-Urpí (Universitat Pompeu Fabra), Francisco Vigier (Universidad Pablo de Olavide) and two team leaders: Carmen Bestué and Mariana Orozco-Jutorán (Universitat Autònoma de Barcelona).

3 The name of the project was "Quality in translation as an element to safeguard procedural guarantees in criminal proceedings: development of resources to help court interpreters of Spanish – Romanian, Arabic, Chinese, French and English" (FFI2014–55029-R). It lasted three years from January 2015 to December 2017 and it received funding from the Spanish State Grant Programme of Research, Development and Innovation related to Social Challenges.

4 The whole process and the difficulties faced by researchers in designing, creating, compiling and transcribing the corpus are explained in Orozco-Jutorán (2018).

5 The list of references would be too long to be included here. See for instance Hale (2004, 2007), Mikkelson (1998), Tipton and Furmanek (2016), Ortega Herráez (2011) and Pöchhacker (ed.) (2015).

6 "(. . .) Second, the claimant of the right must show, assuming it is not a case of a complete denial of an interpreter but one involving some alleged deficiency in the interpretation actually provided, that there has been a departure from the basic, constitutionally guaranteed standard of interpretation. For the purposes of this appeal, I define this standard as one of continuity, precision, impartiality, competency and contemporaneousness" R. *v.* Tran, [1994] 2 S.C.R. 951 [https://scc-csc.lexum.com/scc-csc/scc-csc/en/item/1166/index.do].

7 The first city in terms of population is Madrid, with 3,223,334 inhabitants, followed by Barcelona, with 1,620,343 inhabitants, Valencia with 791,413 and Seville with 688,711 inhabitants. Source: The National Statistics Institute, Spain [www.ine.es/] accessed in Jan. 2019, data from Jan. 2018.

8 The migrant population in the area (provincia) of Barcelona is 711,314. It is the second largest, after Madrid area (provincia), with 795,271 migrants. Source: The National Statistics Institute, Spain [www.ine.es/]; accessed in Jan. 2019, data from Jan. 2017.

9 www.exmaralda.org/en/. We would like to express our gratitude to Bernd Meyer, who suggested the use of this software, and Thomas Schmidt, the developer of the software package, who helped us with the technical aspects of the software.

References

Ahmad, K. and Rogers, M. (2001). Corpus linguistics and terminology extraction. *In*: S.E. Wright and G. Budin, eds. *Handbook of terminology management, Vol. 2: Application-oriented terminology management*. Amsterdam: John Benjamins, pp. 725–760.

Angermeyer, P.S. (2015). *Speak English or what? Codeswitching and interpreter use in New York city courts*. New York: Oxford University Press.

Arumí, M. and Vargas-Urpí, M. (2018). Annotation of interpreters' conversation management problems and strategies in a corpus of criminal trials in Spain: The case of non-renditions. *Translation and Interpreting Studies*, 13 (3).

Bestué, C. (2018). Aproximación empírica a la labor del intérprete en los tribunales de justicia. *In*: M.J. Ariza Colmenarejo, ed. *Derecho de traducción interpretación e información en el proceso penal*. Valencia: Tirant lo Blanch, pp. 139–175.

Biel, Ł. (2017). Researching legal translation: A multi-perspective and mixed-method framework for legal translation. *Revista de Llengua i Dret, Journal of Language and Law*, 68, pp. 76–88.

Calzada Pérez, M. (2017). Corpus-based methods for comparative translation and interpreting studies. Mapping differences and similarities with traditional and innovative tools. *Translation and Interpreting Studies*, 12 (2), pp. 231–252.

Corpas Pastor, G. and Seghiri, M. (2010). Size matters: A quantitative approach to corpus representativeness. *In*: R. Rabadán, *et al.*, eds. *Lengua, traducción, recepción: En honor de Julio César Santoyo/Language, translation, reception: To honor Julio César Santoyo*. León: Universidad de León, pp. 111–145.

Creswell, J.W. (1998). *Qualitative inquiry and research design: Choosing among five traditions*. Thousand Oaks, CA: Sage.

Hale, S. (2004). *The discourse of court interpreting*. Amsterdam: John Benjamins.

Hale, S. (2007). *Community interpreting*. Hampshire: Palgrave Macmillan.

Mikkelson, H. (1998). Towards a redefinition of the role of the court interpreter. *Interpreting*, 3 (1), pp. 21–45.

O'Reilly, M. and Kiyimba, N. (2015). *Advanced qualitative research. A guide to using theory*. London: Sage.

Ormstorm, R., *et al.* (2014). The foundations of qualitative research. *In*: J. Ritchie, *et al.*, eds. *Qualitative research practice: A guide for Social Science students and researchers*. London: Sage, pp. 1–26.

Orozco-Jutorán, M. (2017). Anotación textual de un corpus multilingüe de interpretación judicial a partir de grabaciones de procesos penales reales. *Revista de Llengua i Dret, Journal of Language and Law*, 68, pp. 33–56.

Orozco-Jutorán, M. (2018). The TIPp project: Developing technological resources based on the exploitation of oral corpora to improve court interpreting. *Intralinea*,

20. Available at: www.intralinea.org/specials/article/the_tipp_project [Accessed 5 Sept. 2018].

Ortega Herráez, J.M. (2011). *Interpretar para la Justicia*. Granada: Comares.

Pöchhacker, F., ed. (2015). *Routledge encyclopedia of interpreting studies*. London: Routledge.

Pöchhacker, F. (2016). *Introducing interpreting studies*. London: Routledge.

Pontrandolfo, G. (2016). *Fraseología y lenguaje judicial. Las sentencias penales desde una perspectiva contrastiva*. Roma: Aracne.

Roberts-Smith, L. (2009). Forensic interpreting. Trial and error. *In*: S. Hale, *et al.*, eds. *The critical link 5: Quality in interpreting – a shared responsibility*. Amsterdam: John Benjamins, pp. 13–35.

Saldanha, G. and O'Brien, S. (2013). *Research methodologies in translation studies*. London: Routledge.

Saukko, P. (2003). *Doing research in cultural studies: An introduction to classical and new methodological approaches*. London: Sage.

Tipton, R. and Furmanek, O. (2016). *Dialogue interpreting. A guide to interpreting in public services and the community*. London: Routledge.

Vargas-Urpí, M., 2017. Court interpreting as a shared responsibility: Judges and lawyers in a corpus of interpreted criminal proceedings. *Revista Canaria de Estudios Ingleses*, 75, pp. 139–154.

Vigier, F.J., *forthcoming*. Interpreting at Spanish criminal courts: Preliminary results of the TIPp project. *Translation and Translanguaging in Multilingual Contexts*.

Vigier, F.J. and Sánchez, M. del M. (2017). Using parallel corpora to study the translation of legal system-bound terms: The case of names of English and Spanish courts. *In*: R. Mitkov, ed. *Computational and corpus-based phraseology. Second international conference, europhras 2017 proceedings*. Cham: Springer, pp. 260–273.

Wadensjö, C. (1998). *Interpreting as interaction*. New York: Longman.

Wright, S.E. and Budin, G., eds. (1997). *Handbook of terminology management*. Amsterdam: John Benjamins.

10 An online survey as a means to research the 'outstitutional' legal translation market

Juliette Scott

1 Introduction

Significant volumes of legal texts are translated outside institutions – e.g. as part of cross-border business transactions and disputes; for case-directed access to foreign legislation; or owing to increasing levels of migration and mobility. The area is sorely under-researched, in part due to difficulties that scholars experience gaining entry in order to collect data. In these circumstances, research by experienced practitioners can allow certain hurdles to be overcome and aims to be fulfilled. Recruitment of participants can be facilitated by leveraging the researcher's existing networks; more comfortable and richer dialogues with stakeholders can fine-tune the subject and methods of study; and the impact and utility of findings can be heightened. At the same time, practitioner-researchers must bear in mind the pitfalls of over-involvement, identification with subjects, or skewed perspectives.

This chapter describes an online survey carried out by means of a questionnaire collecting both quantitative and qualitative data. It was designed to investigate the area of outsourced legal translation in a robust way by triangulating input from those outsourcing and those to whom work is outsourced. The intersections and differences between data from this kind of research on two groups with potentially 'opposing' standpoints may be of value to a variety of research projects. Although the project described relates to a specific 'outstitutional' locus, the discussions here should be fully transposable to other fields of legal translation research (Biel and Engberg 2013; Biel 2017). It is important to emphasise the difference between surveys as a method of study and questionnaires as a survey data collection tool among several others – such as interviews or focus groups. In order to collect empirical data in the field of legal translation, online questionnaires can provide an attractive solution for a number of reasons. The data subjects in this case – predominantly legal translators and lawyers – are relatively web-savvy and able to engage with the tool. In addition, both groups are under severe time pressure and unlikely to grant interviews, even when held remotely, or attend focus groups, without financial or other incentives. These features run alongside the attractions of online questionnaires extending across all disciplines, such as relatively non-invasive enquiry; wide potential catchment areas both in terms of numbers and geographical reach; data input effected by respondents,[1] reducing researcher workload; quick turnaround for data collection once subjects are reached; and data analysis facilitated by direct imports from collection tools.

2 Online and offline surveys of and by practitioners

The last twenty years have seen a sea change in Internet usage by many segments of the population, and likewise the legal sector. Electronic document exchange has become the norm. Lawyers and legal translators now have online access to a wide variety of resources such as case-law, legislation and intelligence. We can thus now say that many of these two groups of practitioners are 'Internet-savvy', but they are equally 'time-poor'. In view of these two features, engaging with research subjects in these sectors via online questionnaires rather than interviews, focus groups or other face-to-face research approaches whether in person or remote, can provide more flexibility, more participation, and hence more data than could otherwise be obtained. Online questionnaires can also offer an option to be stopped and started at will if the respondent is interrupted or wishes to enter more details. The design flexibility offered by platforms is considerable, data collection costs are modest and surveys "can serve both qualitative and quantitative research questions" (Toepoel 2015).

In the wider world, surveys have become ubiquitous online on a multitude of subjects. With the 'big data' revolution (Mayer-Schönberger and Cukier 2013), collecting, mining, extracting, analysing, interpreting, reporting and utilising data have become commonplace, not to mention a significant source of income for the business world, both directly for firms such as Cambridge Analytica or BlueLabs and indirectly for a host of companies via the customer and market insights that can be reaped. Participating in surveys, particularly for marketing purposes, is often incentivised – perhaps with vouchers or other kinds of rewards, and even vaunted as a way of making a small extra income. Despite this profit-driven landscape, practice-led research can be attractive to participants for more altruistic reasons – as a way to make their opinions felt, to call attention to bad practices, or to share and advance knowledge.

2.1 Features of practitioner research

As an entry point to the subject of practitioner research,[2] it may be helpful to refer to the tripartite model first proposed by Frayling (1993), which differentiates research "FOR practice, where research aims are subservient to practice aims, THROUGH practice, where the practice serves a research purpose, or INTO practice, such as observing the working processes of others" (Rust *et al.* 2007, original emphasis). In the academic field of professional discourse, a neighbouring discipline to that of Legal Translation Studies, the collection of reflections on the 'ins and outs' of practitioner research edited by Alessi and Jacobs (2015) contains an abundance of approaches, methodologies, case studies and collaborations. The volume illustrates that the interconnections between research and practice are perhaps less clear-cut than the tripartite model might suggest.

Reflective practitioners can provide valuable insights into processes, products and markets that are not necessarily available to academics and may be able to uncover interesting areas for academic research. With regard to data collection, their networks may also facilitate the recruitment of survey respondents, and entry into business and professional workplaces for fieldwork. Nevertheless, these benefits have their downside. The literature warns those embarking upon practitioner research of potential bias and limitations such as: vested interests in findings; lack of detachment from subject matter and/or informants; tunnel vision as a result of insider knowledge; and case- or site-specific data that cannot be generalised or replicated (Denscombe 2007, pp. 129–131). The difficulties do not only relate to academic rigour, however. Despite their professional experience, practitioners may not find it easy to obtain academic funding and may need to juggle paid work and research at the same time. Additionally, in the field of Legal Translation Studies high levels of interdisciplinarity make research stimulating, but can mean that researchers end up in a 'no-man's land' with no clear-cut attachments to either language/translation or law faculties.

2.2 *Online surveys: pros and cons*

The benefits of online surveys for academic research comprise are, in particular: "access to individuals in distant locations, the ability to reach difficult to contact participants, and the convenience of having automated data collection, which reduces researcher time and effort" (Wright 2006, p. 3). Similarly for Hewson, "specialist difficult-to-reach populations can be obtained fairly time and cost effectively" using web-based surveys, while online platforms provide relative consistency in displaying data entry forms, conditional branching of questions or "skip logic" and pop-up help windows (2015, p. 281). In a dedicated "how-to guide", Toepoel (2015) covers the whole process of conducting online surveys from development to processing and reporting from an academic perspective.

As already noted, however, it is important for researchers to bear in mind the disadvantages of online survey research. These include, *inter alia*, limitations brought about by access to, use of and familiarity with the Internet by the target population, data validity, self-reporting (Chan 2009), difficulties in verifying sources, noise, dirty data, representativeness, framing and sampling issues (Hewson 2015; Toepoel 2015; Wright 2006).

Clearly, the online questionnaire does not need to be used alone, and, according to the research project, can be complemented with, say, translation logs, emails, focus groups, polls, panels, interviews (either remote or face-to-face), data gathering from documentary sources or ethnographic methods such as observation and work shadowing (e.g. Denscombe 2007; Robson 2011).

2.3 *Approaches to translator surveys*

Surveys of the translation field have been carried out by individual scholars, by educational consortia (e.g., CIUTI, MeLLANGE), by translators' associations in specific geographical areas (e.g., USA, UK, Germany, France), by institutions (European Commission, Government of Canada) and by commercial organisations (Common Sense Advisory, SDL, TAUS). These groups may also collaborate to produce a survey (ATA 2016 with Industry Insights, Inc.; the European Commission Representation in the UK with CIOL and ITI 2017, PwC with the Government of Canada 2012, Pym *et al.* 2012 with the European Commission). The target populations studied include "freelance" translation and interpreting practitioners, in-house translators and interpreters, employees of translation agencies, students, graduates, members of translators' associations, translation companies and translation-related roles within businesses and institutions. Methods used range from links to online questionnaires emailed to members of associations (BDÜ 2015; ATA 2016) or made available through a number of channels including targeted social media (Gough 2011; Scott 2016), to interviews (Jääskeläinen and Mauranen 2006; Lagoudaki 2006; McAuliffe 2016), work shadowing and participant observation (Drugan 2013; McAuliffe 2016) and focus groups (Lagoudaki 2006). The large-scale survey by Pym *et al.* (2012) even involved collating for analysis large numbers of previous surveys from translators' associations.

Appendix 1 provides a non-exhaustive list of surveys from the last 20 years, particularly in the last decade. Many of them focus on translation technologies (Corpas Pastor *et al.* 2015; Fulford and Granell Zafra 2004; Gaspari *et al* 2015; Gough 2011; Olohan 2011), status and working conditions (Dam and Zethsen 2008, 2009, 2011; Fraser 1997, 2000; Katan 2009, 2011; Monzó 2002; Pym *et al.* 2012) and prices (ATA 2016; BDÜ 2015; CIOL/ITI 2011; SFT 2015; OTTIAQ 2014). Other subjects examined are quality (Drugan 2013; QUALETRA 2013), revision policies (Rasmussen and Schjoldager 2011), project management (Olohan and Davitti 2015) and translator training (CIUTI *et al.* 2015; Orlando 2016, 2018). Some focus on translation companies rather than translators (Ferreira Alves 2012; TAUS 2017). There are also 'industry' overviews: some instigated by institutions such as the Canadian Government (PwC 2012) or the European Commission (Pym *et al.* 2012) and some with underlying commercial aims either to generate revenue from the survey itself (Common Sense Advisory 2010–18) or to provide incidental marketing benefits (SDL 2016, 2017; TAUS 2017). Many surveys of the "industry" overview type are particularly concentrated on forecasting market trends. Overall, the numbers of usable responses vary with the survey aims, from tens to thousands, and geographical and language coverage is often slanted either according to the survey instigator's profile and/or the serendipitous availability of informants who care to respond. Less common are surveys investigating sectors of specialisation in translation practice such as medical, technical (Jääskeläinen and Mauranen 2006) or legal (Hertog and Van Gucht 2008; McAuliffe 2016; Monzó 2002; QUALETRA 2013; Scott 2016). Notwithstanding, some general surveys include and/or segregate data on legal translation and legal translators (translation of official documents in Pym *et al.* 2012; pricing by associations' surveys e.g., CIOL/ITI 2011; SFT 2015).

3 Survey design, structure and content

Once the researcher has made an informed epistemological choice – whether qualitative, quantitative or mixed methods – and having considered carefully whether the research question(s) is (are) an appropriate fit with the online survey approach, including with regard to the target population, survey design can begin.[3] In the case of the project used as an example in this chapter, the aim was:

> to explore the outsourcing of legal translation through two questions related to briefing: "How does the briefing process work within the outsourced legal translation environment?"; "Are legal translation principals and/or translators working as external practitioners satisfied with that process?"; and two questions related to performance: "Do the principals express any issues vis-à-vis the performance of translations received?"; "Do such legal translation principals and/or translators have any suggestions to improve performance?"
>
> (Scott 2016)

In view of its target population – (1) persons procuring/commissioning legal translation and (2) legal translators – and the strong likelihood that they were familiar with Internet-based tools, an online questionnaire was chosen. The wording was adjusted for a primarily non-native speaker audience, since the survey was seeking to collect data from all around the world relating to as many language pairs as possible. For the latter reason and due to budget constraints, translation of the questionnaire into a large number of other languages was rejected in favour of plain language "globish". Separate questionnaires were devised for the two groups, and for triangulation[4] purposes, the questions mirrored each other – as shown in Figure 10.1.

"Triangulation refers to the use of more than one approach to the investigation of a research question in order to enhance confidence in the ensuing findings" (Bryman 2004, pp. 1142–1143). In this project, the mirrored questions were aimed at data triangulation, while closed and open questions provided a measure of methodological triangulation.

The questions themselves were developed using a series of real-world trials over a number of iterations. This staged approach allowed the wording and subject of questions to be progressively refined according to the reactions of trial respondents and the sample data they provided. It is worth noting here that a practitioner-researcher may be in a privileged position to access and converse with respondents in a trial owing to their familiarity with and involvement in the sector, although one must bear in mind the points raised in section 2.1.

Regarding the order of questions, a consensus from the literature (e.g. Bryman 2006; Denscombe 2007; Hewson 2015; Robson 2011) was followed with consideration to the subject matter and target informants. In compliance with recommended practice for ethical research, information on participation, confidentiality, anonymity, researcher details, institutional host and opting in were stated in the header. Moreover, no potentially sensitive personal data was

TRANSLATORS	*PRINCIPALS*
2 What sort of documents do you translate?	14 What type of texts do you commission?
3 Please select below the language pair that you most commonly translate.	16 Does your organisation mainly work in one specific language pair?
4 Who are your MAIN clients for legal translation (or your employer if you work in-house)?	7 Which providers do you use most for legal translation?
5 What information does a translation order usually contain?	10 What information does your firm's translation order usually contain?
6 How often, in practice, are you informed of the intended purpose of the translation when you receive the order?	8 How often, in practice, do you inform translators of the intended purpose of the translation when commissioning?
7 How often, in practice, are you informed of the profile of the final user of the translation when you receive the order?	9 How often, in practice, do you provide the translator with the profile of the final user of the translation when commissioning?
9 During the translation process, how would you describe interaction with clients if questions arise?	11 During the translation process, how would you describe interaction with translation providers if questions arise?
10 Do you find some kinds of documents particularly troublesome? If so, please specify below.	20 Do you find some types of documents particularly troublesome? If so, please specify below.
11 After proofreading/checking, how often do you get feedback from the client?	13 After proofreading/checking, how often do you give translators feedback for their information?
12 Can you describe the worst legal translation situation that you have encountered – the circumstances and the issue?	22 Can you describe the worst translation quality problem that you have encountered – the circumstances and the issue?

Figure 10.1 Triangulation of key questions between respondent groups

requested and no question reply was obligatory. The questionnaire opened with demographic data (name, email, country, organisation, role), and then proceeded to explore the main focus of the survey as per the research questions cited previously, using open, closed and filter or contingency questions. Specifically, multiple-choice questions (scroll-down menus, check boxes and radio buttons, in list form and basic tables), supplemented with free-text boxes for key areas (criticisms of translated documents; details of troublesome legal genres; details of translation insufficiencies/errors, how translations could be improved). The last question of the survey invited feedback concerning the survey itself. Help boxes which appeared upon mouse hover near the relevant question contained clarifications.

When selecting the online platform, after having assessed the widely used SurveyMonkey.com, Wufoo[5] was chosen, owing to its lower cost as the research was self-funded; the options available to the researcher as regards form design, exports and reporting; and its compliance with the US-EU Safe Harbor Framework on the collection, use and retention of personal data.[6] The questionnaire was adapted to the online format, dividing the questions into three screens for ease of readability and use by respondents. The questionnaire text and choice of platform were then submitted to the university ethics committee for approval.

Once ethics approval had been obtained, the questionnaires were piloted with a representative range of stakeholders, as well as academic colleagues for further input. In the light of feedback received from the pilot, the following structural changes were made for the main phase of the survey: the questionnaire was reorganised into a more logical order; and some demographic questions were added or amended. As regards content, the following points were more fully explored: the translation purchase order; the intended purpose and final user of the target text; genres of source texts translated; and in view of the comparative law aspects underpinning legal translation, identifications of the source and target legal systems of respondents' texts. Since the pilot results did not change fundamentally either the survey aims or the data to be collected, I elected to treat both the pilot and main phases as a single dataset, while annotating them separately for the record.

4 Data collection, extraction and analysis

Given that this chapter focuses on the online survey as a research method, in the following section I will focus mainly on the collection and extraction of data using online questionnaires, and will not deal in detail with quantitative or qualitative data analysis, for which a plethora of dedicated literature is available (e.g., Bazeley and Jackson 2013; Bryman 2006; Denscombe 2007; Robson 2011). As already noted, collecting data from and access to professional respondents is a major stumbling block for much research into corporate and legal communication (Alessi and Jacobs 2015, pp. 3–4). Accordingly, multiple strategies were adopted in attempting to recruit survey respondents. Academia proved to be the least successful source of help and no collaborations could be put in place for data gathering. One possible reason is the aforementioned "no-man's land" between language/translation and law faculties. Lawyers' associations and professional bodies in the UK, France and elsewhere in Europe were contacted, without any success. I also attempted, in vain, to enlist the aid of senior figures in such bodies at legal theory lectures and international conferences. Translators' associations were similarly of little help.

In view of these decidedly thin prospects for data collection, I decided to put to use my own network of contacts built up over 25 years in the professional field and to take advantage of my attendance at international conferences. This was far more productive. For example, in the pilot study, one conference alone led to seven commissioners participating. Personally addressed emails sent to potential commissioner-participants produced a further nine responses. Alongside these direct methods, I used a technique known as "snowballing" (Denscombe 2007; Noy 2008) whereby existing respondents are asked whether they can pass on the questionnaire or suggest useful contacts who may be interested. This extended the number of participants still further. One consequence of this "opportunistic" sampling approach is that data may be collected from various geographical locations, and, in the case of this study, pertain to assorted language pairs, jurisdictions and areas of law. Given that the aim of the project was first and foremost to seek out potential evidence to support a hypothesis, grounded in personal experience of the market by the practitioner-researcher – that there might be room for improvements in the briefing of legal translators – the strategy was deemed tenable, to be supplemented in the future, for example by country-, language- or genre-specific studies.

Social media can reap benefits by using a carefully targeted strategy. I approached closed LinkedIn lawyers' groups, without success. On the other hand, an announcement through the LinkedIn Legal Translation Network Group led to large numbers of translator responses. A post on a highly respected legal drafting blog as a result of a personal communication led to ten replies from commissioners in the pilot study alone. Additionally, a multi-channel social media strategy was launched, including, *inter alia*, the author's blog[7] whereby many translator and commissioner participants were recruited – ascertained via click-throughs.

As the study progressed, I observed that lawyers having had problems with translations, or with family ties to translators or interpreters, or working extensively internationally, were far readier to participate. In brief, a "bottom-up" approach, involving contacts at grass-roots level in the market, proved far more successful than a "top-down" approach involving institutions. It also proved important for the researcher to be reactive and flexible when recruitment attempts were unsuccessful, and to find alternative strategies without delay.

Regarding the mechanics of data collection, whilst it is essential to be painstaking in their preparation, design, piloting and set-up, a significant advantage of online surveys is a reduced onus on the researcher at data entry stage, since survey respondents do this themselves. Once the questionnaire is launched, it is a matter of monitoring responses, perhaps initiating new recruitment drives or sending out reminders, until the survey is closed either when "enough" data has been amassed or for other reasons,[8] and extraction and analysis can begin. The Wufoo platform generates useful albeit simple and primarily quantitative-focused reports, but can also export the data in various formats for subsequent data analysis. Once again aiming at increased methodological rigour, and to be able to exploit the data more fully than manual handling would allow, I decided to use data analysis software (Bazeley 2009; Seidel 1998). Given that qualitative data outweighed quantitative data in this project, and having trialled other solutions such as Dedoose, I opted for NVivo owing to its array of tools (Bazeley and Jackson 2013). The coding stage comprised a first automated round of attribute coding, with several further rounds of manual coding: key themes, emergent themes, node reorganisation, in addition to cross-checks, conceptual maps, queries and matrices and supported by corpus linguistics methods (for details of these processes see Scott 2016 for the project under discussion, and more generally Bazeley 2009). The results were then structured using theoretical models that had been developed alongside the fieldwork, to directly address the research questions. Said theoretical models include a multidimensional description of legal translation performance, a tripartite model of legal translation constraints, and a detailed articulation of the legal translation briefing process. I will not attempt to report on the outcomes of this large project in the limited space available here, but interested readers will find extensive discussions in Scott (2016).

5 Conclusions

In the little-researched field of externalised legal translation, the online survey enabled the researcher's net to be cast far and wide, both geographically and in terms of respondent profiles. Insights were gained in a wide range of language pairs, genres, jurisdictions and areas of law. These could be built upon in the future and inform detailed studies with more restricted perimeters. The questionnaire approach seemed to fit the target audience, judging by high completion rates and the rich data obtained. While piloting and meticulous preparation are the *sine qua non* of survey-based research, in this instance triangulation and in-depth multi-perspective data analysis were both crucial to the robustness of project results. In closing this discussion of a project which originated in practice and was carried out by a practitioner-researcher, let me reiterate the importance of treating participants with the utmost respect, recognising the stake they have in our results, and ensuring that as much as possible is made of the outcomes.

Notes

1 Regarding those who kindly accept to provide researchers with insights into their professional worlds, I use in this chapter the terms "respondent", "participant" and "informant". It is worth noting, however, the recommendations of the Association for Qualitative Research regarding the term "respondent": "the research subject is no longer regarded as a passive object to be studied, being kept in the dark about the research and its objectives and simply 'responding', but as a valued partner in an exploratory process". www.aqr.org.uk/glossary/respondent.
2 May also be referred to as "action research", "participatory action research", "practitioner-led inquiry", or "community action research" with various subtleties of focus and meaning according to different authors.
3 SurveyMonkey, used by many researchers as a hosting platform, offers detailed free resources on aspects of creating, running and analysing online surveys that may be consulted in complement to the literature: www.surveymonkey.com/mp/survey-guidelines/?ut_source=header.
4 This measure was taken as a result of feedback from fellow legal translation studies scholar and practising translator, Dr Gianluca Pontrandolfo.

5 During the course of the research, Wufoo was absorbed by the SurveyMonkey Group, but remained operational separately and under its own branding.
6 Potential changes resulted from the CJEU judgment of 6 October 2015 (Case C-362–14, Maximillian Schrems v Data Protection Commissioner [2015] EU:C:2015:650), but project data was collected before that date. At the time of writing researchers in Europe fall subject to the General Data Protection Regulation (GDPR). Data protection and privacy developments are continuing apace worldwide, and it is clearly essential for researchers to keep abreast.
7 www.wordstodeeds.com
8 Depending, for example, on epistemological stance, on representativeness, on data quality, or on the research project's financial or time constraints.

References

Alessi, G.M. and Jacobs, G., eds. (2015). *The ins and outs of business and professional discourse research: Reflections on interacting with the workplace.* Basingstoke: Palgrave Macmillan.

ATA [American Translators Association]. (2016). *ATA translation and interpreting services survey fifth edition.* Alexandria, VA: ATA.

Bazeley, P. (2009). Analysing qualitative data: More than 'identifying themes'. *The Malaysian Journal of Qualitative Research*, 2 (2), pp. 6–22.

Bazeley, P. and Jackson, K. (2013). *Qualitative data analysis with NVivo.* London: Sage.

BDÜ [Bundesverband der Dolmetscher und Übersetzer – German translators' association]. (2015). *Honorarspiegel für Übersetzungs und Dolmetschleistungen.* Berlin: BDÜ.

Biel, Ł. (2017). Researching legal translation: A multi-perspective and mixed-method framework for legal translation. *Revista de Llengua i Dret, Journal of Language and Law*, 68, pp. 76–88.

Biel, Ł. and Engberg, J. (2013). Research models and methods in legal translation. *Linguistica Antverpiensia*, 12, pp. 1–11.

Bryman, A. (2004). Triangulation. *In*: M.S. Lewis-Beck, *et al.*, eds. *The SAGE encyclopedia of social science research methods.* London: Sage, pp. 1142–1143.

Bryman, A. (2006). Integrating quantitative and qualitative research: How is it done? *Qualitative Research*, 6, pp. 97–113.

Chan, D. (2009). So why ask me? Are self-report data really that bad? *In:* C.E. Lance and R.J. Vandenberg, eds. *Statistical and methodological myths and urban legends: Doctrine, verity, and fable in the organizational and social sciences.* New York: Routledge, pp. 309–336.

CIOL/ITI [Chartered Institute of Linguists/Institute of Translation and Interpreting] (2011). *Rates and salaries survey for translators and interpreters.* London: CIOL/ITI.

CIUTI/Schmitt, P.A., *et al.* (2015). *CIUTI survey 2014.* Geneva: CIUTI.

Common Sense Advisory (2010–18). *The language services market. Annual survey.* Cambridge, MA: Common Sense Advisory.

Corpas Pastor, G., Zaretskaya, A. and Seghiri, M. (2015). Translators' requirements for translation technologies: A user survey. *In: New horizons in translation and interpreting studies.* Geneva: Tradulex.

Dam, H.V. and Zethsen, K.K. (2008). Translator status. A study of Danish company translators. *The Translator*, 14 (1), pp. 71–96.

Dam, H.V. and Zethsen, K.K. (2009). Who said low status? A study on factors affecting the perception of translator status. *The Journal of Specialised Translation*, 12, pp. 2–36.

Dam, H.V. and Zethsen, K.K. (2011). The status of professional business translators on the Danish market: A comparative study of company, agency and freelance translators. *Meta*, 56 (4), pp. 976–997.

Denscombe, M. (2007). *The good research guide for small-scale social research projects.* Maidenhead: McGraw-Hill Open University Press.

De Palma, D.A. and Stewart, R.G., (2012). *Trends in translation pricing.* Cambridge, MA: Common Sense Advisory.

Dillon, S. and Fraser, J. (2006). Translators and TM: An investigation of translators' perceptions of translation memory adoption. *Machine Translation*, 20, pp. 67–79.

Drugan, J. (2013). *Quality in professional translation.* London: Bloomsbury.

European Commission/CIOL/ITI [Chartered Institute of Linguists/Institute of Translation and Interpreting] (2017). *UK translator survey.* London: European Commission.

EUATC [European Union of Associations of Translation Companies] (2017). *Expectations and concerns of the European language industry.* Brussels: EUATC.

Ferreira Alves, F. (2012). Translation companies in Portugal. *Anglo Saxonica*, III, (3), pp. 233–263.

Fraser, J. (1997, June). Briefing? What briefing? Findings of a survey on the flow of information between clients, translation agencies or companies and freelance translators. *ITI Bulletin*, pp. 13–16.

Fraser, J. (2000). The broader view: How freelance translators define translation competence. *In:* C. Schäffner and B. Adab, eds. *Developing translation competence.* Amsterdam: John Benjamins, pp. 51–62.

Frayling, C. (1993). Research in art and design. *Royal College of Art Research Papers*, 1 (1), pp. 1–5.

Fulford, H. and Granell Zafra, J. (2004). The uptake of online tools and web-based language resources by freelance translators: Implications for translator training, professional development, and research. *In: Coling 2004: Proceedings of the second international workshop on language resources for translation work, research & training.* Geneva: University of Geneva, pp. 50–57.

Gallego-Hernández, D. (2015). The use of corpora as translation resources: A study based on a survey of Spanish professional translators. *Perspectives*, 23 (3), pp. 375–391.

Gaspari, F., Almaghout, H. and Doherty, S. (2015). A survey of machine translation competences: Insights for translation technology educators and practitioners. *Perspectives*, 23 (3), pp. 333–358.

Gough, J. (2011). An empirical study of professional translators' attitudes, use and awareness of web 2.0 technologies, and implications for the adoption of emerging technologies and trends. *Linguistica Antverpiensia*, 10, pp. 195–217.

Hertog, E. and Van Gucht, J., eds. (2008). *Status quaestionis: Questionnaire on the provision of legal interpreting and translation in the EU.* Antwerp: Intersentia.

Hewson, C. (2015). Research methods on the internet. *In:* L. Cantoni and J.A. Danowski, eds. *Communication and technology.* Berlin: De Gruyter Mouton, pp. 277–302.

Jääskeläinen, R. and Mauranen, A. (2006). Translators at work: A case study of electronic tools used by translators in industry. *In:* G. Barnbrook, *et al.*, eds. *Meaningful texts: The extraction of semantic information from monolingual and multilingual corpora*. London: Continuum International, pp. 48–53.

Katan, D. (2009). Translation theory and professional practice: A global survey of the great divide. *Hermes*, 42, pp. 111–153.

Katan, D. (2011). Occupation or profession: A survey of the translator's world. *In:* R. Sela-Sheffy and M. Shlesinger, eds. *Identity and status in the translational professions*. Amsterdam: Benjamins, pp. 11–30.

Lagoudaki, E. (2006). *Translation memories survey 2006*. London: Imperial College.

Mayer-Schönberger, V. and Cukier, K. (2013). *Big data: A revolution that will transform how we live, work and think*. London: John Murray.

McAuliffe, K. (2016). Hidden translators: The invisibility of translators and the influence of lawyer-linguists on the case law of the Court of Justice of the European Union. *Language and Law/Linguagem e Direito*, 3 (1), pp. 5–29.

MeLLANGE (Multilingual eLearning in LANGuage Engineering), 2006, Apr. 20. *Corpora & e-learning questionnaire results summary*. Available at: http://mellange.eila.univ-paris-diderot.fr/Mellange-Results-1.pdf [Accessed 10 Oct. 2018].

Monzó, E. (2002). *La professió del traductor jurídic i jurat: Descripció sociològica de la professió i anàlisi discursiva del transgènere*. Thesis (PhD). Castelló: Universitat Jaume I.

Noy, C. (2008). Sampling knowledge: The hermeneutics of snowball sampling in qualitative research. *International Journal of Social Research Methodology*, 11 (4), pp. 327–344.

Olohan, M. (2011). Translators and translation technology: The dance of agency. *Translation Studies*, 4 (3), pp. 342–357.

Olohan, M. and Davitti, E. (2015). Dynamics of trusting in translation project management: Leaps of faith and balancing acts. *Journal of Contemporary Ethnography*, 46 (4), pp. 391–416.

Orlando, D. (2016). *The trials of legal translation competence: Triangulating processes and products of translators vs. lawyers*. Thesis (PhD). Trieste: University of Trieste.

Orlando, D. (2018). The problem of legal phraseology. A case of translators vs lawyers. *In:* S. Gozdz-Roszkowski and G. Pontrandolfo, eds. *Phraseology in legal and institutional settings*. Abingdon: Routledge.

OTTIAQ [Ordre des traducteurs, terminologues et interprètes agréés du Québec] (2014). *Sondage de 2014 sur la tarification et les revenus*. Montreal: OTTIAQ.

ProZ (2010–12). *State of the industry*. Syracuse, NY: ProZ.

PwC (2012). *Translation bureau benchmarking and comparative analysis final report*. Available at: https://ailia.ca/dl359 [Accessed 10 Oct. 2018].

Pym, A., *et al.* (2012). *The status of the translation profession in the European Union*. Luxembourg: European Commission.

Qualetra (2013). *Testing, assessment and evaluation on the current legal translation practices in criminal proceedings in the EU*. Brussels: European Commission.

Rasmussen, K.W. and Schjoldager, A. (2011). Revising translations: A survey of revision policies in Danish translation companies. *The Journal of Specialised Translation*, 15, pp. 87–120.

Robson, C. (2011). *Real world research: A resource for social scientists and practitioner-researchers*. Oxford: Blackwell.

Rust, C., *et al.* (2007). *Review of practice-led research in art, design & architecture*. London: Arts and Humanities Research Council.

Scott, J.R. (2016). *Optimising the performance of outsourced legal translation.* Thesis (PhD). Bristol: University of Bristol. [publication Oxford University Press Oct. 2018 as *Legal Translation Outsourced*].

SDL (2016). *Translation technology insights.* Maidenhead: SDL.

SDL (2017). *Corporate translation technology survey.* Maidenhead: SDL.

SDL/AMTA [Association for Machine Translation in the Americas]/EAMT [European Association for Machine Translation] (2010). *Trends in automated translation.* Maidenhead: SDL.

Seidel, J.V. (1998). Qualitative data analysis. Appendix to the *The Ethnograph v4. Manual.* Available at: www.qualisresearch.com [Accessed 10 Oct. 2018].

SFT [Syndicat national des traducteurs professionnels – French translators' association] (2015). *Enquête 2015 sur les pratiques professionnelles des métiers de la traduction.* Paris: SFT.

Slatyer, H. and Napier, J. (2010). *The kaleidoscope of practice.* Sydney: Macquarie University.

TAUS (2017). *The translation industry in 2022.* De Rijp: TAUS.

TAUS, *et al.* (2015). *Translation quality evaluation.* De Rijp: TAUS.

Toepoel, V. (2015). *Doing surveys online.* London: Sage.

Wright, K.B. (2006). Researching internet-based populations: Advantages and disadvantages of online survey research, online questionnaire authoring software packages, and web survey services. *Journal of Computer-Mediated Communication*, 10 (3). doi:10.1111/j.1083-6101.2005.tb00259.x.

Appendix 1

Translator surveys (1997–2017)

The following list is a cross-section of translator surveys carried out by academics, professional associations, institutions and commercial enterprises. The list is not exhaustive and it seeks only to illustrate the variety of types of subject examined, methods and respondent profiles.

Authors/Organisation	*Date(s)*	*Method(s)*	*Subject/title*	*Informants/data sources*
ATA	2016	Online questionnaire	Pricing: "Translation and Interpreting Compensation Survey" (5th edition)	"translation and interpreting professionals worldwide [ATA members . . .] Approximately two-thirds of the respondents reside in the U.S., 15% in Europe, 6% in South America, 4% in Canada, and the remaining 6% in other locations" Numbers not specified for public access. The previous edition in 2008 was drawn from 979 responses.
BDÜ	2015	Online questionnaire	Fees: Honorarspiegel für Übersetzungs und Dolmetschleistungen	1,100 translators and interpreters, BDÜ members
CIOL/ITI	2011	Online questionnaire	"Rates and Salaries Survey for Translators and Interpreters"	1743 translators and interpreters, members of 2 UK translators' associations and other related associations, 2/3 UK-based and others based around the world
CIUTI/Schmitt, Gerstmeyer, & Müller	2015	Online questionnaire	Training & employment	Translation and interpreting graduates "2,813 respondents from 42 institutes in 19 countries"
Common Sense Advisory	2010–2018	Online questionnaire or direct phone & email	The Language Services Market	"our annual survey and report gather information from a representative sample of our validated database of over 18,000 language service and technology suppliers"
Corpas Pastor, Zaretskaya, & Seghiri	2015	Online questionnaire	"Translators' Requirements for Translation Technologies: a User Survey"	736 completed responses from 88 countries, majority of translators were experienced and worked freelance

Dam & Zethsen	2008 2009 2011	Paper-based questionnaire	Translator status	244 professional translators working on the Danish market: 47 company translators, 66 agency translators & 131 freelance translators
De Palma & Stewart/ Common Sense Advisory	2012	Online questionnaire	Trends in Translation Pricing	"translation rates for 222 language pairs from 3,772 providers in 114 countries. Our data includes responses from an online survey and rate tables from freelancer websites"
Dillon & Fraser	2006	Online questionnaire	Translation memory adoption by translators	59 responses: "translators from the main researcher's own cohort at the University of Westminster and from the Peer Mentoring Group and the French, German and Spanish e-groups of the UK-based Institute of Translation and Interpreting, representing a wide span of ages and levels of experience"
Drugan	2013	Interviews, questionnaires completed during visits, work shadowing	Translation quality	"a representative range of LSPs [language service providers], clients and support services"
European Commission Representation in the UK/ CIOL/ITI	2017	Online questionnaire	"UK Translator Survey"	588 respondents (anonymous)
EUATC	2017	Online questionnaire [presumed from report]	"Expectations and concerns of the European language industry"	866 responses from 49 countries, "including many outside Europe": companies, individuals, translation departments, training institutes, others

(*Continued*)

Appendix 1 (Continued)

Authors/Organisation	*Date(s)*	*Method(s)*	*Subject/title*	*Informants/data sources*
Ferreira Alves	2012	Paper-based questionnaire [presumed from Annex to paper]	"a sociological survey of some of the major translation agencies operating in Portugal"	12 "translation companies" in Portugal
Fraser	1997 2000	Paper-based questionnaire	Working conditions and status of freelance translators	296 freelance translators (UK-based and worldwide), 84 UK-based translation agencies and companies
Fulford & Granell Zafra	2004	Paper-based questionnaire	Tools and resources used by freelance translators, ICT adoption	390 UK-based freelance translators
Gallego-Hernández	2015	Online questionnaire	Corpora as translation resources	526 Spanish professional translators, working freelance, at agencies, companies and institutions, and as project managers
Gaspari, Almaghout, & Doherty	2015	Online questionnaire	Machine translation competences	438 responses, most from 21 countries, working for "institutions, companies or organisations of all sizes", many of whom were translators, academics and many fulfilled more than one role
Gough	2011	Online questionnaire	Professional translators' attitudes, use and awareness of Web 2.0 technologies	224 usable responses from 42 countries, professional translators
Hertog & Van Gucht	2008	Online questionnaire	"*Status quaestionis:* Questionnaire on the provision of legal interpreting and translation in the EU".	194 respondents from 27 Member States, some governmental, some professional

Jääskeläinen & Mauranen	2006	Interviews, translation logs, paper-based questionnaire	Use of electronic tools by translators in industry in Finland	Translators (in-house & freelance, small translation agencies): interviews (5), translation logs (10), paper-based questionnaire [no figure]
Katan	2009 2011	Online questionnaire	Translation theory and professional practice: a global survey of the great divide	1151 replies, from translators and interpreters in 25 countries which comprises 98% of respondents
Lagoudaki	2006	Pilot: Interviews, focus group Main survey: Online questionnaire	"Translation Memories Survey"	Pilot: 18 translation professionals Main survey: 874 translation professionals from 54 countries
McAuliffe	2016	Interviews, participant observation, documentary	Lawyer-linguists at the Court of Justice of the European Union	78 interviews, participant interactions in professional and informal contexts. Triangulation with existing literature and comparable studies.
MeLLANGE [university consortium]	2006	Online questionnaire 56% Paper-based questionnaire 44%	Corpora and E-learning	Total 1015 respondents, UK 567, France 125, Germany 25, Italy 19, Spain 4, Undefined 275
Monzó	2002	Questionnaire (paper), sample translations	Status and sociological analysis of the legal translation profession in Spain	400 questionnaires, sample translations
Olohan	2011	Translators' online forums	Use of translation memories	Discussion threads

(*Continued*)

Appendix 1 (Continued)

Authors/Organisation	*Date(s)*	*Method(s)*	*Subject/title*	*Informants/data sources*
Olohan & Davitti	2015	Participant observation, interviews, artefacts from field sites	Translation project management	Sites of ethnography: 2 UK-based translation companies. Field and analytical notes from 150 hours of observation and informal conversations, artefacts (including documents stipulating policies and procedures), transcripts of 7 interviews.
Orlando	2016 2018	Paper-based questionnaire	Legal translator training and competences	"15 MA-level translation trainees with no specialisation in the legal domain", "15 linguistically-skilled postgraduate lawyers with no translation-related qualification"
OTTIAQ	2014	Online questionnaire	Pricing (services, per language pair, according to experience)	394 respondents, OTTIAQ members
ProZ [online translation platform]	2010 2011 2012	Online questionnaire	"State of the industry"	Respondents: ProZ members. Details of data not public.
PwC (PricewaterhouseCoopers LLP)/Government of Canada	2012	Interviews, publications	"Translation Bureau Benchmarking and Comparative Analysis"	Comparative analysis: "five Canadian and three international language services organizations". Benchmarking: overview of global translation market

Pym *et al.*, DGT	2012	Data-gathering from various sources: literature review of other surveys; questionnaire to translators' associations and translation scholars; follow-up exchanges.	"The status of the translation profession in the European Union"	Translators' associations and some 100 experts and informants (EU countries and comparisons with the United States, Canada and Australia)
QUALETRA (Work Stream 4, Assessment)	2013	Electronic	"Testing, Assessment and Evaluation on the Current Legal Translation Practices in Criminal Proceedings in the EU"	464 responses: "Translator trainers, Legal practitioners, Professional associations"
Rasmussen & Schjoldager	2011	Online questionnaire	Revision policies in Danish translation companies	24 translators and related positions (e.g. project managers, proofreaders, language engineers)
Scott	2016	Online questionnaires (2)	Briefing and performance of outsourced legal translation	84 principals, for the most part from leading law firms and corporations, in 33 countries and five continents, and 303 legal translation practitioners from 41 countries and six continents.
SDL/AMTA/EAMT	2010	Online questionnaire	"Trends in automated translation"	"228 individuals in global business"

(*Continued*)

Appendix 1 (Continued)

Authors/Organisation	*Date(s)*	*Method(s)*	*Subject/title*	*Informants/data sources*
SDL	2016	Online questionnaire	"Translation Technology Insights"	"2,784 responses globally from individuals involved in some way with translation or translation technology. Our respondents comprise freelance translators, employees of translation agencies and translation-related roles within business and public-sector organizations".
SDL	2017	Online questionnaire	"Corporate Translation Technology Survey"	"hundreds of organizations in the private and public sector [. . .] 554 respondents, from dozens of countries worldwide"
SFT	2015	Online questionnaire	Pricing (location, supplements, practices, per language pair)	1140 completed, association members (54%) non-members 46%), regions of France 75%, outside France 25%
Slatyer & Napier	2010	Online questionnaire	"The Kaleidoscope of Practice"	"800 surveys [. . .] returned by translator and interpreter practitioners from all over Australia"
TAUS/van der Meer & Görög	2015	Online questionnaire	Translation quality evaluation	"In-house staff" 38%; "translators or academic staff" 33%; "translation companies" [no further details of respondents]
TAUS	2017	"Consultation surveys"	"The Translation Industry in 2022"	Members of TAUS community; "202 responses [. . .] from decision makers, people on director level and business owners"

11 Interviewing legal interpreters and translators

Framing status perceptions and interactional and structural power

Esther Monzó-Nebot

1 The spectrum for sociological approaches to legal interpreting and translation

The different turns in Translation and Interpreting Studies (TIS) have widened the scope of topics and approaches to the issues relevant to translation and interpreting. Such broadened scope has enabled TIS scholars to embrace different research ideologies and strategies and to increase the variety and complexity of data gathering and data analysis methods and techniques. Although there is no strict link between the approaches and turns (linguistic, textual, cultural, social, ethical, activist; see Tymoczko 2007), and the ideologies (positivism, interpretative pragmatism, constructivism, critical and activist approaches, etc.), the strategies (inductive, deductive; focus on specific units and levels of analysis; specific hypotheses), the methods (including survey, experiment, case study, action-research, ethnography, grounded theory, Delphi, mixed methods, etc.), or the techniques (observation, process tracing, interview, narrative analysis, statistics, correlation, etc.), specific combinations may offer more streamlined designs. If, for example, our aim is to study how ergonomics impact interpreting and translation performance, an experimental design would allow for a nuanced distinction of the bearing of the different variables under scrutiny in the final results. However, if we want to analyse how interpreters prioritise their professional duties, a survey or case study method would provide more suitable frameworks for our research.

Sociological approaches to TIS aim to describe and explain how translators and interpreters individually and collectively construct and interact with social structures, that is, their socio-political contexts, as non-geographical boundaries. Such approaches focus on interactions, attitudes and perceptions, exchanges, processes of group formation, coordination mechanisms, norms, power construction, ideological conflicts, on how other actors emerge in their social dynamics, on how other groups interact and impact their social interactions, etc. With this broad scope, sociological approaches may materialise in studies at the level of actors, systems or socio-historic developments, or combine those levels if research questions so require.

A prevalent interest in both sociology and TIS is *power* and the most influential definition is Weber's notion of power as the ability of an individual or group to impose their will and achieve their goals, even when others are trying to prevent them from fulfilling their aims or are pursuing their own competing goals (1922, p. 29). Social power derives from economic, ideological/cultural, political but also physical or, especially since the Cold War, military factors (Mann 1993). Power is socially constructed and recognised and it is contingent on variables such as gender, class, age, race or language, which are culture-bound but also depend on and impact social stratification, relations and mobilities (Hill Collins 1998). In constructing power, translation and interpreting in legal and institutional contexts have long been seen as much more than means for interlinguistic communication and their uses in intercultural and intergroup recognition (Fraser 1995; Kraus 2007, 2018), empowerment (Arendt [1958] 1998) and/or domination (Weber 1958) are a growing interdisciplinary interest (see Sosoni 2005; Martín Ruano 2018). In developing the idea of *ethnolinguistic democracy*, Fishman stressed the role of institutional and diplomatic translation and interpreting in safeguarding cooperation and seeking symmetry by showing respect for other cultures (Fishman 1993). Other authors have focused on asymmetric uses, where translation and interpreting are operated in gatekeeping the ideas of justice entering specific societies (Rodríguez García 2010) or in (re)producing, reinforcing and also contesting dominating power relations (Benrabah 2005; Vidal Claramonte 2013; Martín Ruano 2014). Furthermore, language is also one of the (culture-bound) categories organising society, and legal interpreting and translation (LIT) are determinant in ensuring that the different linguistic groups present within the boundaries of societies can access their rights (Steytler 1993; Erasmus 2000; Mikkelson 2000, p. 48; Reed *et al.* 2001; Valero-Garcés 2007; Abel 2009), including their linguistic human rights (Skutnabb-Kangas 1998; Krausneker 2000; Sanz Moreno 2017). Against the background of growing diversity, studying how the availability and quality of LIT impact social structures and the relations between different (also linguistic) social groups becomes urgent (Monzó-Nebot and Jiménez-Salcedo 2018). The links between LIT and the very notions of justice and democracy may hold the key to the success of our future societies (Monzó-Nebot 2018).

The interaction between cultural and social factors that reveals itself when approaching power is also conspicuous when considering the ethical dimensions of LIT. Conceptions of what is right and what is wrong are central in distinguishing cultures and ethnic groups (Barth 1969), as examined in anthropology, ethnography and cultural studies. Indeed, in establishing the agenda for *Translator* Studies, Chesterman (2009) featured ethics as an interest of the cultural approaches. Nonetheless, ethical ideals and ethical endeavours influence social development and may be considered within the scope of Sociology. The ethical aspects of society concerned sociologists at an early stage (Addams 1902; Hoffding 1905; Mead 1908; Martineau [1838] 1989). Also, Durkheim (1950) developed his thoughts on professional ethics around the same time, and his views have deeply influenced the development of Translation and Interpreting

Profession Studies (TIPS). Durkheim saw professionals as *corps intermédiaires*, closer to human needs and individual interests than governments, and therefore able to assess and take into account their contexts and special circumstances when regulating and providing specific services (Durkheim 1893, p. xxxiii). Under Durkheim's functional views on society, professions are legitimated by their function and their solidarity with the societies they serve to become sources of moral norms (Durkheim 1893, p. xi) and enforceable rules pertaining to their professional field. Although TIS has indeed developed philosophical and cultural reflections on ethics in attempting to define the role of translation and interpreting in modern societies (Chesterman 1997; Tymoczko 2000; Prunč 2005; Inghilleri 2008; Hebenstreit 2018), the research in the field of LIT has prominently focused on the ethics of professional practice from a functionalist view. Professionalisation models (Tseng 1992; Mikkelson 1996; Monzó-Nebot 2002; Witter-Merithew and Johnson 2004; Wadensjö 2007; Pym *et al.* 2012; Chen and Liao 2016; Resta and Ioannidis 2016) are greatly influenced by the *trait approach* in the Sociology of Professions, that is, an early stage of reflection when the main interest was to define the very term and establish distinctions and boundaries between professions and other occupations. In doing so, historically rooted descriptions have been at times taken as models or guidelines for describing or even diagnosing needs – mainly referred to structures and institutions rather than competences or attitudes – but also relations and expectations. From a functionalist approach, codes of ethics are drafted by professional groups to ensure a common set of values and rules guaranteeing that practitioners are free from undue influence in developing their role and duties and that society is protected against malpractice. The values and rules which are deemed necessary and common, however, vary between different translation- and interpreting-specific codes of practice (McDonough 2011).

Beyond a functionalist view, Lambert observes those codes under a neoweberian light (2018), as a tool for translators and interpreters to arrogate authority and create trust, which is essential in ensuring the success of the professional group when facing competition (Monzó-Nebot 2009). In so doing, the neutrality of the professionals and their organisations is questioned, and claiming neutrality for the professionals is seen as a politicised strategy rather than an imperative on practice (Lambert 2018, p. 285). As deeply rooted in LIT codes of practice as they may be, neutrality and impartially in linguistic mediation are increasingly viewed as disguises of the dominating ideologies, therefore serving power (Beaton 2007, 2010), chimeric (Koskinen 2000; Vidal Claramonte 2013; Martín Ruano 2015) and empirically disproven (Angermeyer 2009; Tryuk 2012; Beaton-Thome 2013). Alternative ethical principles are being observed in practice (Inghilleri 2008; Valero-Garcés 2016), and the ambivalence of roles as construed by codes of conduct, practitioners and societies (Hale 2005; Mason 2005) causes a potentially paralysing cognitive dissonance.

Another topic receiving considerable attention in legal TIPS is that of accreditation. Establishing an exclusive jurisdiction over a professional domain of practice is a process requiring both social closure (Weber 1922, p. 177, 1958; Parkin

1974) and the public's trust and recognition (Wilensky 1964; Berlant 1975). Accreditation is one of the mechanisms usually tied to this process. By linking the practice of a particular task to a body of knowledge and the acquisition of that knowledge to training programs or tests of knowledge, credentials provide barriers and boundaries with the lay and untrained public, as well as an external sign that can be readily recognised and valued (Pym *et al.* 2012). Studies in LIT explore how different contexts make different credentials available (Napier 2004; Salvador i Padrosa 2006; Roberts-Smith 2007; Hlavac 2013; Salmi and Kinnunen 2015), highlighting specific issues, such as the limited availability of testing for less translated languages (Fiola 2000), offering insights into the designs of licensing processes (Hertog *et al.* 2007), and suggesting improvements in relevant tests (Roberts 2000; Wallace 2013, 2015), especially in the fields of sworn translation and court interpreting.

From a social microperspective, scholars in LIT have looked into the dynamics of specific workplaces. In describing power relations and practices (Takeda 2008), scrutinising the complex forces at work in identity processes (Koskinen 2008), or studying the implementation of new technologies and its practical consequences (Braun and Taylor 2011), scholars have made use of case studies to shed light on particular and framework conditions impacting the processes, the aims and the results of LIT. The microsocial look has led the way in studies of the role that interpreters and translators can, should, or do actually play in legal settings (Valero-Garcés 2007; Hale 2008; Jacobsen 2009), and the look becomes even more nuanced in studies of *facework* (Jacobsen 2001; Lee 2013, 2015) and *footing* (Wadensjö 1998; Kent 2007), where particular interventions of interpreters and translators are examined in quest of their interpretation and uses of social relations. Also attitudes towards and perceptions of LIT have been analysed by focusing on specific workplaces (Berk-Seligson 1990; McAuliffe 2009) and on specific groups with social entitativity (Napier and Rohan 2007; Napier 2011; Gascón Navarro 2015; Valero-Garcés and Lázaro Gutiérrez 2016). Both this microperspective and the structural macroperspective are combined in studies adopting Bourdieu's practice theory (Bourdieu 1972) to explore the social geographies of translation and interpreting and professionals' understanding and enactment of the social and their possibilities (Monzó-Nebot 2005; Vidal Claramonte 2005; Valero-Garcés and Gauthier 2010).

In studying external social structures and the individuals' subjective experiences, either separately or in interaction, quantitative and qualitative goals may be adopted. A quantitative goal would seek to isolate and define categories and would prefer techniques that allow to determine the relationship between those categories with the greatest possible precision. A qualitative goal would be more suitable when researchers aim at developing analytic frameworks (for instance, when their object of study has not been sufficiently explored and the categories themselves still need to be determined) or when they expect categories to change over time (Glaser and Strauss 1965). The same research project may combine both goals in inquiring, for instance, about individuals' motivations to specialise in legal interpreting or translation. A qualitative design would allow for those motivations to be identified and related to specific categories, such as context or personal-specific variables and interrelationships. Then a quantitative approach may be used to determine whether any or all the motivations identified are widely shared by legal interpreters and translators. A qualitative approach offers a broader vision of any object, which allows complexities to emerge in the course of the research, whereas the quantitative approach narrows down the lens to achieve greater focus and precision.

The diversity characterising the sociological approaches to LIT does not allow to identify a common research agenda, such as those advanced by Toury's norms in Descriptive Translation Studies (Toury 1978, 1995) or Simeoni's subservient habitus hypothesis (Simeoni 1998). Sociological approaches are heterogeneous as to goals, hypotheses, methods and techniques but they can be together understood as a special social science in that they focus on one aspect of human activity, that is, mediated communication, from a sociological stance.

2 Status as a sociological issue in translation and interpreting studies

Status is a common concern in Profession Studies. In TIPS, the lack or loss of status affecting the translation and interpreting professions has been a pervasive topic. Either as the conclusion of empirical studies (Katan 2011; Mirsafian 2012; Pym *et al.* 2012) or as the premise for further elaboration (Morris 1995; Bassnett 1996; Scott 2017), the relative low positions of translators and interpreters within social structures has generally been posed as a challenge to professional development and an actionable issue for researchers and practitioners.

Quantitative, qualitative and mixed-method approaches to status in TIPS have shown a predominant reliance on self-reported methods where translators and interpreters themselves are asked to appraise their relative positions within societies or workplaces. When perceptions are the intended goal (Setton and Liangliang 2009), such an approach can provide key insights and contribute to a number of goals, such as systematising the network of beliefs within the translation and interpreting community. However, using introspective methods to purportedly access a true and accurate reflection of the structural situation being researched (Dam and Zethsen 2012) would be methodologically flawed. Indeed, when approaching social phenomena, correctly identifying subjective (experienced by one person), intersubjective (collectively recognised by individuals within a society or a smaller social group) as well as structural factors and constructs becomes essential in ensuring scientific rigour. The challenge of reconciling external social structures and the individuals' subjective experiences has been addressed by the social sciences, and solutions have been imported into TIS, most notably through Bourdieu's practice theory (Bourdieu 1972, 1997). Self-reported accounts, either as dyadic or monadic exercises but also as polyadic endeavours (such as focus groups), are mediated by values and belief systems, interpretations, biases and commitments. As informative and enriching as such data are, they cannot be taken at face value. Using multiple sources of data to triangulate the findings (Koskinen 2008, pp. 149–150) is an appropriate strategy if the aim is to shed light on structural concepts (both at large, for a society, and for smaller groups, such as workplace contexts).

To successfully determine what research design can provide insights in the selected object of study, developing our conceptual model – that is, the operationalisation of our central concepts – becomes imperative as it has empirical consequences and it impacts the validity of conclusions. A primary concern in defining the conceptual model is the distinction between related terms affecting the object of study. In the case at hand, *status* is particularly prone to confusions. Generally defined as structural ranking of individuals or groups within a common scale of perceived hierarchy, the determinants for having relatively higher or lower status than other groups or individuals are complex and encompass other categories such as power, influence and dominance (Magee and Galinsky 2008; Fiske 2010), reputation (Gould 2002), prestige and respect (Anderson *et al.* 2006; Fragale *et al.* 2011). A first step would be then to operationalise *status*.

2.1 A conceptual model for status

Within TIPS, issues of status usually respond to professionalisation concerns and are generally linked to demands for higher social awareness, visibility, prestige, salaries, or professional ranks. As a central concept to every approach in the study of professions, either as a means of control or as a way to achieve social power, status is indeed an integral part of definitions of *profession* and *professionalisation* (Elliott 1972). The assumption is that society is stratified and that the number of positions at the top of the structure is limited, coveted and contested. Social mobility, however, is possible and higher status may be *attained* by climbing up the ladder (Müller and Pollak 2015) of the hierarchical order (Abbott 1981).

In this sense, status is understood as an objective position within a social structure, which is awarded intersubjectively and defined by the relative rank of individuals and groups, be it within society at large or within confined social spaces such as workplaces. As such, it is distinguishable from *perceived*, self-assessed status, on the one hand, and from *prestige*, on the other. Whereas *objective status* is defined by durable positions in a system, *perceived status* is the personal experience of such positions, part of the agents' system of beliefs, which may or may not find its match in the empirical world and yet looms large in their social experience. The ideas of self, including the relative positions of oneself and one's own group within social structures, are internalised by socialisation through interaction with significant others (Berger and Luckman 1966), and work as a mechanism to align the conduct of members within a group. Indeed, such ideas support one particular orthodoxy, even though this may become invalid and require readapting in different social spheres, workplaces, cultures or periods. Albeit no direct experience might have been acquired in a field, images and expectations of the positions of the different agents may be built at a distance through the narratives circulated within social spaces, in training and personal relations. Such ideas are taken for granted and acted upon as a practical truth – they shape action and reproduce themselves in further interactions. In Einstein's terms, such spooky action at a distance, or "quantum entanglement" (Einstein *et al.* 1935), causes the discipline to continue to operate and be complied with "even when the perception no longer takes place" (Bottici 2014, p. 18).

Prestige is another relevant notion in this conceptual model. If status is rank, and therefore supported by the structure, prestige is "respect freely conferred from others who seek proximity to capable individuals" (Hays 2013); it is acknowledged and allocated by other members of society either backed by or against field forces, and establishes relationships of "deference, acceptance and derogation" (Goldthorpe and Hope 1972, p. 2). A person in any occupation commonly seen as having low-status may garner high levels of prestige and be allocated deference and preference (materialised in decision-making power, interpersonal trust and the like); conversely, any individual from a high-status group may be derogated in interaction, even by those sharing the same social group. Indeed, prestige allocation can be challenged, reassessed, or engendered for specific interactions and sustained subsequently for the same individuals, thereby allowing for prestige and status to depart from each other even without further influencing the social structure. Within TIS, such a distinction has not been adopted and, as pointed out by Ruokonen (2013), prestige has been used as a synonym to structural status (see Dam and Zethsen 2011), or used without providing any specific definition. However, the distinction of these two concepts is key in designing research, as empirical studies have shown that factors such as gender differences impact prestige for specific individuals even though they may share the same occupation and objective status (Powell and Jacobs 2013).

Prestige and status, both structural or objective and perceived or subjective, can be determined *interprofessionally* in relation to other occupational groups and *intraprofessionally*, in relation to colleagues of the same profession. The distinction has proven useful as unlike factors influence intra- and interprofessional interactions and perceptions. Abbott (1981), for instance, found that the higher positions of intraprofessional status were occupied by doctors who withdrew themselves from direct contact with patients, even when contact was seen as the source of high status in interprofessional perceptions. This would provide increased support for the need of rigorous conceptual distinctions.

As important as conceptual borders are in establishing the best method for our research, acknowledging their interactions in constructing social objects and phenomena is equally necessary. These notions share responsibility in the very possibility for groups and individuals to exert power, both in interaction (interpersonal power) and in social organisation (structural power), be it exercising the autonomy to define how a social problem should be addressed, attaining a position that ensures resources, or gaining respect. As stated previously, scholars in TIS consider high status or prestige achievement (depending on the conceptual boundaries used) to be a major concern for the discipline and its professionals to thrive, to negotiate and take decisions that are respected, to be visible. Indeed, there seems to be academic consensus that human beings show a preference for high social status (Frank 1985; Veblen 1994; Wright 1994; Gould 2003;

Brennan and Pettit 2004), even though some individuals and groups accept and perpetuate lower positions (Dumont 1970; Yanagisako and Delaney 1995) and others favour equality (Whitmeyer 2007).

The striving for structural and interpersonal power seems justified as empirical work continues to reveal the beneficial effects of the attainment and enactment of interpersonal power. Both better performance and higher job-related satisfaction have been reported in relation to interactional power: higher action tendencies (Galinsky *et al.* 2003), decreased procrastination (Judge and Bono 2001), improved goal attainment (Guinote 2007), greater creativity (Galinsky *et al.* 2008), optimism (Anderson and Galinsky 2006) and, last but not least, risk-taking attitudes (Anderson and Berdahl 2002; Anderson and Galinsky 2006) have been empirically linked to higher interactional power. Also, structural power shows reasons to be coveted. Power is an organising force within societies (Marx 1867), industries (Borenstein 1989), organisations (Courpasson 2000), teams (Anderson and Brown 2010) and also between social identities (Nadler 2002), individuals (Molm 1990) and personal behavioural options (Keltner *et al.* 2003). Power enables the subjugation, domination and manipulation of some (Gruenfeld *et al.* 2008) as it liberates others (Fleming and Spicer 2014).

Interactional power may be observed through deference and preference practices. These are enacted in interactions, influenced by the discipline acquired in socialisation, through past interactions and narratives, which portray a structure of relative positions and internalise conceptions of our personal and the social self. In turn, present interactions impact predispositions and future granting of interpersonal status; through time, they may impact the structure and result in differing levels of structural status. Status is thus a process and a state, attained and sustained socially (Harper 1988) in professional (Abbott 1981) but also everyday situations (Roscigno *et al.* 2007) through the way agents present themselves, especially through routinised interactive and discourse practices (Atkinson 1995; Sinclair 1997; Fournier 1999). It is also influenced by external characteristics such as signalling (cf. Pym *et al.* 2012) and preconceptions (Berger *et al.* 1972). The widespread image of translators as a low-status occupation may lead us to question the very possibility for translators to enjoy those benefits. However, when considering objective status, several institutions define translators and interpreters as professional staff (rather than support personnel) and confer the highest ranks possible to translation and interpreting positions.

Given the bearing of the perceptions of the relative positions of participants in any given relationship on the way professionals present themselves in interactions, and the impact of those interactions on how professional status evolves or may evolve, insights into translators' and interpreters' individual practices are critical. The question remains whether, as suggested by Gould (2003), the ambiguity between objective status on the one hand, and the perceived status on the other, can counter the benefits of high status in prestige allocation. In this chapter, using data gathered from in-depth interviews with professional translators and interpreters conducted by the author, it will be argued that, whereas objective status may be common to any given group of translators and interpreters within a system, perceived status shows significant individual variations. Additionally, I will put forward the idea that there is a relation between the perceived status and the interactional power enacted resulting in variations in deference granting and the tendencies and possibilities to challenge or perpetuate any given *status quo* and structural power. For the sake of brevity, further complexities examined in the project, such as the impact of the discrepancies between status and perceived status on job satisfaction; the bearing of roles arrogated and attributed to the agents sharing the same workspace; or the influence of the different dimensions of ownership in interactional power, subjective well-being and performance will not be included in this chapter.

3 In-depth interviews as techniques in social research

Finding the relations between perceived status and interactional practices, especially perceived deference and interactional power, requires us to explore a new territory of personal experiences where categories are yet to be determined. A qualitative survey method and techniques allowing for extended accounts of perceptions and experiences would make a suitable design to investigate such relations. Among qualitative techniques, interviews and narratives provide individuals with the space to elaborate their own accounts of social experiences. Interviews further let the researcher prime specific situations and guide the agents' accounts to explore the target areas. Among the different types of interviews (from structured one-time surveys to descriptive and interpretative open-ended questions in longitudinal studies or informal interviews to form hypotheses), in-depth interviews allow for a subject-centred approach and extensive accounts, protected by the necessary degree of confidentiality, which encode a wealth of data on personal experiences, where the subject and their particular views and behaviours are central to the research.

It must be noted that if conclusions were to be generalised in order to develop assumptions (for instance, as to what particular interactional models and *doxas* should inform training agendas), results should be triangulated with other methods, such as workplace observations and quantitative surveys. The data gathered with interviews and other self-reported narratives refer to subjective experiences – in this case, experiences of different social structures. As necessary sources in understanding translators' and interpreters' behaviour, the narratives of the agents themselves can provide the details of *what*, *how* and *why*, and open new avenues for research with designs that can further test the structural validity of the views collected.

In-depth interviews are particularly suitable for researching agents' perceptions and behaviours in social encounters and disentangling the meaning they make from their experiences. In these interviews, open-ended questions are used to explore and build upon the interviewee's experiences. The technique offers a privileged access to the mental constructions of individuals, their logic of practice and the categories on which they operate in the social world. In-depth interviews can open a window into daily lives, their contents and patterns, but also to beliefs, values and understandings of others (Weiss 1995). This enables the mapping of social organisations and, as part of mixed-methods designs, also the understanding and causal explanation of any quantitative study by providing the reasons and motives underlying the data, particularly by revealing how social and cultural experiences mediate human behaviour.

The classic definition of an interview presents this technique as "a face-to-face verbal exchange, in which one person, the interviewer, attempts to elicit information or expressions of opinion or belief from another person or persons" (Maccoby and Maccoby 1954, p. 449). The nature of such "information or expressions" has been subject to quite some debate; whereas neo-positivist approaches believed in the neutrality of the interviewee and the trustworthiness and solidity of their answers, more recent approaches acknowledge the individual's subjectivity. The perception of the role of interviewers has also evolved, from neutral to participatory, and it is now seen as being co-responsible in the resulting discourses or even in the resulting actions (Reinharz and Chase 2002).

Against this background, conducting interviews needs to be practiced and understood as a reflexive exercise (Gubrium and Holstein 2012), that is, acknowledging how the intersubjective experience transforms the research (Finlay 2003, p. 4). This reflexivity goes beyond merely indexing identity features such as gender, national origin or age, and requires a deep understanding of how our identities impact our roles in the interview as a social encounter, and in the eliciting of data as a practice of knowledge co-creation. This endeavour is imbued with ethical and political considerations, requires awareness at every step of the process and the capacity to compare and understand without evaluating. The researcher is required to acknowledge that the research is negotiated and socially constructed, and to describe decisions and dilemmas: "from the questions they ask to those they ignore, from who they study to who they ignore, from problem formulation to analysis, representation and writing" (Hertz 1997, p. viii).

A certain expertise is therefore required on the part of the researcher both in research methods and in interpersonal dynamics. The researcher needs to build rapport and to listen in order to engage the interviewee in a trusting relationship to ensure they enjoy the necessary conditions to share their views:

- For starters, small talk will allow for the particular social situation to be created, and for the interviewee and the interviewer to focus on their interaction.
- Introducing the purpose of the research, using an engaging story when possible, will establish roles and provide interviewees with information to further decide on their participation; any necessary ethical statements should be voiced and agreed on (especially regarding confidentiality, commercial and secondary uses of the data); it is also helpful to give the interviewee an explicit prerogative to discontinue or pause the conversation at any time and to skip specific questions if they do not want to answer.
- Planned questions touching on the topic but focusing on the interaction rather than on key issues will help to get the conversation started as a

negotiated exchange, making the flexibility of the questions evident to the interviewee.

- The rapport will be a priority in the whole conversation: keeping eye contact (when this is culturally convenient) and taking care of non-verbal language, especially expressions and gestures.
- To activate and guide the conversation, researchers use questions and prime specific situations, without forcing or constricting the interviewee's freedom to elaborate.
- After the planned topics have been discussed, the researcher should provide space for the interviewee to ask their own questions and ask them whether they are willing to be contacted again, with advances, results or follow-up questions.

To preserve the integrity of the data for ensuing stages, recording is essential and it is recommended to use two different recording methods or devices. Recording ensures that researchers do not analyse what their own memories recall but the actual narratives, that they can capture further details after the event and that they can focus on keeping the interaction active and creating rapport. Several authors have presented the advantages and disadvantages of video and audio recording (among others, Schilling 2013; Hammersley and Atkinson [1995] 2007), and they highlight the need of taking into account how recording will impact the encounter.

To ensure deep understanding, some authors stress the need for the researcher to be familiar with the community and the object of study. Past or present membership to the same community is no longer stigmatised but actually encouraged (Ellis and Flaherty 1992; Lofland and Lofland 1995; Denzin 1997; Johnson *et al.* 2003) as a means to ease access to layered meanings, details and nuances. However, familiarity with the subject entails the risk of taking knowledge for granted and believing some issues are actually *common sense* instead of community-specific knowledge and values. Addressing these issues requires experience in reflexivity to ensure all the necessary elements are accounted for in planning, analysing and presenting the research.

A remarkable advantage of being a member or a returning member of the community under scrutiny is that this largely eases the process of locating and recruiting informants. Indeed, access to the field is a challenge that can preclude the completion of social research projects. Lack of time, concerns for privacy, mistrust toward the real goals of the research and the researcher, lack of familiarity with ethics processes and requirements may render a research project unfeasible due to the lack of informants. Some measures to mitigate such a risk include planning plenty of time to get involved with the community and acquire member knowledge so that means for reciprocity can be built, including assistance or information. Extended contact and reciprocity also enhance mutual trust and interest of informants for the research, which will benefit the process of co-creation. Time demands, however, are difficult to meet and to reconcile with teaching, administration and other researching obligations, especially when financial constraints are also an issue.

3.1 Interviewing legal interpreters and translators

The research presented here is part of a wider project on legal interpreters' and translators' *habiti*, where they are interviewed about their socialisations, relations to others in professional settings, their subjective well-being and their perceptions on different issues related to their translation-related *doxas* and *illusios* (see Bourdieu 1972).[1] To be able to focus on the methodological issues and due to space requirements, only a subset of interviewees (nine translators working for the same organisation) and a part of the theoretical operationalisations and results were considered for the following description and the ensuing discussion.

All the interviews considered in this contribution were held between November 2013 and September 2015. Nonetheless, the location and recruitment of informants had begun in September 2013. The process was notably eased by the fact that the first subjects had been my colleagues when working as a translator at an international organisation in Geneva, Switzerland. Other interviews with interpreters and lawyers working for the same organisation and translators working for other organisations were held but will not be considered in this study to reduce its scope.[2] The interviewees decided on the time and place of the interviews, which were held at their workplace, their homes, a local pub nearby, a restaurant and a café in the city. All interviews were face-to-face and recorded. Most consisted of only one session, but two interviewees requested a second session to elaborate on specific details.

For the cases presented in this study, it is notable that I used to work at the organisation where the interviewees came from and had knowledge of the community (professional grades, hierarchies, work processes, opportunities for intra- and interprofessional contact and cooperation, meeting points, interpersonal relations). This facilitated the formulation of relevant demographic questions, start-off questions, primers and follow-ups, matching non-verbal language conventions and developing means to create and maintain rapport. After establishing the social situation, the research project was presented and the ethical issues were agreed on. The interviewees were also given the chance to pose any questions or comments and were informed of their entitlement to pause or discontinue the conversation and to skip or add any topics. The demographic questions involved general (country of residence, nationality, age range) to work-specific issues (years of experience, positions held, current position, years in current position and in the organisation) with a view to creating a workplace-related mindset. In this regard, it is worth noticing that the translators and interpreters working for international organisations usually work in a country which is not their own and that, before becoming permanent staff, they tend to work for different organisations located in either the same or other countries. This may have caused that questions pertaining to these aspects, formulated as short-answer questions, actually elicited rather extensive narratives in six cases.

The guiding questions and primers were embedded in open-ended questions. The researcher used a list of topics as guidance and ticked the topics as they were elaborated on, either after a question or without trigger, as part of the agents' narratives. Follow-up questions were developed on the spot. When not occurring spontaneously, primers for intra- and intergroup contacts and conflicts, translation-specific and professional norms, behaviours and views or assessments were produced (*can you imagine/remember a situation where* . . .). For interviews conducted in Spanish, gestures and response tokens were frequently used. For interviews conducted in English, only sparsely.

It is remarkable that all interviewees included in this study asked for further details as to the theoretical approaches used to frame the research and as to other studies on the issue. In some cases, this metaconversation was rather extensive. As a researcher, I shared my own priorities in looking at the data and my views as to how my gender, experience in the institution and social identity was to have an influence on my interpretations, for which awareness-taking and reframing exercises (such as self-priming different roles, interests and theoretical perspectives) would be needed. The post-interview stage of this research was especially rewarding as our respective social identities were made explicit and enacted in a spirit of cooperation and mutual interest.

3.2 Analysing data

A common technique to analyse interview narratives is content analysis (Berelson 1971; Neuendorf 2002; Krippendorff 2013; Mayring 2014), which allows for the examination of any communicative event. Content analysis aims to systematise, objectivise and quantify specific characteristics. A clear advantage is that it renders a great quantity of data more manageable by offering quantitative results, such as category frequencies and ratings, after a process of coding (identifying and tagging specific themes). Content analysis is useful in describing or exploring new areas, establishing patterns, and determining salience. In this study, content analysis was used as a first step. The analysis of the interviews was based on the categories informed by the theoretical framework, which have been partially presented in this contribution. The interviews were initially coded and the presence and salience of such codes were examined. Reflections and comments on first interpretations were drafted and this helped organising codes in the theory-driven categories. Then patterns, relationships and differences, salient themes and sequences were identified and explored (for instance, relations between years of experience and initiative in establishing interprofessional contact). Those were then linked to the theoretical basis of the study and propositions were drafted for further analysis and testing.

The interviews, however, had elicited some interesting issues that were not captured by this first analysis. Some interviewees referred to the same episodes from different perspectives and framed the meaning derived from such events in varying ways. More specially, the same interactions and structural relations were narrated by several interviewees from alternative positions and elaborating diverging interpretations. The meaning of these accounts was not properly explained with a content analysis, so a narrative analysis was selected as a complement to help in disentangling the relevance of the episodes related (Mishler 1995). Such episodes and their intersections were considered against the varying frames and perspectives, the meanings that were derived from them, the reported roles of individuals and the emotions related (Sarbin 1986; Polkinghorne 1988; Bruner 1990; McAdams 1993). Relations with the categories and results from the content analysis were then established and further elaborated.

4 Results and discussion

Results suggest that, by framing themselves as high-status or low-status translators, the subjects of this study created a projected social reality which they enacted in interaction. Such mental conception of the structure enables individuals to elucidate, understand and articulate the internal reality governing their views of their selves and of their relationships with others. In-depth interviews allowed us to reconstruct such conception.

As for the relation between perceived status and prestige (deference and preference granted both interprofessionally and intraprofessionally), four out of the five subjects with the highest objective status (subjects A–D) consistently provided narratives and cues of high intraprofessional prestige. The fifth case (subject E) was not consistent in accounts of intraprofessional encounters, but did provide more examples of high prestige than of low prestige in those interactions. Subjects A to D also provided narratives of high interprofessional prestige (three male, one female), three (A–C) in absolute terms and one (D) in relative terms, as D's appraisal of other professional groups' prestige within the institution was lower than A, B and C had reported. A and C were the translators having reported the highest perceived status in the sample, D reported a relatively high status (as status for other professions within the institution was perceived as lower by D than by other individuals in this group), B reported a satisfactory level of status, even though comparatively lower to other groups (acquiescence), and E arrogated a high intraprofessional status but a low interprofessional status. This subject, the only one with a degree in translation in this group, reported the lowest perceived interprofessional status among the individuals with highest objective status and also the lowest intra- and especially interprofessional prestige.

Among these individuals with higher objective status, those reporting the highest perceived status (A and C) conveyed narratives where they had been able to impact institutional processes and advance their translation *doxa* within the institution. Such structural power was perceived to be out of reach for translators by the rest of individuals in this group. This research does not allow to determine whether higher interactional power is a result of higher perceived status or whether it is the success in changing a disadvantageous situation within the institution that increases perceived status. A study of perceptions before the narrated event would be necessary to that end. What is certain is that their trying to introduce changes within the institution is the trigger of such a change, which may suggest that perceptions of status work at a motivational level to act upon the structure. It is also interesting to highlight that reported interactional power did not relate to objective status, as individuals sharing the same professional group (occupying the highest positions intraprofessionally) did not report the same experiences in interprofessional prestige allocation, although they did report intraprofessional prestige in relation to translators in lower ranks.

Among those translators with lower objective status, both perceived status and prestige were also reportedly low, both inter- and intraprofessionally. However, the one translator who provided narratives of impact on work processes also reported a higher perceived status in relative terms as the subject assessed the status of other professions within the institutions as lower than the rest of translators. This same translator also arrogated more active roles and felt more meaningful and productive in the workplace than all other co-workers with the same rank. This parallelism with the perceptions reported by D seems to suggest that the motivational effects of perceived status are based on upward social comparison: it shows positive effects in interactions as long as the arrogated status is among the highest in the workplace, even though the distance with lower ranking positions is short.

Using status and prestige to explain interactional and structural power brings some interesting results and trends, but finer grained explanations and more consistent relations can be developed integrating new concepts that can help see new interactions. For instance, when analysing the wording used to refer to translators and other professionals, it was observed that those who arrogated more active (less invisible) roles as translators felt more productive. Among those, the subjects reporting higher perceived prestige were actually able to have an impact on the structure by attuning processes to their *doxas*, even when reporting low perceived status. When they stated being attuned with the translation *doxa* (self-reportedly) operating in the institution structure, translators with lower objective status reported less active roles.

5 Conclusions

Although the results presented here are only partial, some useful insights were gained, notably that it seems ill-informed to consider the different dimensions of status as one single construct, as these distinct dimensions have varying impacts on prestige and interactional power. Indeed, higher perceived status shows a relation with high prestige, especially interprofesionally, but also intraprofessionally, even when objective status remains equal for all subjects. Also, the motivational effects of perceived status and their dependence on upward social comparison are worth further exploration, as are the impact of disparities between perceived and objective status on individuals' influence in the structure.

When considering what in-depth interviews can do for legal TIS, complexity is a keyword. They enable insights into a complex network of interactions that resists simplification. The theoretical approach presented here was not adequate to explain all the interactions and episodes revealed by the interviewees' narratives. When working with in-depth interviews, researchers are offered the opportunity to reframe their research, the theoretical assumptions and the participants, including themselves, in order to systematise and represent the social meanings found. More specifically, the study presented here led to widening the theoretical basis of the project to include *psychological ownership* as the framework for the analysis, with potentially more clarifying and consistent results to help explain the interactions between the different dimensions of status and prestige and their impact on interactional and structural power. At any rate, the exploratory nature of the study and its limited goal (determinants of interactional power) must be taken into account. If the purpose is to obtain generalisable results, in-depth interviews should be integrated within more complex research designs that combine qualitative and quantitative approaches.

Notes

1 The complete theoretical framework and the results derived from the first nine interviewees were presented at the Transfiction 3 Conference held at Concordia University, Canada, in May 2015. Results from a wider sample of 17 interviews encompassing translators and interpreters' experiences were presented at the EST Congress 2016 held at Aarhus University, Denmark, in September 2016. The project has since increased the number and professional profiles of agents interviewed.

2 At that time, I was working at the University of Graz, Austria, to which I am indebted for granting the necessary research leaves (four one-week periods between 2013 and 2015). No funding was received for this research.

References

Abbott, A. (1981). Status and status strain in the professions. *American Journal of Sociology*, 86, pp. 819–835.

Abel, L. (2009). *Language access in state courts.* New York: Brennan Center for Justice, New York University School of Law.

Addams, J. (1902). *Democracy and social ethics.* New York: Palgrave Macmillan.

Anderson, C. and Berdahl, J.L. (2002). The experience of power: Examining the effects of power on approach and inhibition tendencies. *Journal of Personality and Social Psychology*, 83 (6), pp. 1362–1377.

Anderson, C. and Brown, C.E. (2010). The functions and dysfunctions of hierarchy. *Research in Organizational Behavior*, 30, pp. 55–89.

Anderson, C. and Galinsky, A.D. (2006). Power, optimism, and risk-taking. *European Journal of Social Psychology*, 36 (4), pp. 511–536.

Anderson, C., *et al.* (2006). Knowing your place: Self-perceptions of status in face-to-face groups. *Journal of Personality and Social Psychology*, 91 (6), pp. 1094–1110.

Angermeyer, P.S. (2009). Translation style and participant roles in court interpreting. *Journal of Sociolinguistics*, 13 (1), pp. 3–28.

Arendt, H. [1958] (1998). *The human condition.* 2nd ed. Chicago: University of Chicago Press.

Atkinson, P. (1995). *Medical talk and medical work: The liturgy of the clinic.* London: Sage.

Barth, F. (1969). *Ethnic groups and boundaries. The social organization of culture difference*. Boston: Little, Brown and Co.
Bassnett, S. (1996). The meek or the mighty: Reappraising the role of the translator. *In:* R. Álvarez and Á. Vidal, eds. *Translation, power, subversion*. Clevedon: Multilingual Matters, pp. 10–24.
Beaton-Thome, M. (2007). Interpreted ideologies in instutional discourse. The case of the European Parliament. *The Translator*, 13 (2), pp. 271–296.
Beaton-Thome, M. (2010). Negotiating identities in the European Parliament: The role of simultaneous interpreting. *In:* M. Baker, *et al.*, eds. *Text and context: Essays on translation and interpreting in honour of Ian Mason*. Manchester: St. Jerome Publishing, pp. 117–138.
Beaton-Thome, M. (2013). What's in a word? Your *enemy combatant* is my *refugee*: The role of simultaneous interpreters in negotiating the lexis of Guantánamo in the European Parliament. *Journal of Language and Politics*, 12 (3), pp. 378–399.
Benrabah, M. (2005). The language planning situation in Algeria. *Current Issues in Language Planning*, 6 (4), pp. 379–502.
Berelson, B. (1971). *Content analysis in communication research*. New York: Glencoe.
Berger, J., Cohen, B.P. and Zelditch, M. (1972). Status characteristics and social interaction. *American Sociological Review*, 37 (3), pp. 241–255.
Berger, P. and Luckman, T. (1966). *The social construction of reality: A treatise in the sociology of knowledge*. Garden City and New York: Anchor Books.
Berk-Seligson, S. (1990). *The bilingual courtroom: Court interpreters in the judicial process*. Chicago and London: Oxford University Press.
Berlant, J.L. (1975). *Professions and monopoly: A study of medicine in the United States and Great Britain*. Berkeley: University of California Press.
Borenstein, S. (1989). Hubs and high fare: Dominance and market power in the U.S. airline industry. *The Rand Journal of Economics*, 20 (3), pp. 344–365.
Bottici, C. (2014). *Imaginal politics: Images beyond imagination and the imaginary*. New York: Columbia University Press.
Bourdieu, P. (1972). *Esquisse d'une théorie de la pratique, précédée de trois études d'ethnographie kabyle*. Geneva: Librairie Droz.
Bourdieu, P. (1997). *Méditations pascaliennes*. Paris: Seuil.
Braun, S. and Taylor, J.L., eds. (2011). *Videoconference and remote interpreting in criminal proceedings*. Guildford: University of Surrey.
Brennan, G. and Pettit, P. (2004). *The economy of esteem: An essay on civil and political society*. Oxford: Oxford University Press.
Bruner, J. (1990). *Acts of meaning: Four lectures on mind and culture*. Cambridge: Harvard University Press.
Chen, Y. and Liao, P. (2016). A revised model for the professionalization of court interpreting in Taiwan. *Compilation and Translation Review*, 9 (2), pp. 137–164.
Chesterman, A. (1997). Ethics of translation. *In:* M. Snell-Hornby, *et al.*, eds. *Translation as intercultural communication*. Amsterdam: John Benjamins, pp. 147–157.
Chesterman, A. (2009). The name and nature of translator studies. *Hermes. Journal of Language and Communication Studies*, 42, pp. 13–22.
Courpasson, D. (2000). Managerial strategies of domination. Power in soft bureaucracies. *Organization Studies*, 21 (1), pp. 141–161.
Dam, H.V. and Zethsen, K.K. (2011). The status of professional business translators on the Danish market: A comparative study of company, agency and freelance translators. *Meta: Translators' Journal*, 56 (4), pp. 976–997.

Dam, H.V. and Zethsen, K.K. (2012). Translators in international organizations: A special breed of high-status professionals? Danish EU translators as a case in point. *Translation and Interpreting Studies*, 7, pp. 212–233.

Denzin, N.K. (1997). *Interpretive ethnography: Ethnographic practices for the 21st century.* Thousand Oaks: Sage.

Dumont, L. (1970). *Homo hierarchicus: An essay on the caste system.* Chicago: University of Chicago Press.

Durkheim, É. (1893). *De la division du travail social.* Paris: Félix Alcan.

Durkheim, É. (1950). *Leçons de sociologie: Physique des mœurs et du droit.* Paris: Les Presses universitaires de France.

Einstein, A., *et al.* (1935). Can quantum mechanical description of physical reality be considered complete? *Physical Review*, 47, pp. 777–780.

Elliott, P. (1972). *The sociology of professions.* London: Palgrave Macmillan.

Ellis, C.S. and Flaherty, M.G., eds. (1992). *Investigating subjectivity: Research on lived experience.* Newbury Park: Sage.

Erasmus, M. (2000). 'Community Interpreting' in South Africa. Current trends and future prospects. *In:* R. Roberts, *et al.*, eds. *The critical link 2: Interpreters in the community. Papers from the 2nd international conference on interpreting in legal, health, and social service settings, Vancouver, BC, Canada, 19–23 May, 1998.* Amsterdam: John Benjamins, pp. 191–206.

Finlay, L. (2003). The reflexive journey: Mapping multiple routes. *In:* L. Finlay and B. Gough, eds. *Reflexivity. A practical guide for researchers in health and social sciences.* Oxford: Wiley-Blackwell, pp. 3–20.

Fiola, M. (2000). The challenge of accrediting aboriginal interpreters. *In:* R.P. Roberts, *et al.*, eds. *The critical link 2: Interpreters in the community. Selected papers from the second international conference on interpreting in legal, health and social service settings, Vancouver, BC, Canada, 19–23 May 1998.* Amsterdam: John Benjamins, pp. 121–127.

Fishman, J.A. (1993). Ethnolinguistic democracy. Varieties, degrees and limits. *Language International*, 5 (1), pp. 11–17.

Fiske, S.T. (2010). Interpersonal stratification: Status, power, and subordination. *In:* S.T. Fiske, *et al.*, eds. *Handbook of social psychology.* Hoboken: Wiley-Blackwell, pp. 941–982.

Fleming, P. and Spicer, A. (2014). Power in management and organization science. *The Academy of Management Annals*, 8 (1), pp. 237–298.

Fournier, V. (1999). The appeal to 'professionalism' as a disciplinary mechanism. *The Sociological Review*, 47 (2), pp. 280–307.

Fragale, A.R., Overbeck, J.R. and Neale, M.A. (2011). Resources versus respect: Social judgments based on targets' power and status positions. *Journal of Experimental Social Psychology*, 47 (4), pp. 767–775.

Frank, R.H. (1985). *Choosing the right pond: Human behavior and the quest for status.* Oxford: Oxford University Press.

Fraser, N. (1995, July–Aug). From redistribution to recognition? Dilemmas of justice in a 'postsocialist' age. *New Left Review*, 212, pp. 68–93.

Galinsky, A.D., *et al.* (2003). From power to action. *Journal of Personality and Social Psychology*, 85, pp. 453–466.

Galinsky, A.D., *et al.* (2008). Power reduces the press of the situation: Implications for creativity, conformity, and dissonance. *Journal of Personality and Social Psychology*, 95 (6), pp. 1450–1466.

Gascón Navarro, F.A. (2015). *La percepción de los abogados de oficio de las actuaciones de intérpretes judiciales en el partido judicial de Zaragoza: Análisis cualitativo de un grupo focal [Legal-aid lawyers' perceptions of judicial interpreters in the courtroom, with a focus on the judicial district of Zaragoza: A qualitative analysis of a focus group].* Thesis (MA). Castelló de la Plana: Universitat Jaume I.

Glaser, B.G. and Strauss, A.L. (1965). Temporal aspects of dying as a non-scheduled status passage. *American Journal of Sociology*, 71 (1), pp. 48–59.

Goldthorpe, J.H. and Hope, K. (1972). Occupational grading and occupational prestige. *Social Science Information*, 11 (5), pp. 17–73.

Gould, R.V. (2002). The origins of status hierarchies: A formal theory and empirical test. *American Journal of Sociology*, 107 (5), pp. 1143–1178.

Gould, R.V. (2003). *Collision of wills: How ambiguity about social rank breeds conflict.* Chicago: University of Chicago Press.

Gruenfeld, D.H., *et al.* (2008). Power and the objectification of social targets. *Journal of Personality and Social Psychology*, 95 (1), pp. 111–127.

Gubrium, J.F. and Holstein, J.A. (2012). Narrative practice and the transformation of interview subjectivity. *In:* J.F. Gubrium, *et al.*, eds. *The SAGE handbook of interview research. The complexity of the craft.* Thousand Oaks: Sage, pp. 27–43.

Guinote, A. (2007). Power and goal pursuit. *Personality and Social Psychology Bulletin*, 33, pp. 1076–1087.

Hale, S.B. (2005). The interpreter's identity crisis. *In:* J. House, *et al.*, eds. *Translation and the construction of identity.* Seoul: IATIS, pp. 14–29.

Hale, S.B. (2008). Controversies over the role of the court interpreter. *In:* C. Valero-Garcés and A. Martin, eds. *Crossing borders in community interpreting: Definitions and dilemmas.* Amsterdam: John Benjamins, pp. 99–121.

Hammersley, M. and Atkinson, P., [1995] 2007. *Ethnography principles in practice.* London: Routledge.

Harper, R. (1988). *An ethnography of accountancy.* Thesis (PhD). Manchester: University of Manchester.

Hays, N.A. (2013). Fear and loving in social hierarchy: Sex differences in preferences for power versus status. *Journal of Experimental Social Psychology*, 49 (6), pp. 1130–1136.

Hebenstreit, G. (2018). Translating and interpreting cultures. Discussing translation and interpreting ethics in a postmonolingual age. *In:* E. Monzó-Nebot and J. Jiménez-Salcedo, eds. *Translating and interpreting justice in a postmonolingual age.* Delaware: Vernon Press, pp. 61–75.

Hertog, E., *et al.* (2007). From aequitas to aequalitas. Establishing standards in legal interpreting and translation in the European Union. *In:* C. Wadensjö, *et al.*, eds. *The critical link 4: Professionalisation of interpreting in the community. Selected papers from the 4th international conference on interpreting in legal, health and social service settings, Stockholm, Sweden, 20–23 May 2004* Amsterdam: John Benjamins, pp. 151–165.

Hertz, R. (1997). *Reflexivity and voice.* Thousand Oaks: Sage.

Hill Collins, P. (1998). Toward a new vision: Race, class and gender as categories of analysis and connection. *In:* R.F. Levine, ed. *Social class and stratification: Classic statements and theoretical debates.* Boston: Rowman & Littlefield, pp. 231–247.

Hlavac, J. (2013). A cross-national overview of translator and interpreter certification procedures. *The International Journal for Translation & Interpreting Research*, 5 (2), pp. 32–65.

Hoffding, H. (1905). On the relation between sociology and ethics. *American Journal of Sociology*, 10 (5), pp. 672–685.

Inghilleri, M. (2008). The ethical task of the translator in the geo-political arena. From Iraq to Guantánamo Bay. *Translation Studies*, 1, pp. 212–223.

Jacobsen, B. (2001). Court interpreting and face: An analysis of a court interpreter's strategies for conveying threats to own face. *In:* D. Russell and S. Hale, eds. *Interpreting in legal settings*. Washington, DC: Gallaudet University Press, pp. 51–71.

Jacobsen, B. (2009). The community interpreter: A question of role. *Hermes. Journal of Language and Communication Studies*, 42, pp. 155–166.

Johnson, J.M., *et al.* (2003). Victim protection orders and the stake in conformity thesis. *Journal of Family Violence*, 18 (9), pp. 317–323.

Judge, T.A. and Joyce, E.B. (2001). Relationship of core self-evaluations traits-self-esteem, generalized self-efficacy, locus of control, and emotional stability-with job satisfaction and job performance: A meta-analysis. *Journal of Applied Psychology*, 86, pp. 80–92.

Katan, D. (2011). Occupation or profession: A survey of the translators' world. *In:* R. Sela-Sheffy and M. Shlesinger, eds. *Identity and status in the translational professions*. Amsterdam: John Benjamins, pp. 65–87.

Keltner, D., *et al.* (2003). Power, approach, and inhibition. *Psychological Review*, 110 (2), pp. 265–284.

Kent, S.J. (2007). Why bother? Institutionalisation, interpreter decisions and power relations. *In:* C. Wadensjö, *et al.*, eds. *The critical link 4: Professionalisation of interpreting in the community*. Amsterdam: John Benjamins, pp. 193–204.

Koskinen, K. (2000). *Beyond ambivalence. Postmodernity and the ethics of translation*. Tampere: University of Tampere.

Koskinen, K. (2008). *Translating institutions: An ethnographic study of EU translation*. Manchester: St. Jerome Publishing.

Kraus, P.A. (2007). Intercultural recognition and linguistic diversity in Europe. *In:* D. Castiglione and C. Longman, eds. *The language question in Europe and diverse societies. Political, legal and social perspectives*. Oxford and Portland, OR: Hart, pp. 61–80.

Kraus, P.A. (2018). Between minority protection and linguistic sovereignty. *Revista de Llengua i Dret*, 69, pp. 6–17.

Krausneker, V. (2000). Sign languages and the minority language policy of the European Union. *In:* M. Metzger, ed. *Bilingualism and identity in deaf communities*. Washington, DC: Gallaudet University Press, pp. 142–158.

Krippendorff, K. (2013). *Content analysis. An introduction to its methodology*. Los Angeles: Sage.

Lambert, J. (2018). How ethical are codes of ethics? Using illusions of neutrality to sell translations. *The Journal of Specialised Translation*, 30, pp. 269–290.

Lee, J. (2013). A study of facework in interpreter-mediated courtroom examination. *Perspectives: Studies in Translatology*, 21 (1), pp. 82–99.

Lee, J. (2015). Evaluation of court interpreting: A case study of metadiscourse in interpreter-mediated expert witness examinations. *Interpreting*, 17 (2), pp. 167–194.

Lofland, J. and Lofland, L.H. (1995). *Analyzing social settings*. Belmont: Wadsworth.

Maccoby, E.E. and Maccoby, N. (1954). The interview: A tool of social science. *In:* L. Gardner, ed. *Handbook of social psychology*. Cambridge: Addison-Wesley, pp. 449–487.

Magee, J.C. and Galinsky, A.D. (2008). Social hierarchy: The self-reinforcing nature of power and status. *The Academy of Management Annals*, 2 (1), pp. 351–398.

Mann, M. (1993). *The sources of social power, Vol. 2. The rise of classes and nation-states, 1760–1914.* Cambridge: Cambridge University Press.

Martineau, H. ([1838] 1989). *How to observe morals and manners.* New Brunswick: Transaction Publishers.

Martín Ruano, M.R. (2014). From suspicion to collaboration: Defining new epistemologies of reflexive practice for legal translation and interpreting. *The Journal of Specialised Translation*, 22, pp. 194–213.

Martín Ruano, M.R. (2015). (Trans)formative theorising in legal translation and/ or interpreting: A critical approach to deontological principles. *The Interpreter and Translator Trainer*, 9 (2), pp. 141–155.

Martín Ruano, M.R. (2018). Unveiling and redressing inequality dynamics in legal and institutional translation: From symbolic violence to symbolic recognition. *In:* E. Monzó–Nebot and J. Jiménez-Salcedo, eds. *Translating and interpreting justice in a postmonolingual age.* Delaware: Vernon Press, pp. 35–59.

Marx, K. (1867). *Das Kapital. Kritik der politischen Oekonomie. Erster Band.* Hamburg: Otto Meissner.

Mason, I. (2005). Projected and perceived identities in dialogue interpreting. *In:* J. House, *et al.*, eds. *Translation and the construction of identity.* Seoul: IATIS, pp. 30–52.

Mayring, P. (2014). *Qualitative content analysis. Theoretical roundation, basic procedures and software solution.* Klagenfurt. Available at: http://nbn-resolving.de/urn:nbn:de:0168-ssoar-395173 [Accessed 10 Oct. 2018].

McAdams, D.P. (1993). *Personal myths and the making of the self.* New York: William Morrow.

McAuliffe, K. (2009). Translation at the Court of Justice of the European Communities. *In:* F. Olsen, *et al.*, eds. *Translation issues in language and law.* New York: Palgrave Macmillan, pp. 99–115.

McDonough, J. (2011). Moral ambiguity: Some shortcomings of professional codes of ethics for translators. *The Journal of Specialised Translation*, 15, pp. 28–49.

Mead, G.H. (1908). The philosophical basis for ethics. *International Journal of Ethics*, 18, pp. 311–323.

Mikkelson, H. (1996). Community interpreting. An emerging profession. *Interpreting*, 1 (1), pp. 125–129.

Mikkelson, H. (2000). *Introduction to court interpreting.* Manchester: St. Jerome Publishing.

Mirsafian, L. (2012). Inferiority of translation. Governmental publishing houses in Iran. *Interdisciplinary Journal of Contemporary Research in Business*, 4 (1), pp. 744–750.

Mishler, E.G. (1995). Models of narrative analysis: A typology. *Journal of Narrative and Life History*, 5, pp. 87–123.

Molm, L.D. (1990). Structure, action, and outcomes: The dynamics of power in social exchange. *American Sociological Review*, 55 (3), pp. 427–447.

Monzó-Nebot, E. (2002). *La professió del traductor jurídic i jurat. Descripció sociològica de la professió i anàlisi discursiva del transgènere [Sworn legal translation as a profession: A sociological approach to the profession and a genre-based analysis of a transgenre].* Thesis (PhD). Castelló de la Plana: University Jaume I.

Monzó-Nebot, E. (2005). Being ACTIVE in legal translation and interpreting: Researching and acting on the Spanish field. *Meta: Journal des traducteurs*, 50 (4), doi:10.7202/019922ar.

Monzó-Nebot, E. (2009). Legal and translational occupations in Spain: Regulation and specialization in jurisdictional struggles. *Translation and Interpreting Studies*, 4, pp. 135–154.

Monzó-Nebot, E. (2018). Translators and interpreters as agents of diversity. Managing myths and pursuing justice in postmonolingual societies. *In:* E. Monzó Nebot and J. Jiménez-Salcedo, eds. *Translating and interpreting justice in a postmonolingual age*. Delaware: Vernon Press, pp. 9–34.

Monzó-Nebot, E. and Jiménez-Salcedo, J., eds. (2018). *Translating and interpreting justice in a postmonolingual age*. Delaware: Vernon Press.

Morris, R. (1995). The moral dilemmas of court interpreting. *The Translator*, 1 (1), pp. 25–46.

Müller, W. and Pollak, R. (2015). Mobility, social. *In:* N.J. Smelser and P.B. Baltes, eds. *International encyclopedia of the social & behavioral sciences*. 2nd ed. Amsterdam: Elsevier, pp. 640–646.

Nadler, A. (2002). Inter-group helping relations as power relations: Maintaining or challenging social dominance between groups though helping. *Journal of Social Issues*, 58 (3), pp. 487–502.

Napier, J. (2004). Sign language interpreter training, testing, and accreditation: An international comparison. *American Annals of the Deaf*, 149 (4), pp. 350–359.

Napier, J. (2011). Signed language interpreting. *In:* K. Malmkjær and K. Windle, eds. *The Oxford handbook of translation studies*. Oxford: Oxford University Press, pp. 353–372.

Napier, J. and Rohan, M. (2007). An invitation to dance: Deaf consumers' perceptions of signed language interpreters and interpreting. *In:* M. Metzger and E. Fleetwood, eds. *Translation, sociolinguistic, and consumer issues in interpreting*. Washington, DC: Gallaudet University Press, pp. 159–203.

Neuendorf, K. (2002). *The content analysis guidebook*. Thousand Oaks: Sage.

Parkin, F. (1974). Strategies of social closure in class formation. *In: The social analysis of class structure*. London: Tavistock Publications.

Polkinghorne, D.E. (1988). *Narrative knowing and the human sciences*. New York: State University of New York Press.

Powell, B. and Jacobs, J. (2013). Gender differences in the evaluation of prestige. *The Sociological Quarterly*, 25 (2), pp. 173–190.

Prunč, E. (2005). Translationsethik. [Translation ethics]. *Informatologia*, 38 (pp. 1–2), 9–21.

Pym, A., *et al.* (2012). *The status of the translation profession in the European Union*. Brussels: European Commission.

Reed, M., *et al.* (2001). Working paper on access to justice for deaf people. *In:* F. Harrington and G.H. Turner, eds. *Interpreting interpreting: Studies and reflections on sign language interpreting*. Coleford: Douglas McLean, pp. 168–216.

Reinharz, S. and Chase, S.E. (2002). Interviewing women. *In:* J.F. Gubrium and J. Holstein, eds. *Handbook of interview research: Context and method*. Thousand Oaks: Sage, pp. 221–238.

Resta, Z. and Ioannidis, A. (2016). A sociological approach to the professionalization of court interpreting in Greece. *In:* M, Bajčić and K. Dobrić Basaneže, eds. *Towards the professionalization of legal translators and court interpreters in the EU*. Newcastle upon Tyne: Cambridge Scholars, pp. 66–82.

Roberts, R.P. (2000). Interpreter assessment tools for different settings. *In:* R.P. Roberts, *et al.*, eds. *The Critical Link 2: Interpreters in the community. Selected papers from the second international conference on interpreting in legal, health and social service settings, Vancouver, BC, Canada, 19–23 May 1998*. Amsterdam: John Benjamins, pp. 103–120.

Roberts-Smith, L. (2007). Forensic interpreting. Trial and error. *In:* S. Hale, U. Ozolins and L. Stern, eds. *The critical link 5. Quality in interpreting – a shared responsibility*. Amsterdam: John Benjamins, pp. 13–35.

Rodríguez García, J.M. (2010). The regime of translation in Caro's Colombia. *In: The city of translation. Poetry and ideology in nineteenth-century Colombia*. New York: Palgrave Macmillan, pp. 39–84.

Roscigno, V.J., *et al.* (2007). Social closure and processes of race/sex employment discrimination. *Annals of the American Academy of Political and Social Science*, 609, pp. 16–48.

Ruokonen, M. (2013). Studying translator status: Three points of view. *In:* M. Eronen and M. Rodi-Risberg, eds. *Haasteena näkökulma, Perspektivet som utmaning, Point of view as challenge, Perspektivität als Herausforderung. VAKKI-symposiumi XXXIII 7. – 8.2.2013*. Vaasa: VAKKI Publications, pp. 327–338.

Salmi, L. and Tuija, K. (2015). Training translators for accreditation in Finland. *The Interpreter and Translator Trainer*, 9 (2), pp. 1–14.

Salvador i Padrosa, S. (2006). Les proves d'habilitació per a la traducció i la interpretació jurades [Licensing tests for sworn translators and interpreters]. *In:* E. Monzó Nebot, ed. *Les plomes de la justícia. La traducció al català dels textos jurídics*. Barcelona: Pòrtic, pp. 67–89.

Sanz Moreno, R. (2017). La audiodescripción. O la desminorización como derecho [Audiodescription. Or the right to deminorization]. *In:* E. Monzó-Nebot and J. Jiménez-Salcedo, eds. *Les llengües minoritzades en l'ordre postmonolingüe*. Castelló de la Plana: Universitat Jaume I, pp. 121–136.

Sarbin, T.R. (1986). *Narrative psychology: The storied nature of human conduct*. New York: Praeger.

Schilling, N. (2013). *Sociolinguistic fieldwork*. Cambridge: Cambridge University Press.

Scott, J. (2017). The pernicious effects of terms used for and by the legal translation profession. *Revista de Llengua i Dret*, 68, pp. 57–75.

Setton, R. and Liangliang, A.G. (2009). Attitudes to role, status and professional identity in interpreters and translators with Chinese in Shanghai and Taipei. *Translation and Interpreting Studies*, 4 (2), pp. 210–238.

Simeoni, D. (1998). The pivotal status of the translator's habitus. *Target*, 10, pp. 1–39.

Sinclair, S. (1997). *Making doctors: An institutional apprenticeship*. Oxford: Berg.

Skutnabb-Kangas, T. (1998). Human rights and language wrongs – a future for diversity. *Language Sciences*, 20 (1), pp. 5–27.

Sosoni, V. (2005). Multilingualism in Europe. Blessing or curse? *In:* A. Branchadell and L.M. West, eds. *Less translated languages*. Amsterdam: John Benjamins.

Steytler, N.C. (1993). Implementing language rights in court: The role of the court interpreter. *South African Journal on Human Rights*, 9 (2), pp. 205–222.

Takeda, K. (2008). Interpreting at the Tokyo war crimes tribunal. *Interpreting*, 10 (1), 1978.

Toury, G. (1978). The nature and role of norms in literary translation. *In:* J.S. Holmes, *et al.*, eds. *Literature and translation. New perspectives in literary translation.* Leuven: Acco, pp. 83–100.

Toury, G. (1995). *Descriptive translation studies and beyond.* Amsterdam: John Benjamins.

Tryuk, M. (2012). The judge, the doctor, the immigration officer and the interpreter. Community interpreters' role perception – a polish perspective. *The Interpreters' Newsletter*, 17, pp. 117–138.

Tseng, J. (1992). *Interpreting as an emerging profession in Taiwan – a sociological model.* Thesis (MA). New Taipei: Fu Jen Catholic University.

Tymoczko, M. (2000). Translation and political engagement. *The Translator*, 6 (1), pp. 23–47.

Tymoczko, M. (2007). *Enlarging translation, empowering translators.* Manchester and Kinderhook: St. Jerome Publishing.

Valero-Garcés, C. (2007). Challenges in multilingual societies. The myth of the invisible interpreter and translator. *Across Languages and Cultures*, 8 (1), pp. 81–101.

Valero-Garcés, C. (2016). Aproximaciones desde la ética en la interpretación en casos de violencia de género [Ethics-based approaches to interpreting in cases involving gender-based violence]. *Babel*, 62 (1), pp. 67–85.

Valero-Garcés, C. and Gauthier, L. (2010). Bourdieu and public service interpreting and translation: Towards a social theory in PSIT. *MonTI*, 2, pp. 97–117.

Valero-Garcés, C. and Lázaro Gutiérrez, R. (2016). Perceptions from the outside in cases of gender violence. 'What are you [the interpreter] doing here?'. *European Journal of Applied Linguistics*, 4 (1), pp. 57–72.

Veblen, T. (1994). *Theory of the leisure class.* New York: Penguin.

Vidal Claramonte, Á.M.C. (2005). Re-presenting the 'real': Pierre Bourdieu and legal translation. *The Translator*, 11 (2), pp. 259–275.

Vidal Claramonte, Á.M.C. (2013). Towards a new research model in legal translation: Future perspectives in the era of asymmetry. *Linguistica Antverpiensia NS-TTS*, 12, pp. 182–196.

Wadensjö, C. (1998). *Interpreting as interaction.* London and New York: Longman.

Wadensjö, C. (2007). Interpreting professions, professionalisation, and professionalism. *In:* C. Wadensjo, *et al.*, eds. *The critical link 4: Professionalisation of interpreting in the community.* Amsterdam: John Benjamins, pp. 1–8.

Wallace, M. (2013). Rethinking bifurcated testing models in the court interpreter certification process. *In:* D. Tsagari and R. Van Deemter, eds. *Assessment issues in language translation and interpreting.* Bern: Peter Lang, pp. 67–84.

Wallace, M. (2015). A further call to action: Training as a policy issue in court interpreting. *The Interpreter and Translator Trainer*, pp. 173–187.

Weber, M. (1922). *Grundriß der Sozialönomik. III. Abteilung. Wirtschaft und Gesellschaft.* Tübingen: Mohr.

Weber, M. (1958). Class, status, party. *In:* H. Heinrich Gerth and C. Wright Mills, eds. *From Max Weber: Essays in sociology.* Oxford: Oxford University Press, pp. 180–195.

Weiss, R.S. (1995). *Learning from strangers. The art and method of qualitative interview studies.* New York: Simon & Schuster.

Whitmeyer, J.M. (2007). The acceptance of low prestige. *Politics and the Life Sciences*, 26 (2), pp. 33–45.

Wilensky, H.L. (1964). The professionalization of everyone? *The American Journal of Sociology*, 70, pp. 137–158.

Witter-Merithew, A. and Johnson, L. (2004). Market disorder within the field of sign language interpreting: Professionalization implications. *Journal of Interpretation*, 14, pp. 19–55.

Wright, R. (1994). *The moral animal: Evolutionary psychology and everyday life.* New York: Pantheon Books.

Yanagisako, S. and Delaney, C. (1995). *Naturalizing power: Essays in feminist cultural analysis.* New York and London: Routledge.

Index

Note: page numbers in *italic* indicate a figure. Page numbers in **bold** indicate a table.

For Product Safety Concerns and Information please contact our EU representative GPSR@taylorandfrancis.com
Taylor & Francis Verlag GmbH, Kaufingerstraße 24, 80331 München, Germany

www.ingramcontent.com/pod-product-compliance
Ingram Content Group UK Ltd.
Pitfield, Milton Keynes, MK11 3LW, UK
UKHW011007180926
475701UK00004B/603
9780367730000